Beijing to Beijing+5
Review and appraisal of the
implementation of the Beijing
Platform for Action

Beijing to Beijing+5
Review and appraisal of the implementation of the Beijing Platform for Action

Report of the Secretary-General

United Nations, New York, 2001

NOTE

The designations employed and the presentation of the material in this publication do not imply the expression of any opinion whatsoever on the part of the Secretariat of the United Nations concerning the legal status of any country, territory, city or area or of its authorities, or concerning the delimitation of its frontiers or boundaries. The term "country" as used in the text of this publication also refers, as appropriate, to territories or areas.

Symbols of United Nations documents are composed of capital letters combined with figures.

Division for the Advancement of Women
Department of Economic and Social Affairs
Two United Nations Plaza, 12th Floor
New York, NY 10017, USA
Fax: (212) 963-3463
E-mail: daw@un.org

UN2
ST/ESA/DAW
2001 B23

Contents

Abbreviations and Acronyms

ACC	Administrative Committee on Coordination
AECI	Agency for International Cooperation
AFD	Agency for Development
AMINA	African Development Fund Microfinance Initiative for Africa
CAS	Country Assistance Strategy
CCAQ	Consultative Committee on Administrative Questions
CCAs	common country assessments
CCPOQ	Consultative Committee on Programme and Operational Questions
CDF	Comprehensive Development Framework
CDFI	Community Development Financial Institutions Fund
CIDA	Canadian International Development Agency
CNDIST	National Centre on Documentation and Scientific and Technical Information
CONFINTEA	Fifth International Conference on Adult Education
CPC	Committee for Programme and Coordination
CPIA	Country Policy and Institutional Assessment
CRIPT	Research Centre for Initiating Technology Projects
CSN	country strategy note
DAC	Developmental Assistance Committee
DANIDA	Danish International Development Agency
DFID	Department for International Development
EC	European Commission
ECA	Economic Commission for Africa

ECE	Economic Commission for Europe
ECLAC	Economic Commission for Latin America and the Caribbean
EFA	Education for All
ENACT	Environmental Action
ESCAP	Economic and Social Commission for Asia and the Pacific
ESCWA	Economic and Social Commission for Western Asia
EU	European Union
FAO	Food and Agriculture Organization of the United Nations
FEMSA	Project to Educate Women and Young Girls in Mathematics and Science
GAIN	Gender in Africa Information Network
GAINS	Gender Awareness Information and Network System
GMMP	Global Media Monitoring Project
GMS	gender management systems
GNP	gross national product
GTZ	German Development Cooperation Agency
HIV/AIDS	human immunodeficiency virus / acquired immune deficiency syndrome
IACWGE	Inter-Agency Committee on Women and Gender Equality
ICSC	International Civil Service Commission
ICTs	information and communication technologies
ILO	International Labour Organization
IMF	International Monetary Fund
INSTRAW	United Nations International Research and Training Institute for the Advancement of Women
IPU	Inter-Parliamentary Union
ISTAT	Italian National Statistical Institution
IWMF	International Women's Media Foundation
MERCOSUR	Southern Core Common Market
NATO	North Atlantic Treaty Organization
NGOs	non-governmental organizations
OAS	Organization of American States
OAU	Organization of African Unity

ODA	official development assistance
OECD	Organisation for Economic Cooperation and Development
PEARL	Programme for the Enhancement of Adolescent Reproductive Health
PfA	Platform for Action
PIMS	Policy Information Marker System
PNAE	National Action Programme on Environment
PROGRESA	Programa de Educación, Salud y Alimentación
SADC	Southern African Development Community
SAPs	structural adjustment programmes
SBA	Small Business Administration Programme
SIDA	Swedish International Development Agency
STDs	sexually transmitted diseases
TWIB	Technology for Women in Business
UEMOA	West African Economic and Monetary Fund
UNCTAD	United Nations Conference on Trade and Development
UNDAF	United Nations Development Assistance Framework
UNDCP	United Nations International Drug Control Programme
UNDG	United Nations Development Group
UNDP	United Nations Development Programme
UNESCO	United Nations Educational, Scientific and Cultural Organization
UNFPA	United Nations Population Fund
UNHCR	Office of the United Nations High Commissioner for Refugees
UNHCR	United Nations High Commissioner for Human Rights
UNICEF	United Nations Children's Fund
UNIFEM	United Nations Development Fund for Women
UNV	United Nations Volunteers
USAID	United States Agency for International Development
WDF	Women Development Fund
WHO	World Health Organization
WMW	Women's Media Watch

Introduction

"We hereby adopt and commit ourselves as Governments to implement the following Platform for Action, ensuring that a gender perspective is reflected in all our policies and programmes. We urge the
United Nations system, regional and international financial institutions, other relevant regional and international institutions and all
women and men, as well as non-governmental organizations, with
full respect for their autonomy, and all sectors of civil society, in
cooperation with Governments, to fully commit themselves and
contribute to the implementation of this Platform for Action."

Beijing Declaration (1995), para. 38

The present publication prepared by the United Nations Division
for the Advancemant of Women, is a review and appraisal of the
progress made towards the implementation of the Beijing Platform
for Action adopted by Governments at the Fourth World Conference on Women in Beijing in 1995. It consists of three parts. Part
One provides the background to the Beijing Conference, its context,
the intergovernmental process since Beijing and an overview of the
major trends in implementation of the Platform for Action. Part
Two consists of an analysis of implementation in each critical area
of concern and the institutional and financial arrangements as
called for in the Platform for Action. Part Three picks up on some
of the trends of political, economic, social and cultural changes
identified in the Platform for Action that have become particularly
pronounced since the Beijing Conference and that pose new challenges for the full implementation of the Platform for Action.

Parts One and Two are based on an analysis of reports received from governments in response to a questionaire on the implementation of the Platform for Action. The analysis of the 135 responses initially received by the end of December 1999 was forwarded to the third session of the Commission on the Status of Women acting as the preparatory committee for the special session of the General Assembly entitled "Women 2000: gender equality, development and peace for the twenty-first century" (E/CN.6/2001/PC/2). Reports from an additional 19 Member States were subsequently received and included in the present publication.[1] Achievements and obstacles cited in these additional reports have also been reflected in the publication.

Notes

[1] Reports received after 31 December 1999 are from the following Member States: Bangladesh, Brazil, Bulgaria, Cambodia, Costa Rica, Cyprus, Estonia, Fiji, Haiti, Ireland, Malta, Mauritius, Papua New Guinea, Romania, San Marino, Sierra Leone, Slovak Republic, Thailand and Turkmenistan.

Part One

I. Background

A. The mandate

The General Assembly, in its resolutions 52/100 of 12 December 1997, and 52/231 of 4 June 1998, decided to convene a special session to review and assess the progress achieved in implementing the Nairobi Forward-looking Strategies for the Advancement of Women[2], and the Beijing Declaration[3] and Platform for Action (PfA).[4] The review and appraisal of progress was initiated at the forty-third session of the Commission on the Status of Women, in keeping with the Commission's multi-year work programme established in Economic and Social Council resolution 1996/6 of 22 July 1996. In that resolution, the Council also requested a report on the implementation of the Platform for Action, on the basis of national reports, taking into account the Nairobi Forward-looking Strategies for the Advancement of Women.

In its resolution 54/142 of 17 December 1999, the General Assembly reaffirmed the request of the Economic and Social Council and requested the Secretary-General to prepare, in time for the next session of the Commission on the Status of Women acting as the preparatory committee for the special session of the Assembly entitled "Women 2000: gender equality, development and peace for the twenty-first century" in the year 2000, *inter alia*, comprehensive reports on progress made in the implementation of the Platform for Action nationally, regionally and internationally, taking into account all relevant information and inputs available to the United Nations system, including national action plans, reports of the States parties to the Committee on the Elimination of Discrimination against Women under article 18 of the

Convention on the Elimination of All Forms of Discrimination against Women,[5] replies of Member States to the questionnaire of the Secretary-General,[6] statements made by delegations at relevant forums of the United Nations, reports of the regional commissions and other entities of the United Nations system and follow-up to recent global United Nations conferences. This report is an integral part of the review and appraisal of the progress made in implementing the Beijing Platform for Action and should be read in conjunction with document E/CN.6/2000/3, which represents the input of the United Nations system of organizations in achieving the goals of the Platform for Action.

B. Context of the Beijing Declaration and Platform for Action

The first United Nations World Conference on Women which was held in Mexico City in 1975, was followed by the United Nations Decade for Women: Equality, Development and Peace (1976-1985). The second conference (World Conference of the United Nations Decade for Women: Equality, Development and Peace), held in Copenhagen in 1980, adopted a Programme of Action for the Second Half of the United Nations Decade for Women: Equality, Development and Peace,[7] while the third conference, hosted by Kenya in 1985, adopted the Nairobi Forward-looking Strategies for the Advancement of Women to the Year 2000. The Fourth World Conference on Women held in Beijing in 1995 adopted the Beijing Declaration and Platform for Action. The successive United Nations conferences on women drew a growing number of women and men as active partners in respect of the global agenda for gender equality. Besides stimulating research, advocacy and policy efforts in promoting women's advancement, these conferences helped to increase awareness of the gender dimensions of equality, development and peace. "The women of the world have been the driving force to shape this agenda and move it forward" (thirteenth paragraph of closing statement by Boutros Boutros-Ghali, Secretary-General of the United Nations, at the Fourth World Conference on Women).[8]

The Beijing Declaration and Platform for Action were built on the consensus of 189 countries and constitute an agenda for fundamental change in the 12 critical areas of concern for achieving gender equality.

They are the product of a systematic process of dialogue and exchange within and among Governments, international organizations and civil society. The Platform for Action builds on commitments made during the United Nations Decade for Women, 1976-1985, *inter alia*, at the Nairobi Conference, as well as on the other related commitments and agreements achieved in the series of United Nations global summits and conferences held in the 1990s. These included the World Summit for Children (1990), the United Nations Conference on Environment and Development (1992), the World Conference on Human Rights (1993), the International Conference on Population and Development (1994) and the World Summit for Social Development (1995). It provided a strong framework for mainstreaming a gender equality dimension into the agenda of the conferences that followed, such as the United Nations Conference on Human Settlements (Habitat II) (1996) and the World Food Summit (1996).

The Beijing Platform for Action identifies strategic objectives for action and assigns responsibility to various actors. Governments are accorded primary responsibility for implementation, *inter alia*, in the creation of an enabling policy environment. The United Nations, including the regional commissions, and the organizations of the United Nations system, international organizations and institutions, women's groups and other non-governmental organizations (NGOs), and the private sector are also invited to contribute to the effective achievement of goals. The implementation of the Beijing Platform for Action requires interventions at international, regional and national levels, with clear linkages between actions at each level.

C. Intergovernmental mechanisms for the follow-up to the Beijing Conference

The General Assembly endorsed the Beijing Declaration and Platform for Action, and established a three-tiered intergovernmental mechanism, consisting of the Assembly, the Economic and Social Council and the Commission on the Status of Women to play the primary role in overall policy-making and follow-up, and in coordinating the implementation and monitoring of the Platform for Action.

The General Assembly, in addition to its targeted attention to the advancement of women and follow-up to the Beijing Platform for Action, continues to elaborate its overall emphasis on gender equality both as a means to the realization of the goals of other global conferences, and as an end in itself. To that end, the Assembly has directed all of its committees and bodies to mainstream a gender equality perspective. It has also drawn the attention of other bodies of the United Nations system to this strategy, and its practical implications for normative and policy developments and operational activities, in areas such as macroeconomic policy formulation, poverty eradication, human rights, humanitarian assistance, disarmament and peace.

The functional commissions of the Economic and Social Council, and the Council itself, have taken steps to contribute to the implementation of the Platform for Action and, in particular, to mainstream a gender equality perspective in their work. The Council, in exercising its overall coordination and management role, especially with regard to coordinated and integrated follow-up to United Nations conferences and summits, has provided clear guidance, and areas for further improvements, with respect to achieving the goals of the Beijing Declaration and Platform for Action.

Since 1996, the Commission on the Status of Women has reviewed each of the 12 critical areas of concern, making recommendations on concrete measures and effective instruments of public policy and planning to accelerate the implementation of the Platform for Action. In response to calls by both the World Conference on Human Rights and the Fourth World Conference on Women, the Commission elaborated an Optional Protocol to the Convention on the Elimination of All Forms of Discrimination against Women,[9] that is to say, a complaints mechanism thereto, which was adopted by the General Assembly at its fifty-fourth session and signed by 23 States on 10 December 1999. The Optional Protocol went into force on 22 December 2000 upon ratification by ten States parties.

D. Approaches underpinning the Platform for Action

A number of approaches were highlighted in the Platform for Action as important strategies for the promotion of women's advancement and achievement of gender equality. These include the mainstreaming strategy, the life-cycle approach, partnership between women and men, promotion and protection of human rights and integration of gender concerns in policies and programmes for sustainable development.

1. Gender mainstreaming

Mainstreaming a gender perspective into all areas of societal development was established as a global strategy for promoting gender equality in the Platform for Action. Mainstreaming involves ensuring that attention to gender equality is a central part of all interventions—analyses, policy development, advocacy, legislation, research, and the planning, implementation, monitoring and evaluation of projects and programmes.

The strategy of mainstreaming was further defined in Economic and Social Council agreed conclusions 1997/2[10] of 18 July 1997 (sect. I.A): "It is a strategy for making women's as well as men's concerns and experiences an integral dimension of the design, implementation, monitoring and evaluation of policies and programmes in all political, economic and societal spheres so that women and men benefit equally and inequality is not perpetuated. The ultimate goal is to achieve gender equality." These agreed conclusions established guiding principles for mainstreaming. Within the United Nations system, further impetus was given to the mainstreaming strategy through a letter of the Secretary-General dated 13 October 1997 addressed to the heads of all United Nations entities stressing the importance of mainstreaming and providing concrete directives. The General Assembly, in its resolution 52/100 of 12 December 1997, provided, *inter alia*, guidance on mainstreaming gender equality perspectives into programme budgets within the United Nations system.

Gender analysis was established as a basic requirement for the mainstreaming strategy. The current situation of women and men in relation to different issues/problems and the impact of planned policies, legislation, and projects and programmes on women and men respectively—and on the relations between them—should be analysed before any decisions are made. Gender analysis should go beyond cataloguing differences to identifying inequalities and assessing relationships between women and men. Gender analysis needs to be carried out at household and community levels. Within organizations, gender analysis is also required to assess the extent to which values, cultures, structures and procedures support promotion of gender equality.

Effective mainstreaming requires strong political commitment to the promotion of gender equality, in particular through the development of accountability mechanisms. The allocation of sufficient resources for mainstreaming, including, if necessary, additional financial and human resources, is important for the implementation of the strategy. Mainstreaming requires that attention to gender equality be explicit throughout processes and documents. The attention to gender equality should be coherent and sustained. The mainstreaming strategy is not limited to the social sectors or to some "soft" components of programmes and projects where women's contributions and needs are well established. It applies to all types of interventions, for example, economic policies and programmes, infrastructure development, urban development, poverty eradication, promotion of human rights and good governance—and at all levels: advocacy, analysis, policy development, legislation, and planning, implementation and monitoring of projects and programmes. Mainstreaming also recognizes that not only is achieving gender equality about providing assistance to women and incorporating women into existing structures, but it also requires transformative change.

The mainstreaming strategy does not exclude but rather complements the efforts and resources specifically targeted to women for promoting gender equality. Specific structures such as women's organizations, gender focal points and/or gender units continue to be necessary to support implementation of the mainstreaming strategy.

2. Life-cycle approach

The life-cycle approach considers life a continuum embodying phases within the life course and their distinct realities and needs. The life-cycle approach is used in the Platform for Action to capture the prevalence and incidence of discriminatory practices that affect women at different stages of life, and it has been widely applied in the areas of health and education.

The life-cycle approach provides a powerful analytical tool for capturing: (a) the common conditions that surround women's lives at a specific stage of life and, in this regard, the girl-child has been included in the Platform for Action among the critical areas of concern requiring special attention; (b) the transformations in the conditions and attributes of various stages of life as a result of changes in values, lifestyles, technology and so forth; for example, technological advances in bioengineering have had great impact on women's fertility patterns and medical advances have reversed adverse health conditions in all age groups and have increased life expectancy across the globe; (c) emerging new areas associated with specific life stage that may have been previously neglected or overlooked.

3. Partnerships between women and men

The attention to men in the Platform for Action is an indication of the important shift from an exclusive focus on women to a gender approach that focuses on both women and men and the relationships between them. A gender perspective is consistently utilized to compare the position and situation of women and men and the differences and disparities between them. The relationships between women and men are given specific attention, particularly in relation to sexuality and reproduction. Efforts to reduce negative gender stereotyping of women and men are encouraged and the Platform for Action calls for promotion of public debate on the new roles of women and men.

The need to ensure equal rights and opportunities for both women and men is a key focus in the Platform for Action. Particular emphasis is given to the sharing of family responsibilities by men. The Platform for Action calls on Governments to "... promote the equal sharing of responsibilities for the family by men and women, including through appropriate legislation, incentives and/or encouragement ..." (PfA, para. 179 (c)).

The Platform for Action also emphasizes the importance of equal partnerships between women and men in all areas of societal development.

The Platform for Action states clearly that "a transformed partnership based on equality between women and men is a condition for people-centred sustainable development" (PfA, para. 1). Men are encouraged to become more active advocates for gender equality. The Beijing Declaration states that Governments are determined to "encourage men to participate fully in all actions towards equality" (PfA, para. 25). Activities targeted specifically to men are also recommended in many areas to promote change in male attitudes and behaviour, as well as foster greater commitment of men to gender equality, particularly in the area of reproductive rights and health.

While it took a significant step forward in adopting a gender approach, the Platform for Action nevertheless does focus exclusively on women in much of its discussion. Greater attention to the role of men is critical since effective promotion of gender equality cannot be achieved unless men are brought along in the process of change. Effective inputs in the area of reproductive rights and health, family welfare and violence against women, for example, will be achieved only with changes in the attitudes and behaviour of men. Efforts to work with men must, however, always be put in the overall context of promoting gender equality and eliminating the adverse social and cultural values, institutional structures and processses that produce inequalities between women and men. Increased attention to men should not mean a deviation from committed support to women by reducing the funding available for women-targeted inputs. Nor should it suggest the abandonment of support to women's individual or collective initiatives.

4. Human rights

The Platform for Action reaffirms the fundamental principles of the Programme of Action adopted by the World Conference on Human Rights[11] held in Vienna in 1993, namely, that the human rights of women and the girl-child are an inalienable, integral and indivisible part of universal human rights. In addition to identifying the human rights of women as one of its critical areas of concern, as an agenda for action, the Platform for Action seeks to promote and protect the human rights and the fundamental freedoms of all women throughout their life cycle (PfA, para. 2). Towards this end, the Governments participating in the Fourth World Conference on Women recognized, in the Beijing

Declaration, that women's rights are human rights (PfA, para. 14) and committed themselves to ensuring the full implementation of the human rights of women and of the girl-child (PfA, para. 9).

The Platform for Action highlights the gains to be realized by society as a whole from increased equality between women and men. It states, that "the advancement of women and the achievement of equality between women and men are a matter of human rights and a condition for social justice ... They are the only way to build a sustainable, just and developed society" (PfA, para. 41). At the same time, the Platform for Action acknowledges that full enjoyment by women of all human rights is an important end in itself and critical to their empowerment and autonomy, and the improvement of their political, social, economic and health status. Recognizing that the elimination of discrimination on the basis of sex and women's equal enjoyment of human rights and fundamental freedoms on the same basis as men do not occur automatically, the Platform for Action advocates an approach where these goals are addressed explicitly at all stages of their implementation. This approach—the rights-based approach—informs the Platform for Action and is also the subject of one of its critical areas of concern, namely, the human rights of women, and it has become, since Beijing, an overarching goal embracing all critical areas of concern.

5. Development

The Beijing Platform for Action underscored the need for a holistic approach to all aspects of development: growth, equality between women and men, social justice, conservation and protection of the environment, sustainability, solidarity, participation, peace and respect for human rights (PfA, para. 14). The Platform for Action also underlined the importance of a continued search for ways of assuring people-centred sustainable development (PfA, para. 17).

The Platform for Action's understanding of development corresponds to the approach of the United Nations Development Programme (UNDP) Human Development Reports of the 1990s. These reports focused on development as a process that aims to enlarge people's choices and enhance equal access to opportunities, ensure sustainability of physical, human, financial and environmental resources, enhance a people-centred macroeconomic environment and empower people to take initiative in activities, events and processes that shape their lives. The linkages between development and peacekeeping and reconstruction in conflict areas were also highlighted in the Platform for Action. A stronger focus on security of people, or their freedom from fear and freedom from want, is essential for full implementation of the Platform for Action.

Notes

[2] *Report of the World Conference to Review and Appraise the Achievements of the United Nations Decade for Women: Equality, Development and Peace, Nairobi, 15-26 July 1985* (United Nations publication, Sales No. E.85.IV.10), chap. I, sect. A.

[3] *Report of the Fourth World Conference on Women, Beijing, 4-15 September 1995* (United Nations publication, Sales No. E.96.IV.13), chap. I, resolution 1, annex I.

[4] Ibid., annex II.

[5] General Assembly resolution 34/180, annex.

[6] A/54/264, para. 49.

[7] *Report of the World Conference of the United Nations Decade for Women: Equality, Development and Peace, Copenhagen, 14-30 July 1980* (United Nations publication, Sales No. E.80.IV.3 and corrigendum), chap. I, sect. A.

[8] *Report of the Fourth World Conference on Women, op. cit.*, annex III.

[9] General Assembly resolution 54/4, annex.

[10] ECOSOC Agreed Conclusions 1997/2, *Official Records of the General Assembly, Fifty-second Session, Supplement No. 3* (A/52/3/Rev.1 and Add.1), chap. IV, sect. A, para. 4.

[11] A/CONF.157/24 (Part I), chap. III.

II. Overview of trends in the implementation of the Beijing Platform for Action

A. Introduction

The Platform for Action invited Governments to develop strategies or plans of action for its implementation (PfA, para. 297). The United Nations Secretariat has received national action plans from 116 Member States, two observer States and five regional or subregional groups. Syntheses of these plans were provided to the Commission on the Status of Women in 1998 and 1999.[12] The areas most frequently described in national action plans were education and training (86 per cent), followed by power and decision-making (85 per cent) and health (80 per cent).

Four years after the Beijing Conference, Governments were asked to report on their actions to implement the Platform for Action in each of 12 critical areas of concern. As indicated above, as of 29 December 1999, a total of 133 out of 185 Member States, and two observers had responded to the questionnaire prepared by the Secretariat in collaboration with the five regional commissions and sent out in October 1998. Since that time, responses have been received from an additional 19 Member States, bringing the total responses to 154. Lists of countries that responded and their regional distribution are included in the Annex. In order to include the experience of as many Member States as possible, the overview incorporates information from other reports to the Division for the Advancement of Women, where relevant. It also incorporates evaluation reports prepared by the secretariats of the Economic Commission for Africa (ECA), the Economic Commission for Europe (ECE) and the Economic Commission for Latin America and the Caribbean (ECLAC), the Economic and Social Commission for Asia and the Pacific (ESCAP) and the Economic and Social Commission for Western Asia (ESCWA) on the basis of the replies to the questionnaire.

The responses are diverse in terms of the nature and content of information provided, with some Member States providing comprehensive sex-disaggregated statistical annexes or background papers in their reports, and others including some data disaggregated by sex in discussions of critical areas of concern, particularly decision-making and education. In the responses to the questionnaire, the most prevalent priorities were the areas of power and decision-making and health (84 per cent), which ranked high in all regions, followed by women and poverty (80 per cent), especially among African countries (98 per cent). The area of violence against women was an additional priority (79 per cent), especially among countries in transition (91 per cent), as were education and training of women (79 per cent) and women and the economy (77 per cent).

The present overview summarizes the main trends in implementation of the Platform for Action, in terms of changes in policy, legislation, institutions and programmes initiated by Governments to comply with the strategic objectives set forth in the 12 critical areas of concern of the Platform for Action. It draws primarily on the government responses to the questionnaire. Part Two of this report contains analyses of developments, including indicative country examples, in each of the 12 critical areas of concern.

Profound changes in the status and role of women have occurred in the years since the start of the United Nations Decade for Women in 1976, some more markedly since the Fourth World Conference on Women. During that time, women have entered the labour force in unprecedented numbers, actually or potentially increasing their ability to participate in economic decision-making at all levels, starting with the household. Women, individually and collectively, have been major actors in the rise of civil society throughout the world, stimulating pressure for increased awareness of the gender equality dimensions of all issues, and demanding a role in national and global decision-making processes.

As the responses from Governments indicate, progress in terms of benchmarks for women's status, including fertility rates, rates of infant and maternal mortality, immunization rates, women's literacy and school enrolment, has been uneven. Although these benchmarks showed improvements in many cases, there was also stagnation and even decline in some countries, particularly in those experiencing conflicts or political or economic transition. However, even where women were most adversely impacted by such factors, there was growing recognition among Member States that the promotion of gender equality was essential to finding solutions to development challenges.

Change in the way societies view the issue of gender equality was evident in almost all of the responses received, frequently as a result of the high level of attention given to the outcome of the Beijing Conference by Governments, non-governmental organizations, the international community and the media. In particular, many specific awareness-raising campaigns about the issue of violence against women were undertaken by Member States following Beijing. As a result, in most regions domestic violence, once regarded as a private matter, has become a public issue and therefore a concern of the State, although public opinion may lag behind legislation and governmental policies. Perhaps most positively, in many countries women's equality with men is now seen as a prerequisite for the achievement of sustainable human development.

A major factor in putting the concerns of women and gender equality on to the national and international agenda has been the recognition of non-governmental organizations, especially women's non-governmental organizations, as partners in national development. In some cases, this has come about in response to gaps in Governments' ability to provide basic services. In others, non-governmental organization networks have taken on national-level challenges, particularly in terms of advocacy for policy or legislative changes. In some countries, women's national peace networks have been created in response to ongoing conflicts. In some regions where civil society has historically been weak, the Beijing Conference spurred the emergence of a large number of women's non-governmental organizations committed to putting the concerns of women and gender equality in the national agenda. In other regions, this process began earlier, during the United Nations Decade for Women, and accelerated after the Nairobi Conference; and the period since Beijing has been characterized by a shift from a primarily advocacy role by many non-governmental organizations to one of cooperation and partnership with Governments. The important role of non-governmental organizations, including women's non-governmental organizations, in monitoring progress and implementation was recognized in the actions and policies of Member States in all regions. In addition, the non-governmental organization role in raising awareness of gender issues in areas such as health, education, employment, media and family relations was recognized and appreciated.

Some responses from Member States note that the existence of an improved understanding of gender equality does not necessarily automatically translate into gender equality in practice. Despite progress, the persistence of traditional and stereotypic gender roles, often reinforced by legal and/or institutional structures, impedes women's empowerment. Promotion of gender equality continues to be relegated to a lower level of national priority, with the result that resources for activities to implement the Platform for Action, are often in short supply. Much more work needs to be done, at every level, to create the enabling environment envisioned in the Platform for Action, in which women's rights are recognized as an indispensable part of human rights and women as well as men have the opportunity to realize their full potential.

B. Achievements in implementation

The initiatives for achieving progress in the implementation of the Platform for Action are reviewed under the following categories: 1. policy change; 2. legal change; 3. institutional change; 4. programme-level changes; 5. the generation and dissemination of knowledge; and 6. resource allocation.

1. Policy change

An important shift in government policy following the Beijing Conference has been the recognition of a gender equality approach to policy design, formulation and implementation, and consequent efforts to refocus policies in order to achieve gender equality in all sectors. This policy shift was reflected in the responses of many reporting countries in their efforts to mainstream a gender equality perspective into national policies for poverty eradication as well as to review macroeconomic policies from a gender equality perspective.

Responses indicated that policy makers have started to operate within the broad framework of sustainable human development, taking account of the need for equal opportunities and choices for women and men so as to ensure a healthy, long and creative life that can be enjoyed in freedom and dignity. Policies tend to be defined more in terms of the needs and interests of women and men, and with a view to contributing to the improvement of their lives. These shifts in policy design and implementation have required greater attention to gender equality issues and made them more visible. Recognizing disparities resulting from gender-based inequalities within households, Governments have sought to transform social and economic norms leading to women's social subordination or economic exclusion. Responses indicate that policy formulation now focuses on gender differences and disparities in various areas including basic education, health services and life expectancy. Policies also focus on the socially constructed constraints on the choices of various groups of women and men, and have become more diverse in that they target different groups of women. Many countries reported on their efforts to implement more comprehensive policies directed to the achievement of gender equality in education, training and employment, as well as the provision of equal access to capital and productive resources.

Policies to increase women's equal participation in all levels of political and economic decision-making were undertaken in many countries, including the setting of quotas for women's representation in State and municipal bodies and civil service occupations. Although in some cases, such quotas were guaranteed by law, more typically they reflected government policy commitments and institutional change. In some cases, Governments also encouraged political parties to recruit more women and consider quotas in the selection of candidates for office.

Other policies adopted by Governments included the establishment of national data banks for the recruitment of women or efforts to strengthen the capacity of women's non-governmental organizations to encourage greater participation by women in public life.

Some countries reported on policy measures to encourage the entry of women into decision-making in the private sector. These included use of a policy of "flexible quota regulations" implemented in the civil service as a model for the private sector, and preferential allocation of government contracts to agencies or firms with a specific percentage of women employees and women in decision-making positions.

In many regions, the shift away from State-regulated trade and investment to market-led development has necessitated the formulation of new policies to influence or regulate the private sector, in particular in regard to income and employment opportunities for women. Several Governments have reviewed existing policies, but only a few have introduced concrete incentives, such as subsidies for businesses that establish childcare facilities, or special equality allowances as part of national income policy agreements.

Employment policies in many countries have sought to address the increased participation of women in the labour force. Some Member States have introduced new opportunities for part-time, flexible and informal sector work, while others have initiated efforts to regulate such work, which typically lacks health, pension and other work-related benefits.

2. Legal change

Legislative reforms have been among the most visible actions taken by Governments following Beijing. Since September 1995, 19 States have ratified the Convention on the Elimination of All Forms of Discrimination against Women, bringing the total number of States parties to the instrument to 166 as of 31 December 2000. On 6 October 1999, in further implementation of the Platform for Action (PfA, para. 230 (k)), the Optional Protocol to the Convention was adopted by the General Assembly.[13]

Several countries have incorporated the Convention in their constitutions, a number stipulating that the Convention takes precedence over national legislation. Sex equality provisions were incorporated in several constitutions while, in others, the constitution was amended to direct the inclusion of a gender equality perspective in national planning. Legislation has been reviewed and/or amended to address discriminatory provisions in areas ranging from civil, family and marriage law to criminal, labour, social security, health and education legislation.

The elimination, prevention, and punishment of violence against women were a major focus of attention. The Inter-American Convention on the Prevention, Punishment and Eradication of Violence Against Women (Convention of Belém do Pará)[14] as of 31 December 2000 has been ratified by 25 of the 35 Member States of the Organization of American States (OAS), ten since Beijing. In their responses, six Latin American and Caribbean States specifically cited the signing of this Convention as an achievement. Also, two Member States from the African region noted among their achievements the signing of the African Charter on Human and Peoples' Rights.[15]

A significant number of countries amended criminal codes or introduced legislation recognizing domestic violence as a crime, with several defining marital rape as a crime, and specifying punishment for perpetrators. Penalties for rape and sexual assault have been increased in several countries, and procedural and evidentiary reforms with regard to these crimes were introduced to ensure prosecution and to protect victims.

States noted that they had introduced legislation outlawing trafficking in women and prohibiting the sexual exploitation of children. Several States, including some with large immigrant and refugee populations, introduced legislation to address traditional practices harmful to women and girls, including female genital mutilation and sexual servitude. Several countries recognized gender-based persecution as a basis for refugee status.

Legislation was amended in several countries to provide for the equal division of marital property between both spouses, to increase the legal age of marriage for women and/or to grant women equal rights with men with respect to conveying their nationality to children.

Several Member States in all regions introduced or amended legislation to address sex discrimination in employment. New measures included prohibition of sex-specific employment advertisements, of the requirement of proof of sterilization or infertility as a condition of employment and of dismissal on the grounds of pregnancy, and provisions to confront sexual harassment in the workplace. Laws were also introduced providing for paid maternity and/or parental leave, and regulating conditions of part-time work, wages and hours for women working in private homes, and public sector contracts.

Several countries established provisions requiring the same standard of working conditions afforded to women nationals to be extended to immigrant and migrant women workers, as well as the same protection against gender-based violence.

Social security legislation was reviewed and/or modified in several countries to eliminate gender inequalities for women who took time away from the workforce to raise children or to provide for widows who remarried.

Women's property and ownership rights, *inter alia,* with regard to land tenure, were introduced, reviewed and/or revised in several different regions with a view to their achieving equality with men. Laws relating to education were revised to enshrine sex equality, incorporate human rights into the curriculum and/or prevent sexual harassment in schools. In several regions, laws were introduced to entitle pregnant school girls to remain in, or return to, school.

Legal provisions were introduced in many countries to ensure or expand women's access to quality health care, including prenatal and post-partum care as well as family planning. Several countries have reviewed punitive provisions relating to termination of pregnancy.

Laws designed to increase women's political participation were introduced in many countries. The constitutions of several States were amended to guarantee a specified percentage or proportion of seats for women in parliament, and in local and municipal government.

Several Member States introduced legislative measures that, although not targeted directly to women, are expected to greatly benefit them. For example, laws increasing the minimum wage should improve the status of women because of women's tendency to be clustered in low-wage jobs. Laws increasing the number of years of compulsory education should especially benefit girls, as girls more often leave school after fulfilling compulsory education requirements.

3. Institutional change

National machineries were restructured or upgraded in many countries in an effort to make them stronger and more coherent. Several were upgraded from bureaux or desks to departments within Governments. Others were upgraded from departmental to ministerial or cabinet level. In some cases, women's organizations urged governments to designate a separate ministry of women's affairs, a status already enjoyed by the national machinery in some countries. A few Member States reported on the designation of an established women's non-governmental organization as the official national machinery, with the authority to develop and implement national action plans. Women's advisory committees were set up in the legislatures or national planning departments of some countries.

Inter-ministerial committees, often including representatives of political parties and non-governmental organizations, were established to mainstream a gender equality perspective within development planning or to review aspects of gender inequality in targeted areas, such as health and employment.

In several countries, units were established in different ministries at federal or state level to focus on eliminating inequality in specific areas, for example, in national planning offices, in ministries of trade and industry, and in ministries of education and justice.

Monitoring bodies, independent of the national machinery and typically including women's non-governmental organizations, were set up to monitor implementation of national plans of action in some countries, and training courses on monitoring and appraisal of national plans of action were introduced.

The gender balance in legislative institutions and judicial bodies has improved in several countries, *inter alia,* through the establishment of quotas for women. The number of women justices on several supreme courts has increased. There have been affirmative action measures for promoting women in the public service in some countries, and similar measures have been set in others with regard to faculty members in schools and universities. Educational quotas have been instituted in other countries to increase the enrolment of girls, *inter alia*, in tertiary institutions and in centres for non-formal education and literacy training.

Several countries have initiated awareness-raising and gender aware-ness training in an effort to change institutional culture in agencies and departments. In particular, efforts to sensitize the police and the judici-ary to gender equality concerns, such as violence against women, have been implemented.

Women's police desks were established in several countries in order to encourage women to report incidents of sexual assault or domestic violence. A number of countries set up or strengthened women's police stations or located women's rights offices or domestic violence units within their police forces.

Ombudsperson's offices were established in a number of countries, especially in Latin America, *inter alia*, with authority to deal with hu-man rights complaints. Some have separate offices or ombudspersons on women's human rights.

Some countries established family courts to deal with gender equality issues, including domestic violence. In some cases, these courts have been given the authority to join related litigation so as to reduce pres-sures on women plaintiffs.

Microfinance institutions were established or restructured in many countries, especially in Africa and in Asia, to facilitate the extension of loans and credit to women operating microenterprises or to women who intended to launch small enterprises. The requirement that women ob-tain consent from male relatives as a condition of receiving credit has been abolished in several countries, while in others credit alternatives have been made available.

4. Programme-level changes

Programmes were initiated in many Member States to implement all critical areas of concern of the Platform for Action. These consisted of special programmes for women, and of efforts to mainstream gender equality perspectives in programmes.

Steps were taken to assist women in translating legal rights into reality in many countries. These included the introduction of courses to im-prove women's legal literacy or awareness of their rights, the estab-lishment of legal clinics and the provision of legal assistance for women on a wide range of issues, including domestic violence. Governments increased their support for women's shelters, crisis centres and legal assistance clinics.

Childcare centres were established and childcare subsidies and services introduced. Programmes to support single parents and/or women heads of households, including income and childcare support, were launched in several countries. Evening schools for young mothers were also created.

Training programmes on domestic violence were conducted for health professionals, law enforcement personnel and other officials. Awareness-raising campaigns were carried out in developed and developing countries, while long-term research into the incidence and types of violence as well as its causes and consequences was initiated.

Member States in all regions launched public awareness campaigns and other measures to counter persisting gender-biased attitudes and beliefs, as well as discriminatory cultural norms. Among these were campaigns to change the negative representation of women in the media, zero tolerance campaigns against violence against women, and campaigns emphasizing the importance of education for the girl-child.

Countries launched programmes to counteract gender-role stereotypes of women and men in the media, including entertainment, news and/or advertisements. Several used the media to change values and perceptions of women and encourage the participation of men in childcare and household responsibilities. Various efforts were made to counter gender socialization in education. Measures were introduced to increase girls' participation in science and technology. School curricula or textbooks were revised to eliminate gender stereotypes, and materials designed to increase gender awareness of teachers and educators were introduced.

Efforts were made to encourage women to voice their concerns and interests as matters of public importance in a number of countries through television and radio programmes as well as journals and magazines devoted to women's issues and concerns.

Several Member States introduced programmes directed at men, including several to increase male involvement in health and reproductive decision-making and to encourage them to take parental leave in order to care for children. Several States set up programmes emphasizing the education and participation of both women and men in efforts to eliminate sexual assault and/or domestic violence.

Programmes to improve the status of women in rural areas, often in connection with programmes to safeguard the environment, were set up in countries in all regions. These focused on research and training, technical and financial assistance, food security programmes and/or support for the recognition of women's traditional knowledge. Some States opened secondary schools in rural areas, in order to improve rural women's opportunities for education.

Programmes focused on improving women's small business ownership were set up in many countries, including training in business and microenterprise management and marketing, as were programmes to improve women's access to credit. Revolving funds and non-governmental organization-supported credit and loan schemes for women were supported by Governments in many countries. Women's business centres were created.

Programmes to assist women refugees and displaced persons were established. Programmes to protect the rights of immigrant women and migrant women workers, especially regarding labour rights and working conditions, have been set up, as have programmes to improve nutrition of agricultural day labourers, particularly women, children and the elderly. Training programmes for embassy and consular staff, especially those involved in immigration, have been introduced by several States in order to protect immigrant and migrant women workers.

The mainstreaming strategy, an approach for incorporating both women's and men's experiences, concerns and needs as an integral part of the design and implementation of policies and programmes, was discussed in many responses to the questionnaire. A number of Member States have stipulated that gender equality perspectives should be incorporated into their planning and development of administrative frameworks and budget allocations. Other countries have tested the mainstreaming strategy in specific priority areas, such as health, education and employment, as well as in national budgeting. Some Member States mandated mainstreaming gender equality within the State machinery.

Some of the responses to the questionnaire discussed issues relating to the methodologies utilized in the mainstreaming strategy. Several Commonwealth countries, for example, have adopted a technique for mainstreaming developed by the Commonwealth Secretariat called the

Gender Management System. Within the European Union (EU) the use of specific EU guidelines on mainstreaming was also reported.

Many responses suggested that the concept of mainstreaming was still not well understood, and that its advantages were not made sufficiently clear. In some cases, it was stated that the concept had been understood more clearly at the theoretical level than in practice.

Some Member States indicated that utilization of the mainstreaming strategy had helped to reduce previous assumptions that some areas of development had no gender equality implications and the tendency to simply ignore the specific concerns and needs of women, for example, in the area of poverty elimination and in health policies.

Little information was available on the financial implications of the mainstreaming strategy. It is therefore not possible to assess the impact on women and on men of budget allocations that are not specifically targeted to increasing gender equality. In recent years, however, there have been concerted efforts in a number of countries to examine the impact of national budget allocations on women and men and the promotion of gender equality.

5. Generation and dissemination of knowledge

Government-supported research institutes and documentation centres were set up in many countries in all regions to further the knowledge and dissemination of information and research on women, including gender equality as well as the gender equality dimension of economic and social issues, thereby legitimizing the importance of women's studies.

Women's studies programmes and/or departments were set up in colleges and universities in countries worldwide. Members of these departments are engaged in research, data gathering and publishing on specific gender equality issues. They also participate in efforts to review and revise school curricula and textbooks.

Governments directed ministries to collect and disseminate sex-disaggregated data in specific areas of concern, including education, health, employment and the reduction of poverty, as well as to focus attention on immigrants and refugees. Plans to revise national income statistics to include unpaid labour in the household have been initiated in some countries.

Research projects on the gender equality dimensions of political, social and economic issues were inaugurated in different countries, some focusing on images of women in art, culture and television, and others on the health and well-being of children, including girls. Several addressed conflict and peace, including the role of women in peace-making and how the conflict resolution process affects women and men differently. Studies on the situation of refugee women, on the impact of structural adjustment on women, on the relationship of women and power, and on women and natural resource management have been initiated.

6. Resource allocation

The allocation of resources to implement national plans of action is one of the most difficult areas to assess. Enormous differences in wealth and resources between countries, particularly those hard hit by natural disasters, disease and famine, as well as economic transition, financial crises and armed conflicts, make comparisons impossible. With regard to resource allocation strategies, however, three trends could be seen in the responses of Member States.

In some responses to the questionnaire, there were no indications of separate allocation of budget resources for achievement of Platform for Action goals. While this constrained implementation in many critical areas of concern, some progress was reported in situations where measures were taken to improve women's access to services provided within the existing national budgets, such as State-supported education, child-care, health care and old-age benefits.

In some countries, resources were targeted to specific projects or to improve the status of women within a specific sector. Such allocations included, for example, the provision of housing and other services to women heads of household, the creation of women's health programmes in many countries in both the North and the South, the provision of financial and technical resources to women, and the extension of credit and loans to women's small businesses in countries at all levels of development.

In a few countries, efforts were made to mainstream gender equality perspectives throughout the budget process in all spending areas, not just certain sectors. Countries that fell into this category structured gender equality perspectives into their budgets in different ways. These ranged from a government mandate that all departments allocate a minimum of 5 per cent of their total annual budget to programmes and projects promoting gender equality, to government instructions that all ministries take gender equality perspectives into consideration and initiate and fund projects designed to implement gender equality.

Member State responses showed that the methodology for measuring resource allocation varied greatly. Many countries reported the amounts allocated to the national machinery and others cited total allocations to women's programmes overall. Some countries also reported allocations for several years, thereby showing how these had increased or decreased since Beijing. There was no comprehensive discussion of how budget allocations that had not been specifically targeted to promotion of gender equality affected women and men respectively. Recently, however, in response to pressure from both international and national women's non-governmental organizations, preliminary efforts to examine the impact of such budget allocations on both women and men have been initiated in some countries.

In order to make their figures more meaningful, a few States also endeavoured to estimate the percentage of the national budget allocated to the implementation of the Platform for Action. In countries that reported the percentage of the national budget allocated to the national machinery the figure was well under 1 per cent in every case except one, where it was 1.61 per cent. In those countries that estimated the percentage of national budget allocated to women's programmes, the estimates were higher, ranging from 0.5 to 2.6 per cent.

Among those Member States that experienced great difficulties in finding new resources, a number of measures have been taken to increase allocations in support of gender equality. These include women's component plans that aim to ensure that set percentages of development funds flow to women, special women's development funds that mandate government departments to support women's organizations, and social funds established to cushion the effects of structural adjustment policies on the poor, in particular through specific allocations to women's programmes.

In a significant number of developing countries, much of the programmatic implementation of the Platform for Action commitments was done through funds from United Nations organizations or other international development agencies. Without such assistance, few resources would have been available for improving the status of women.

C. Obstacles to implementation

As stated in most of the responses to the questionnaire, the decade of the 1990s has been characterized by profound political, social and economic changes, many of which impacted negatively on women and impeded efforts to implement the Platform for Action. Challenges to implementation included: 1. conflict and human displacement; 2. economic instability and change; 3. institutional discrimination against women; 4. the persistence of gender stereotypes and negative attitudes towards women; 5. the absence of targets, data and monitoring mechanisms; and 6. the shortage of financial and technical resources.

1. Conflict and human displacement

Ethnic and national conflicts, especially of an intra-State nature, hampered progress in the achievement of gender equality, and full health and well-being for women and girls. The traumatic effects of these conflicts were exacerbated by sexual violence. That these conflicts also generated large flows of refugees and displaced persons, the majority of whom were women and children, placed financial burdens on States already suffering from resource constraints. Ongoing political instability was also cited as an obstacle to implementation of the Platform for Action in several countries, as human and financial resources in time of such conflicts tended to be diverted from other important sectors.

2. Economic change and instability

Economic change and instability were reported as an obstacle to improving the status of women in several regions. Many countries reported on the negative impact of the Asian financial crisis. For example, rising prices and falling household incomes greatly increased women's difficulties in providing for their families, increasing poverty and causing them to migrate in search of employment. The feminization of poverty, often aggravated by natural disaster and crop failure, was cited by several Member States in Africa and Asia as an obstacle to improving gender equality.

Social problems resulting from economic crises and structural adjustment policies, including the elimination of protective tariffs and cuts in government spending on social services, were cited by several Member States as obstacles to implementation. Women were especially affected by the resulting loss of jobs in the State sector, and incurred increased responsibility for household caregiving. Debt repayment obligations consumed as much as 40-45 per cent of the annual budgets of some countries, limiting the resources available for internal needs, including women's. Trade liberalization also had a negative impact on women owing to falling prices and declining job opportunities in sectors where women had been employed.

The shift from centrally planned to market-oriented economies, resulting in loss of jobs and declining wages in many sectors, was cited as a major obstacle to Governments' ability to bring about positive change in the status of women. Countries in transition reported increases in women's unemployment and a decline in women's income along with a decline in women's political participation, often as a result of the elimination of electoral quotas. Some countries noted deterioration in indicators on women's status, including rising maternal and infant mortality rates, declining female literacy rates and declining educational enrolment of girls. Increased dependency by women on partners or spouses, and an increase in cases of violence against women were also noted.

3. Discriminatory practices

Countries in all regions pointed to the persistence of institutionalized gender discrimination as an obstacle to the implementation of the Platform for Action. Specific manifestations included occupational discrimination and segregation, which contribute to a persistent wage gap between women and men, the failure to promote women to higher levels of authority or decision-making, and the expectation in the family and the workplace that women will retain primary responsibility for household and reproductive tasks.

Among Member States in the developing world, it was noted that women's inability to access financial credit and loans for small businesses, owing to lack of assets and resources, was due to persistent legal, social and economic discrimination against women, and that this thus undermined women's economic enterprises as well as government efforts to support them.

4. Attitudes, beliefs and stereotypes

The persistence of cultural and social norms, traditional beliefs and negative gender stereotypes was the most frequently cited obstacle to the achievement of gender equality in all regions. Examples range from the continued devaluation of women's labour in the home to the belief that women are the responsibility of the husband or male relative. These attitudes and beliefs impede the transformation of legal rights into practical reality for women, and serve to keep women ignorant of their rights.

These attitudes also perpetuate traditional practices, customs, and social and cultural norms prejudicial to women, such as violence against women, polygamy, forced marriage, son preference and so-called honour killings. These attitudes also create a pervasive climate of discrimination, incorporating rigid social codes that entrench stereotypic ideas relating to the roles of women in the family and their participation in public life as well as to appropriate work for women.

Economic, social and cultural changes in many countries have caused a strengthening of stereotypic attitudes towards women. Values overemphasizing the traditional role of women as wives and mothers have reasserted themselves, as have those recognizing men as the breadwinner and head of the family. These attitudes and beliefs perpetuate existing gender discrimination in the labour market, and have also led to the introduction of protectionist legislation that operates to disadvantage women in a market economy. They have perpetuated, or led to the introduction of, policies that discourage the participation of fathers in family life, childcare and the equal sharing of family responsibilities. Moreover, the persistence of stereotypic attitudes and beliefs discourages women from asserting their rights through legal and political processes.

The reported cases of a hardening of attitudes towards women as a result of their growing visibility in public life and the increased recognition of the value of their work, are a cause for serious concern. For example, some countries cited that negative reactions to the advancement of women in the area of employment had led to increased harassment in the workplace, including sexual harassment. Fears were raised that laws on equal pay could lead to reduced employment opportunities for women. The clear cases of resentment towards women in public office that have been reported may have impeded the ability of some Member States to bring about significant change in political participation. An example was cited where a law mandating quotas for women's representation in local and national government had to be repealed owing to negative reactions; in other cases, proposals to introduce similar legislation failed. The reported increase in negative stereotypes of women in the media by several Member States was identified as another cause for concern.

5. Targets, data and monitoring mechanisms

In many countries, implementation of the Platform for Action was impeded by absence of specific targets or the widespread assumption that gender equality is the exclusive responsibility of the national machineries. Several of the responses stated that gender equality was seen as peripheral to government concerns or was pushed off the agenda by other urgent priorities.

The need for monitoring and accountability measures to ensure effective implementation of all policies and programmes was noted in the responses of many Member States, and their absence was considered an obstacle to improving the status of women in many countries, especially developing countries.

Although many countries undertook new surveys and data collection in different areas of concern, lack of data disaggregated by sex and age was frequently mentioned as an obstacle.

6. Resource shortages

The problem of insufficient resources was cited by Member States in all regions, especially those in the developing world. Such problems delayed the development of infrastructure as well as the implementation of new initiatives in all areas of concern, and were particularly acute in rural areas. In education and health especially, resource problems—including, for example, lack of transport, shortages of supplies and lack of capacity—were frequently cited.

It was also noted in some responses that the apparent declining priority given to gender-sensitive programmes by the United Nations system and other international agencies in recent years had resulted in cutbacks in funds earmarked for gender equality and development and that this in turn had meant few resources were available for implementation of the Platform for Action in Member States.

D. Conclusions

A major issue that emerges from the government reports on efforts to implement the Platform for Action is the challenge posed by the multi-faceted impact of globalization. The reorganization of world economic relations, new structures of economic decision-making and international finance that transcend national borders, and resulting financial crises, have seriously challenged the ability of Governments, particularly those in the least developed countries, to direct financial and human resources to the implementation of Platform for Action commitments. A major concern for many Member States is that they continue to be obliged to allocate large portions of their national budgets to debt repayments, requiring cutbacks in spending for public services. This situation presents a new challenge to the international community to make available adequate financial resources to enable States to implement the commitments to the promotion of gender equality made at Beijing and at other United Nations conferences.

The frequent references to a lack of national resources to implement Platform for Action commitments and declining development assistance make it imperative that innovative approaches to the allocation of existing resources be employed, not only by Governments but also by their partners in the non-governmental organization and private sectors and within the international community. Gender analysis of national budgets, including national security and defence, needs to be carried out to determine the impact of budget expenditure on women and men separately. Such analyses are necessary if budget processes are to address gender equality and existing resources are to be utilized in a gender-sensitive manner.

Governments in all regions reported that efforts to improve women's participation in the public sphere had been undermined by women's disproportionate domestic responsibilities. The lack of sharing of responsibilities between women and men in the private sphere needs to be addressed as a serious constraint on women's advancement in the public sphere. In countries that lack the resources to offer household and family support services, such as State-funded childcare centres, incentives need to be devised to encourage men to take more responsibility for household and reproductive tasks. Addressing the deep-seated stereotypes built up around masculine and feminine roles is also a priority repeatedly cited by Member States as obstacles to implementation of the Platform for Action.

The reports re-emphasized the importance of multifaceted approaches and of developing enabling policy environments as well as specific programmes on gender equality. The ways in which progress or decline in one area of concern affects the status of others highlight the importance of a more holistic approach. For example, the fact that, as poverty increases, household strategies rely more heavily on child labour, has implications for the effectiveness of legislation and policies on school enrolment.

The lack of clear time-bound targets for all areas except education, health, poverty and human rights suggests that Governments and non-governmental organizations should cooperate to devise realistic targets and ways of measuring progress for all the critical areas of concern. Despite observations on the "feminization of poverty", for example, the methodologies for measuring poverty among women respective to men are still inadequate. A number of countries reported that they had begun to study the measurement and valuing of unpaid labour in the household. An important next step is the translation of the knowledge gained into policies in the public and private sectors.

One area requiring increased attention is the gender dimensions of human immunodeficiency virus/acquired immunodeficiency syndrome (HIV/AIDS). The increasing toll of the disease among women has become an issue of global importance. Female-controlled methods of prevention need to be developed. The fact that caregiving responsibilities are required of women worldwide needs to be taken into account in the development of policies and strategies.

Overall, analysis of the implementation of the Platform for Action revealed that there had been no major breakthroughs with regard to equal sharing of decision-making in political structures at national and international levels. In most countries of the world, representation of women in decision-making structures remains low. Even in countries where a "critical mass" in decision-making positions within the public sector has been achieved, there are few women on boards of directors of major business corporations. There is need for more careful monitoring of progress in ensuring women's equitable participation in these positions of economic power.

Notes

[12] E/CN.6/1998/6 and E/CN.6/1999/2/Add.1, respectively.

[13] DAW website http://www.un.org/womenwatch/daw/cedaw/sigop.htm for updated information on signatories and ratifications/accessions of the Optional Protocol to the Convention on the Elimination of All Forms of Discrimination against Women.

[14] *Human Rights: A Compilation of International Instruments*, vol. II, *Regional Instruments* (United Nations publication, Sales No. E.97.XIV.1), sect. A.7.

[15] United Nations, *Treaty Series*, vol. 1520, No. 26363.

Part Two

I. Critical areas of concern of the Platform for Action

A. Women and poverty

1. Introduction

In 1995, at the World Summit for Social Development in Copenhagen, and at the Fourth World Conference on Women in Beijing, Governments committed themselves to implementing concrete actions in order to eradicate poverty. In Beijing, the international community recognized expressly that women and men experienced poverty differently and unequally and became impoverished through different processes. If these differences are not taken into account, the causes of poverty cannot be understood or dealt with by public actions. Women are in a more disadvantaged position because they have the dual need of making a living and providing care for family members, tasks that are not equally shared by men.

The Beijing Platform for Action specifically emphasized that the application of gender analysis to a wide range of policies and programmes is critical to the elaboration and successful implementation of poverty reduction strategies. The Platform for Action included the issue of poverty in its 12 critical areas of concern, and under critical area of concern A, "Women and poverty", identified four strategic objectives that it would be important to take into account. These include: to review, adopt and maintain macroeconomic policies and development strategies that address the needs and efforts of women in poverty; to revise laws and administrative practices to ensure equal rights for women and access to economic resources; to provide women with access to savings and credit mechanisms and institutions; and to develop gender-based methodologies and conduct research to address the feminization of poverty.

The Beijing Platform for Action indicates that the development of goals to eradicate poverty is closely connected with the advancement of women and gender equality. Low levels of education, high levels of illiteracy, and the poor health and nutritional status that prevail among women, as well as their limited access to productive resources and remunerative employment, negatively affect the well-being of a large number of women throughout the world, and impede efforts to eradicate poverty. The Platform for Action therefore recommends that poverty eradication strategies should be comprehensive and should address the multidimensional nature of poverty which includes both income poverty and such factors as autonomy, dignity and lack of violence.

To accelerate the implementation of action in the critical area of concern on women and poverty, the Commission on the Status of Women, at its fortieth session in 1996, adopted resolution 40/9[16] wherein it was further emphasized that the eradication of poverty was both a complex and a multidimensional issue, and fundamental to promoting equality between men and women as well as to reinforcing peace and achieving sustainable development. The Commission reaffirmed the need to mainstream a gender perspective into all policies and programmes for the eradication of poverty and to take into consideration the links between eradication of poverty and other critical areas of concern.

By mid-1999, the Division for the Advancement of Women of the United Nations Secretariat had received 116 national action plans, and more than half reported having established policies and programmes for the eradication of poverty among women by promoting employment and income-generating activities, providing basic social services and improving social security systems. The issue of economic and political empowerment was regarded by Governments as a crucial factor in breaking the cycle of poverty.

2. Current trends in poverty situation

There is awareness in the international community that the worst forms of poverty must be eliminated. During the World Summit for Social Development, 186 representatives of countries including 117 heads of State made a strong commitment to eradicating poverty and to setting national time-bound targets for eradicating absolute poverty. However, the Summit did not set a global, time-bound goal. Since then, the Development Assistance Committee (DAC) of the Organisation for Economic Cooperation and Development (OECD), in cooperation with the World Bank and the United Nations, has produced a set of global targets for development. These targets include reducing extreme poverty by one half by the year 2015 as well as achieving universal primary education and the elimination of gender disparities in education, and reducing infant and child mortality by two thirds and maternal mortality by three quarters, while providing universal access to reproductive health services.

At present, not only is poverty a grave concern for developing countries, but it affects industrialized societies as well, and it is growing in countries with economies in transition. It is generally agreed that millions of people are living in poverty and their number is increasing in spite of certain efforts to eradicate the problem. According to the World Bank *World Development Report 1999/2000: Entering the 21st Century*, in spite of some progress in the area of development "the absolute number of those living on 1 dollar a day or less continues to increase. The worldwide total rose from 1.2 billion in 1987 to 1.5 billion in 1999 and, if the recent trend persists, will reach 1.9 billion by 2015."[17]

The situation is serious in South and East Asia, Africa and Latin America. The recent East Asian crisis increased the poverty rates and the inequality in the distribution of income in that region. Indonesia, for example, reported that the result of the crisis was an increase of the number of poor by up to 40 per cent in 1998. According to the latest World Bank figures, between 1987 and 1998, the number of poor in South Asia increased by 10 per cent.

In Latin America, poverty has been increasing in absolute figures. Statistics from the World Bank and ECLAC have shown that the number of poor people increased by about 3 million per year during the first half of the 1990s.

In African regions, it has been estimated that 44 per cent of Africans as a whole and 51 per cent of those in sub-Saharan Africa live in absolute poverty.[18] The world's poorest countries tend to have the highest population growth rates. Although the use of family planning services has increased, a large portion of women still do not have access to quality reproductive health services. Maternal morbidity and mortality remain unacceptably high, especially in developing countries. For example, the maternal mortality rate for sub-Saharan Africa is 971 deaths per 100,000 live births, which is almost double the rate of any other region in the world.[19]

In Central and Eastern European countries, the collapse of socialist economies has contributed greatly to the increase of poverty. The process of transition to market economies has undermined the previous combination of guaranteed jobs, low wages and various compensatory State benefits that had ensured, to a certain extent, an appropriate standard of living. Now the gap is widening rapidly between a rather small portion of the population with a high standard of living and a much larger one that can hardly make ends meet.[20]

Industrial restructuring and changed employment patterns are important factors that aggravate poverty in the developed countries of Europe and in the United States of America. The decline of traditional industries, the transfer of jobs to the developing countries where there are less strict social and ecological standards, a cheaper labour force, lower taxes and massive reductions in public spending have caused two phenomena that have increased the number of poor. These are unemployment, which has reached alarming proportions, and the proliferation of low-paid jobs that are often insufficient to allow the workers to remain above the poverty line. The groups most affected are women, young people and pensioners. For example, in accordance with the 1997 report of the Italian National Statistical Institution (ISTAT), in Italy the number of women in poverty exceeds the number of men: 12.8 per cent of the female population compared with 10.6 per cent of the male population.

We are also witnessing the emergence of a "new poor" who are different, because they do not inherit poverty. Instead, they fall into that category owing to the combination of such factors as inadequate incomes, lack or difficult access to welfare services, and the deterioration of the economic, social and ecological environment. As a result of circumstances, people in that group find themselves lacking sufficient resources to conform to the established standard of living.

3. Achievements in the implementation of strategic objectives

For many countries in all regions of the world, the issue of poverty eradication has been one of the main priorities in development policies. However, the poverty eradication strategies, policies and programmes were predominately considered to be gender-neutral and did not spell out the differences between men and women in respect of their experiencing poverty and undergoing the process of becoming impoverished. Hence, the important achievement after the Beijing Conference has been the recognition by many Governments of a gender dimension of poverty and their efforts to refocus the poverty eradication policies and programmes so as to address the needs and concerns of women in poverty. The overwhelming majority of countries that responded to the questionnaire on the implementation of the Beijing Platform for Action have reported on their concrete activities and initiatives in that area.

The national policy shift in many reporting countries was reflected either in the efforts to mainstream a gender perspective into the national programmes for poverty eradication or in an increase in the number of projects and programmes aimed directly at poverty eradication among women. In Uganda, there is an understanding that the goal of the National Poverty Eradication Action Plan to eradicate mass poverty by the year 2017 may be achieved only if a gender perspective is mainstreamed in all planned activities. In view of that, the plan for 1999/2000-2003/2004 is focusing on addressing women's needs and concerns. To mainstream a gender perspective into sectoral development planning, the Government of Senegal has conducted gender training for senior decision makers. Since 1996, the Government of Madagascar has undertaken a regular review of the ongoing projects from a gender perspective. Niger has reported on the mainstreaming of a gender perspective into national poverty reduction programme.

In Palestine, for example, in 1998, the Ministry of Social Affairs increased its capacity to create special projects for the development of entrepreneurial skills among women. A gender-specific poverty reduction strategy is the goal of the Danish development assistance policy. Country strategies and sector policies are designed with a view to mainstreaming a gender perspective in all activities. The Government of Singapore, following the recommendations of the Beijing Platform for Action to mainstream a gender perspective into all policies and pro- grammes, has implemented the Small Families Improvement Scheme. The purpose of that initiative is to help low-income families secure access to education and housing. The Government of Cameroon identi- fied women as a specific target group in the national poverty eradica- tion programme for 1998/99-2000/01.

The analysis of the Governments' replies has revealed that they have started to operate within the broader definition of poverty. Traditionally poverty has been defined as a lack of access to resources, employment and income that results in a state of material deprivation. Now, it in- cludes the denial of opportunities and choices for living a long, healthy, creative life, and enjoying an appropriate standard of living, freedom and dignity. This approach to human poverty takes into account more than minimum basic needs and focuses the policy discussion on gender differences in basic education, health services and life expectancy and on the socially constructed constraints on the choices of various groups of women and men. From a gender perspective, broader definitions of poverty allow for a better understanding of the relative poverty or well- being of each member of the household.

There are encouraging signs that Governments are becoming more aware of disparities that result from gender-based inequalities within the households and are trying to change various social norms that lead to women's social exclusion or economic subordination.

In 1996, the Government of Tunisia introduced new legislation ex- panding women's rights with respect to accessing housing credit. In India, the Government is expanding literacy campaigns for widows so that they can use their entitlements to various forms of State support.

The globalization of the world's economy presents new challenges and opportunities for sustained economic growth and development as well as risks and uncertainties in respect of the future of that economy. The situation has been aggravated by the growing inequality between re- gions, countries, income groups and the sexes. The caution expressed in the Beijing Platform for Action that women might bear disproportion- ately the negative cost of the transformation in the world economy has been confirmed by the analysis of the Governments' replies.

In addition, a certain number of Governments went beyond pure recognition of the problem and, in accordance with the strategic objective of the Platform for Action, have undertaken concrete steps aimed at reviewing macroeconomic policies from a gender perspective. In Georgia, for example, in 1998-1999 the Government conducted an analysis of the impact of macroeconomic investments and taxation policies on women. The findings of this analysis will help formulate more efficient policies so as to minimize the negative impact of economic transformations on women.

In trying to achieve progress in minimizing the negative impact of structural adjustment programmes and globalization on vulnerable and disadvantaged groups, many Governments were focusing on a two-pronged strategy, while others took a one-pronged approach. The two-pronged strategy included promoting employment and income-generating activities for women both in urban and in rural areas, providing basic social services, including childcare facilities, and improving the social security systems. The one-pronged approach dealt primarily only with either one or the other of these strategies.

Certain progress has been achieved in eliminating poverty among women in those countries that are trying to implement a comprehensive two-pronged approach. For example, in Finland, owing to the existing comprehensive social security system based on individual needs, and employment programmes for women, there is no significant difference in poverty risks for men and women. A slightly lower standard of living among women is due to the existing wage differentials between the sexes. The Ministry of Social Affairs and Health, which directs policies regarding social security, social welfare and health care, has the biggest budget compared with that of other ministries. By 1998, the introduction of the national minimum wage in the United Kingdom and of the federal minimum wage in the United States of America has benefited 1.3 million women and 5.7 million women, respectively. In the United Kingdom, this measure was accompanied by the introduction of the first national childcare strategy which was aimed at assisting women in the reconciliation of their family and professional responsibilities. In 1997, Germany successfully completed a pilot project entitled "Assistance for single homeless mothers" by integrating these women into society and providing them with employment.

Several countries focused on establishing social safety net programmes aiming not only to increase the income of women but also to improve their education, health and nutritional status.

In Latin America, for example, several countries launched programmes that transfer income in cash or in kind to poor households with children, mainly through women, on condition that the household spend it for the health or educational needs of family members, especially children. The Programa de Educación, Salud y Alimentación (PROGRESA) in Mexico, created in 1997 under the Ministry of Social Development, is the most complete in terms of the range of interventions in the area of employment, education, health and nutrition that it offers to women in poverty. In addition, the programme provides training in managerial aspects, self-administration and leadership in order to improve the economic performance of women. The focus on labour-intensive development together with support for social services has also benefited women in Chile.

In Africa, most countries are focusing on cushioning the short-term negative impact of the structural adjustment programmes (SAPs) among women. The Zambian Government, for example, is implementing a Social Action Programme that envisions, among other measures, payment for women's education and health. In 1997, the Government of Burkina Faso conducted an impact assessment of structural adjustment measures on households.

In several countries, the comprehensive approach to poverty eradication among women that combined measures to promote women's remunerative employment and the provision of social safety nets and access to basic services has resulted in a decrease in the number of women in poverty. China reported that the poverty-stricken population had dropped from 65 million in 1995 to 42 million in 1998 with the decrease in the number of poor women accounting for almost 60 per cent of that reduction. In Viet Nam, according to the report, the number of poor households had been cut from 23.3 per cent in 1994 to 17.4 per cent in 1998.

The success of anti-poverty policies and programmes depends on the extent to which these policies and programmes empower people living in poverty in general and women in particular. The Beijing Platform for Action emphasized that "empowerment of women is a critical factor in the eradication of poverty" (PfA, para. 49).

Empowerment of women implies, *inter alia*, that women should have entitlements and capabilities that would allow them to move out of poverty. Analysis of entitlements in poverty analysis has come from the literature on hunger and famines. It focuses on access to commodities and resources. Enhancement of women's entitlements that will contribute to the elimination of their dependency and vulnerability relies upon an increase of their access to land ownership and use, credit and other productive resources. Poverty involves not only the lack of basic necessities but also the denial of opportunities to live a normal life. The goal is to expand human capabilities—what people are capable of doing to move out of poverty through education, training and good health.[21]

Many countries have reported that, after the Beijing Conference, credit, especially microcredit, has become a very popular and successful type of poverty eradication programme which is contributing to women's economic empowerment (Belize, Botswana, Canada, El Salvador, Fiji, Ghana, the Islamic Republic of Iran, Japan, Mexico, Nigeria, Palestine, Papua New Guinea, Sierra Leone, Trinidad and Tobago, the United States of America, Vanuatu, Yemen, Zambia and others). Romania has initiated a project to create a Guaranteed Fund for Small- and Medium-Sized Enterprises Managed by Women, designed to encourage women's entrepreneurship and assist unemployed women to reintegrate into the labour market. The Krygyz Republic reports that microcredit has enabled some of the women who lost their jobs in the course of the transition to a market-based economy to establish microenterprise operations.

In 1997, the United States of America, for example, granted more than 10,000 loans, totalling 67 billion dollars to women business-owners. In Belize, the Small Farmers and Business bank provided 29 per cent of its overall funds to women (during December 1998 to April 1999). Japan gave interest-free loans to 27,000 rural women. In Palestine, since 1994, 96 per cent of women who participated in agricultural projects have benefited from the implementation of loan programmes. In Trinidad and Tobago, the Small Business Development Company which is used by the Government to stimulate the micro- and small-enterprise sector has distributed 65 per cent of its loans for women.

According to the *UNDP Poverty Report 1998: Overcoming Human Poverty*, at present some 10 million women around the world, are reached by systems of small loans. Moreover, at the Microcredit Summit held in Washington, D.C., in February 1997, the participants pledged that by the year 2005 this number would reach 100 million.[22]

The Beijing Platform for Action has recommended that countries "undertake legislative and administrative reforms to give women full and equal access to economic resources, including the right to inheritance and to ownership of land". However, the progress observed since the Beijing Conference in providing women with land rights and access to land, including the elimination of discriminatory inheritance laws, has remained very slow. Only a small number of countries, including Bolivia, Malaysia, the United Republic of Tanzania and Zimbabwe, actually changed laws to make it possible for women to inherit land.

The overwhelming majority of the countries have reported progress in breaking the vicious circle of poverty through the expansion of women's capabilities, *inter alia*, by eradicating illiteracy and increasing the educational level among women and girls. Investing in the schooling of women directly affects the quality of the lives of children. Returns of female education also affect the level of fertility by slowing population growth. A woman with at least seven years of education has 2.2 fewer children than a woman with no schooling.[23] In addition, every year of a mother's schooling leads to a decrease of up to 9 per cent in the mortality rate of children under age 5.[24] (The progress in the area of education and training is described in more detail under the relevant critical area of concern.)

There is a growing perception around the world that the feminization of poverty has been increasing. The most compelling argument used in support of this perception is the increase in the percentage of female-headed households, and the assumption that they are generally much poorer than male-headed households. However, owing to the differences in the conceptualization of the "female-headed household", there is some ambiguity and disagreement concerning the meaning of "feminization of poverty" and its extent.[25] In addition, "the evidence on the comparative poverty of female-headed households *vis-à-vis* their male-headed counterparts is not universal".[26] This does not exclude an association between female-headship and poverty, but rather requires a shift of emphasis away from the static indicator of poverty to the process through which the households become, first, female-headed and, second, poor.

A review of Governments replies has shown that more and more countries are conducting a comprehensive analysis of the situation of female-headed households focusing on the reasons for the increase in their numbers and on the process of their impoverishment. The increase of female-headed households in developed countries is largely due to a higher life expectancy among women, an increase in the number of divorces and a declining marriage rate.

Several countries in Africa, Asia, Central America and Europe have identified military conflicts and civil strife as factors contributing to the increase of female-headed households and their impoverishment.

Many developed countries with rather comprehensive welfare systems have determined that the economic disadvantage of households headed by women in comparison with the households headed by men has been the result of the fact that women are the primary wage earners in an atmosphere of increasing underemployment and unemployment. For example, in Canada the poverty rate for female-headed households rose from 57.2 per cent in 1995 to 61.4 per cent in 1998, with declining employment being a key factor.

The developing countries explained the negative situation of female-headed households by the long-term decline of government spending on welfare programmes and basic social services, as well as by the high rates of indirect taxation, minimum-wage policies and inadequate social security systems. Probably the combination of these and historical factors has resulted in Jamaica's having one of the highest number of female-headed households in the world, with one third of them living below the poverty line.

All countries that reported on the status of female-headed households emphasized that the lack of equality in education and training between men and women was contributing to poverty among female-headed households by putting women at a disadvantage in the labour market and limiting their access to productive resources. The findings of the survey conducted in Trinidad and Tobago confirmed that poverty was more widespread among female-headed households in which the woman had a low educational level.

Many replies contained comparative statistical data on female-headed households that had been unavailable before the Beijing Conference. The more accurate data and analysis have provided a better framework for policy design and ensured its more efficient implementation.

The efforts undertaken by the Governments to address the needs and interests of female-headed households focused on integrating women in productive employment and introducing various systems of allowances, child and woman benefits, and improvement of the social security system. For example, in its 1998 Budget Law, Italy allocated 250 million lire to guaranteeing a basic income for poor families, most of which were headed by women. Greece has established the first normative framework to identify the eligibility for a minimum allowance that would benefit female-headed households. In San Marino the Government provides single women with children with subsidized housing, employment opportunities, social assistance and nursery schools. Colombia identified women heads of households as one of the groups to which priority must be given in provision of services while Costa Rica adopted a programme of basic education for single women with children.

Several countries described special measures to assist female-headed households in rural areas. For example, in the Islamic Republic of Iran and Japan, the Governments allocated additional funds to developing special programmes to integrate the rural female-headed household into productive employment.

After the Beijing Conference, evident progress was achieved in many countries in the research on gender aspects of poverty, the development of conceptual tools and practical methodologies for conducting gender impact assessment and the improvement of data collection. About one third of the countries have reported the launching of research on gender aspects of poverty. Many countries have reported on the establishment of institutions responsible for collecting data disaggregated by sex.

For example, Norway has conducted a research project on poverty in Nordic countries. Belize has conducted a national poverty assessment that, in 1996, determined that 33.1 per cent of the female population lived in poverty. On the basis of this assessment, the Government has developed several poverty alleviating programmes for women and youth. In Yemen, the Government has established a directorate in the central statistical organization responsible for collecting data disaggregated by sex, especially in the area of poverty. It is also focusing on the elaboration of statistical indicators for the evaluation of women's contribution in the national economy. The 1999 *National Human Development Report* of Madagascar provided statistics disaggregated by sex and gender-sensitive indicators that contributed to the understanding of gender inequalities in the country. Kenya has established a computerized database that contains disaggregated data for policy and planning purposes.

4. Obstacles in the implementation of strategic objectives

The analysis of the Governments' replies has confirmed that one of the reasons for the persistence and growth of poverty among women is the lack of a holistic gender approach to policy-making and especially implementation in practice. Other reasons mentioned by the countries include the persistent discrimination against women in the labour market, the existing gap in their wages, their unequal access to productive resources and capital as well as education and training, and the sociocultural factors that continue to influence gender relations and preserve the existing discrimination against women. Many countries emphasized the negative impact of women's low participation in decision-making at all levels.

Some countries, especially those with economies in transition, reported that the high rate of female unemployment, together with the erosion of social safety nets, was a key factor that contributed to the increase of poverty among women (Armenia, Belarus, Estonia, Latvia, the Republic of Moldova, the Russian Federation, Ukraine and Uzbekistan). Cutbacks in public spending, *inter alia*, for childcare, education, health care and other services, along with existing protectionist legislation that prohibits women working in certain jobs, negatively affected women's ability to compete in the labour market. In most of these countries, women constitute the majority of the unemployed.

In Latin America, as a result of the 1980s debt crisis and structural adjustment policies, women also dominate the ranks of the unemployed. According to the 1998 *Social Watch Report*, out of 15 countries surveyed, only Bolivia and El Salvador had developed employment plans for women since 1995 and showed some level of plan implementation.

There was a similar situation in industrialized countries. Many countries reported a higher level among women of unemployment that substantially affected their standard of living. Women in Canada and the United States of America, for instance, have suffered massive lay-offs and a loss of benefits. This is especially true for women from ethnic and indigenous minorities. In Denmark, in 1998, the unemployment rate for women was 7.9 per cent; for men, 5.5 per cent.

Cuts in government spending on basic social services have also had a negative impact on the efforts to eliminate poverty. For example, in India, a 14 per cent cut in government expenditures for primary education resulted in an increase in the number of private schools, which are non-accessible for poor women. Also, a 17 per cent cut in expenditures for non-formal education has led to the closure of many night schools and adult educational programmes for working women.

The replies from some countries showed that women were disproportionately affected by, and often played the role of shock absorbers in, the structural adjustment efforts. During structural adjustments, countries, in order to improve the efficiency of the market system, are forced to reduce public investments in infrastructure, public subsidies and social expenditures on education, health and public services. In view of this, women who are responsible for satisfying the needs of the family absorb the reduction in basic social services by working longer and harder both inside and outside the household, for example, in India, Jamaica, Trinidad and Tobago, Uganda and the United Republic of Tanzania. In addition, as became obvious in many countries of the Asian region during the financial crisis, women are the first to be fired and girls are the first to drop out of schools. The Philippines and Indonesia also mentioned a decrease of food intake among women and girls and a rise in prostitution and violence.

A review of the countries' replies to the questionnaire shows that in many countries the measures aimed at combating poverty among women are still not consistent and comprehensive. In spite of certain progress achieved regarding the understanding of the gender dimension of poverty and efforts undertaken by a number of countries to mainstream a gender perspective into poverty eradication policies and programmes, the precise nature of the nexus between gender and poverty still requires clarification. It also requires operationalization of the gender dimension into policies and programmes at the national, regional and international levels. Though some countries are more advanced in terms of policy formulation, many are still lacking real implementation.

Another difficulty involves the almost complete absence of sex-disaggregated statistics on poverty. The importance and urgency of that problem are reflected in the future plans of the many countries that are planning to conduct surveys and research projects and establish databases in order to receive more accurate information in that area so as to inform the policy makers.

The issue of measurement, as was mentioned by several countries, is important for policy-making of any kind, especially as a justifying concern in the context of competing claims for resources. Economic and social indicators provide a static snapshot of poverty without revealing the processes and mechanisms that are creating poverty and the fact that it might be different for men and women. This is also true when poverty is measured on the basis of household expenditure data that ignores the intra-household distribution. In most countries, it is very difficult to find standard surveys that explore the intra-household distribution of resources. However, without capturing the gender differentials in intra-household distribution relations, the data will not be useful in measuring the gender dimension of poverty. Hence, the design and the formulation of gender-sensitive policies and programmes require that data collection probe the intra-household arena.

The other serious obstacle to the implementation of action in this critical area of concern mentioned by many developing countries is the growing balance of payments deficits and increasing burden of debt. In the 1990s, many developing countries were encountering great difficulty in meeting their payment obligations for the loans they had undertaken in the past to finance their development. While in Ecuador foreign debt consumed 15 per cent of the annual government budget, in the United Republic of Tanzania, for example, it consumed 40 per cent. In Jamaica, 62 per cent of projected expenditures for the reported 1999 financial year were allocated for debt-servicing. This situation has been further aggravated by a reverse flow of capital from the South to the North, annual decreases in developing countries' income from trade, lower prices for raw materials, increasing protectionism and continual cuts in the development aid budgets of the developed countries.

Under these circumstances, women's burden (in their roles as producers, human resources reproducers and maintainers and community managers) increased tremendously, as they were obliged to find ways to cushion the detrimental effects of the debt crisis on themselves and on their families. In that respect, it is worth mentioning the proposal made by Rwanda to transform all of the country's external debt into a fund to assist poor women.

An important indicator of political will and commitment to the eradication of poverty among women is the allocation of resources to implementing the proclaimed policies and programmes. However, very few countries have provided information regarding the allocation of funds or the increasing of resources allocated for gender-sensitive poverty eradication strategies. In addition, the review of the Governments' replies showed that many programmes aimed at poverty eradication among women are under the rubric of the departments of social ministries that usually have meagre allocations in the budget. Levels of development assistance have also fallen very low —to less than half of the recommended 0.7 per cent of gross national product (GNP).

5. Conclusions and further actions

The commitments to eradicate poverty made by Governments through global United Nations conferences, including the World Summit for Social Development in Copenhagen and the Fourth World Conference on Women in Beijing, were reinforced by the launching in 1997 of the first United Nations Decade for the Eradication of Poverty and General Assembly resolution 53/198 of 15 December 1998 the decade called upon the whole United Nations system to undertake all efforts to eradicate poverty. The eradication of poverty remains the responsibility of the national Governments, and it requires an international partnership in which the efforts of all countries can be supported in a sustained and consistent manner. It also requires the whole United Nations system's advocacy of the mobilization of the political will and resources to combat poverty.

The goals of economic growth, development of human capabilities and non-discrimination need to be kept central to development strategies and macroeconomic policy-making at national and international levels. It is also important that the benefits of growth and investments in human capital be gender-sensitive and thus take into account different needs and interests of both men and women. In view of this, a gender perspective offers a powerful tool as regards the efforts to eradicate poverty. Such an approach will contribute to the systematic reduction of disparities in income and wealth and gender inequalities in all walks of life.

In this regard, the following objectives are of particular importance for future actions and initiatives:

- To promote and strengthen the practical implementation of mainstreaming a gender perspective into all developmental policies and programmes; to enhance the development of gender analysis tools and methodologies; to expand gender training and this in its turn will require an improvement in the collection of sex-disaggregated data and national accounting that should include unremunerated labour;

- To create a favourable political and macroeconomic environment, including efforts to relieve foreign debt and to mobilize human and financial resources;

- To promote women's political and economic empowerment and participation in decision-making. It is important to address women's deprivation in basic capabilities such as education and health as well as in their entitlements such as access to capital and productive resources, including access and ownership of land;

- To set the concrete national, regional and international targets for the eradication of poverty among women and establish monitoring procedures and mechanisms.

In conclusion, special efforts were to be made during the Millennium Assembly in September 2000 to endorse a gender-sensitive global poverty eradication strategy.

B. Education and training of women

1. Introduction

The Platform for Action considers education a human right and an essential tool for achieving the goals of equality, development and peace. It established a number of targets under critical area of concern B, "Education and training of women" in line with the 1990 World Declaration on Education for All and the Framework for Action to Meet Basic Learning Needs.[27] In line with the targets established by the International Conference on Population and Development (1994) and the World Summit for Social Development (1995), the Platform for Action recommended that Governments provide, by the year 2000, universal access to basic education and ensure completion of primary education by at least 80 per cent of primary school-age children; close the gender gap in primary and secondary school education by the year 2005; and provide universal primary education in all countries before the year 2015 (PfA, para. 80 (b)). It also recommended that the female illiteracy rates be reduced to at least half their 1990 level, with emphasis on rural women, migrant, refugee and internally displaced women and women with disabilities (PfA, para. 81 (a)). Access to all levels of education, including vocational training, and science and technology and the development of non-discriminatory education and training were also addressed.

The International Consultative Forum on Education for All (EFA) acknowledged at the Mid-Decade Meeting in 1996 that there was widespread support for the goals and principles embodied in the World Declaration on Education for All and its Framework for Action.[28] It noted that, despite progress in some areas, the closing of the gender gap was the area where least progress had been made. The World Education Forum (Dakar, Senegal, 26 to 28 April 2000) assessed the overall progress achieved. The EFA assessment is based on 18 core indicators of which 8 indicators are of direct relevance to the education of women and girls. The assessment will show in detail how the targets set in the Platform for Action, which are identical to the EFA targets, have been achieved.

Specific efforts to achieve education for all have been made in nine of the world's most populous countries (E-9): Bangladesh, Brazil, China, Egypt, India, Indonesia, Mexico, Nigeria and Pakistan which together account for half the world's population and 70 per cent of the world's illiterates. The Second E-9 Ministerial Review Meeting of the nine high- population countries placed priority on the education of women and girls. It recommended that all E-9 initiatives pay particular attention to the education of girls and women and accelerate efforts to make education available to all girls and women and, in particular, ensure that girls completed the full cycle of basic education, and that curricula and teaching-learning materials included a gender perspective.[29]

The General Assembly in 1997 reiterated the importance of literacy as a human right and indispensable element for economic and social progress while appealing to all Governments to redouble efforts to achieve their own goals of education for all by setting targets and timetables, where possible, including gender-specific education targets and programmes to combat the illiteracy of women and girls.

Since the Fourth World Conference on Women, education and training of women, in particular access to decision-making and science and technology, have been addressed at two global conferences organized by the United Nations Educational, Scientific and Cultural Organization (UNESCO). At the World Conference on Higher Education (Paris, 1998) and the World Conference on Science (Budapest, 1999), efforts were made to include a gender perspective and reference was made to the role of women.

The importance of education and training of women has been recognized by many Member States. In their national action plans, established after the Fourth World Conference on Women, 98 out of 116 have considered education and training of women and girls a priority. Several countries established national benchmarks or set specific targets.

In its agreed conclusions 1997/4,[30] the Commission on the Status of Women reconfirmed the recommendations of the Platform for Action, in particular the benchmarks set on education and training of women. The Commission addressed the issue of donor assistance for basic social programmes and the mobilization of additional funds from all sources for education. It recommended that an active and visible policy of mainstreaming a gender perspective be pursued in all policies and programmes in the educational sector, emphasizing the interlinkage between education and training on the one hand and the labour market on the other, as the responsibility of educational planners and policy makers. It asked for more research and information on employment trends, income and future employment opportunities. The importance of gender-sensitive training material and non-discriminatory education and training was highlighted.

The Committee on the Elimination of Discrimination against Women emphasized education and training in its concluding comments pursuant to the presentation of the periodic reports of States parties to the Convention on the Elimination of All Forms of Discrimination against Women. Recommendations deal, *inter alia*, with eradication of illiteracy, education for minority groups, teenage pregnancies and school-drops outs and, most frequently, with the elimination of stereotyped attitudes, prejudices and discriminatory social and traditional practices that remain the root causes for all forms of discrimination against women.[31]

2. Achievements in the implementation of strategic objectives

In their replies to the questionnaire on the implementation of the Platform for Action, all Member States provided information on policies, programmes and projects or good practices that had been undertaken to improve the status of women with regard to education since the Fourth World Conference on Women.

(a) Reform and financing of education
The establishment of an institutional framework for the development of the educational system in general and equitable distribution of resources have minimized gender gaps in education and were beneficial to the education of girls. Some countries have taken specific measures such as the elaboration of a political plan on gender equality in education or the appointment of a coordinator for activities on gender equality.

The links between political will, allocation of resources and results achieved are visible in the field of education. Countries that invested more resources in education have seen an increase in the enrolment number of girls. Algeria, for example, achieved equal access at secondary and higher levels owing to measures taken, such as opening of schools in rural and isolated areas, increase of school meals, coverage of costs for boarding schools to limit the dropping out of girls, and transport and scholarships for students from poor families.

(b) Eradication of illiteracy
The female illiteracy rate remains high and is increasing, in particular in sub-Saharan Africa. Illiteracy is particularly high among adult women as a result of lack of education in younger years. Literacy training has been offered in many countries, although not in a sufficient number. Often such training is targetted to women. In Sierra Leone, for example, the Ministry of Youth, Education and Sports collaborated with UNESCO to establish 47 literacy centres for women. In some countries—for example, in Botswana—more women than men are involved in literacy classes, functional literacy projects and distance education. There is an indication that the gains made by women are higher than those by men. In India, the female literacy rate rose from 39.3 per cent in 1991 to 50.3 per cent in 1997, and these gains are higher than those made by men. A direct link can be established between the increase in female literacy and the increased enrolment rate of girls, since literate women are more likely to send their daughters to school. Sene-

gal, for example, reports that the reduction in female illiteracy has increased the enrolment rate of girls from 35 to 52.9 per cent.

In many instances, the Governments' anti-illiteracy drives are combined with efforts to promote the acquisition of life skills, such as knowledge on health and reproductive health, study of agricultural sciences and technology and legal literacy. In Mali, for example, literacy training is provided for women leaders and members of associations who are simultaneously trained in specific topics such as accounting and crafts. Emphasis is also put on post-illiteracy training, *inter alia*, in different national languages to sustain the knowledge acquired.

(c) Universal access to basic education

Basic education is education intended to meet basic learning needs and includes instruction at the first level, on which subsequent learning can be based. It encompasses early childhood and primary education for children, as well as literacy, general knowledge and life skills for youth and adults. High-quality early years of education are the basis for life-long learning. Enrolment rates for girls and boys at the primary and secondary level combined have increased in almost all regions of the world, although at different paces and starting from different levels. However, in many countries in all regions, enrolment at primary and secondary level has stagnated or declined owing to adverse conditions, often more for boys than for girls.

Countries that report an increase in the enrolment of girls see this as a result of specific measures taken to improve the schooling of all children. Since the Beijing Conference in 1995, significant empirical and analytical knowledge and information have been generated on girls' education. In some countries—as reported, for example, by Turkey—the national demand for education, especially for girls, has become increasingly vocal. Donor support, at the bilateral and multilateral level, for girls' education has been strong.

The importance of secondary education for girls and its completion is increasingly recognized, since the gender gap widens at this level. Low levels of secondary school enrolment for girls have been one of the main shortcomings in respect of women's empowerment, since knowledge is solidified with years of schooling. Secondary schooling has been found to enhance opportunities and freedom of choice of tertiary education and vocational training and is therefore the key to future challenges. Increased years of secondary schooling also correlate with older age at marriage and first childbirth. Some countries, for instance, started a campaign to educate communities on the importance of secondary education for girls. Benin, for example, is better equipping secondary schools so that they can cater for girls.

When there is commitment at the highest level to ensuring basic education and allocation of resources, significant gains are made through reduction of classroom backlogs, provision of additional classrooms and teachers and the creation of multigrade classes in rural areas. Some countries provide specific benefits to teachers working in rural or remote regions. In Georgia, the Parliament adopted a law on high mountain regions establishing benefits for doctors, teachers and other government employees. Others have constructed schools in villages and improved school environments through the addition of libraries or the construction of latrines for girls. For example, Chad reports that it built 6,000 separate latrines for girls.

Many countries recognize the importance of special incentives to promote girls' education. Specific measures that have been taken to improve girls' enrolment and retention in schools include the creation of specific national funds for girls' education and the recruitment of volunteers and auxiliary teachers. Uganda has established the universal primary education policy which meets tuition costs for four children per family and all orphans, indicating that two of the four sponsored children should be female. Some Member States, including, for example, Nepal, provide scholarships for girls from poor families or rural areas. Incentives are given to successful female students from rural areas to become teachers and return to their villages. The establishment of boarding schools free of charge in rural and nomadic areas, for example, in Algeria and the Islamic Republic of Iran, is also a means to reach out to girls in particular. To raise family awareness about the importance of girls' education, girls receive exemption from, or reduction of costs for, schooling, food and other necessities. The priority groups for specific educational programmes are rural girls, girls from indigenous communities and girls with disabilities.

Changes in class schedules and elasticity in the curriculum have been introduced to adjust to the needs of students especially girls, for example, in China and Yemen. In Burkina Faso, the Ministry for Education and some non-governmental organizations launched a campaign entitled "A school bag for my daughter" and awarded a prize to the best students in primary and secondary schools with special mention of girls.

Several countries, including, for example, Argentina, Ghana, Indonesia and Seychelles, have taken legal action to ensure equal access to free and compulsory education for periods of up to 10 years. There is general agreement that opportunities have been provided to girls and women through compulsory education. Turkey reports that one of the most significant steps towards the empowerment of women since Beijing has been the increase of compulsory basic education from five to eight years. A few Member States have adopted laws that guarantee gender equality in the educational system. In Belgium, the French community adopted a decree on positive discrimination in schools as a response to inequalities faced by women and girls, such as, for example, violence. In some countries, for example, Peru, and Venezuela, laws were passed to prohibit the expulsion of pregnant girls from school, while in others, for example, Burkina Faso, Saint Vincent and the Granadines, Seychelles and Zambia, measures were taken to facilitate their re-entry into school following childbirth.

Many countries have taken specific measures to counter female dropping out which occurs mostly at the secondary level. Changes in the curriculum at secondary level were introduced to include family planning and awareness on the implications of early pregnancy and parenthood, for example, in Mexico. In the Caribbean, assistance and scholarships are provided to young mothers to enable them to stay in school. In Jamaica, pilot projects encourage young fathers to continue their education, and receive counselling and instruction in good parenting and family planning habits. Mauritius is opening additional secondary schools in underserved regions, in an effort to improve access and thus reduce drop-outs. In addition, a programme for school leavers is now being run by the Ministry of Women, Family Welfare and Child Development. Community mobile schools for single mothers have been established in some parts of Kenya.

In some countries, non-formal education was introduced that targeted out-of-school children in age group 6-14, ensuring universal access, retention and achievement at the primary level, in particular in districts with low female literacy rates. Alternative non-formal education systems are considered a means to reach out to indigenous communities and disadvantaged groups. In Burkina Faso, quotas of 50 per cent of girls were introduced in satellite schools, non-formal education centres and literacy-training centres. Bhutan reports that 70 per cent of non-formal programme beneficiaries are women.

(d) Achievements in tertiary education

Over the past 20 years, significant progress has been achieved with regard to women in tertiary education. In general, women's enrolments have improved and often exceed those of men.[32] Women's enrolment has reached more than 50 per cent or higher in many countries, according to UNESCO's *1998 Statistical Yearbook.*[33] This is the case in many countries of Eastern and Western Europe, Canada, the United States of America and New Zealand, as well as in some countries in Latin America and the Caribbean. Namibia has 50 per cent more women in higher education. In countries where tertiary education has considerably expanded, the school attendance rate for females has increased more than that for males. Quotas have been established when women's enrolment is lagging behind. Ghana, for instance, introduced affirmative action, *inter alia*, in tertiary institutions and reserved 40 per cent of admissions for girls. That more and more women remain longer at university is the case, for example, in Algeria where 86.6 per cent of female students choose long cycles of studies. The Libyan Arab Jamahiriya reports that more women go abroad for higher education than men. In Norway, the number of female students passing the doctorate examination has increased to 34 per cent. In several countries, rates of drop-out from university studies are often lower for females than for males. Increasingly, women study law, economics, mathematics and other non-traditional programmes. Many women have now higher qualifications than men, but overqualification of women can necessitate retraining in less specialized fields in order that they may find employment especially in countries in transition.

*(e) Vocational training and science and
    technology*

In many countries, special initiatives have been taken, by the Ministry of Employment, the Ministry of Education or the National Machinery for the Advancement of Women, to direct girls to non-traditional fields of study and vocational training and improve access to science and technology. These include career counselling, establishment of boarding schools, provision of scholarships and cooperation with the private sector, complemented by affirmative action in some cases. In Austria, for example, special computer and Internet courses are offered to increase the number of girls in higher-secondary technical schools. In the Netherlands, a "Women and Technology Action Plan 1995-1998" was designed to encourage more girls and women to opt for careers in engineering and technology. In Malta, an existing Technology in Education Programme was restructured to allow girls to have the same opportunities as boys in this field. Some countries established counselling programmes to encourage girls to choose careers in the sciences and technological fields. Saint Vincent and the Grenadines, for example, reports that the introduction of guidance counsellors in schools has increased the number of girls in non-traditional subjects. Zambia, for example, introduced affirmative action in science and technology to encourage the participation of female students. Ghana established science clinics for girls, while Turkmenistan established Centres for Computer Literacy and Languages, specifically targetted to women.

Public campaigns have been launched in many countries, including the organization of conferences or film projection showing women in scientific professions. Some countries are striving to increase the interest of girls in technical subjects and natural sciences already at the primary level. They also support young women researchers so as to make their work visible in the research world. Examples of such efforts are the "Female Researchers in Joint Action" in Denmark and a promotion programme for young female scientists entitled "Herta Firnberg positions" in Austria. The link between education and the labour market is highlighted by a few countries. Cuba, for example, introduced nationwide training programmes in universities to integrate career and skill development for women.

(f) Adult education

The Platform for Action highlights the importance of lifelong education and training for girls and women. In a society of knowledge, there is a transition towards lifelong learning and recognition that school education is becoming the initial phase of a much larger learning process. In many countries, adult education has come to be understood as a tool for increasing competitiveness in the international markets. The Fifth International Conference on Adult Education (CONFINTEA1997) promoted the culture of learning through the "one hour a day for learning" movement and addressed specific recommendations to ensure women's access to adult learning.[34]

Some countries report that women represent the majority of persons enrolled in continuing education classes interested in advancing themselves economically and professionally. In Madagascar, for example, the increase in adult training centres is mostly benefiting women. A few countries are removing obstacles to women's continuous education. Mexico, for example, has eliminated the age limit of 40 years for women in postgraduate admission. Chile is incorporating a gender perspective in its adult education programmes. In Estonia, the Women's Training Centre has initiated training and capacity building projects in entrepreneurial knowledge and skills.

(g) Eliminating gender discrimination from education

Considerable efforts have been deployed in all regions to remove gender bias from textbooks and curricula. As a first step in some countries, decision makers are made aware of the existing bias in education. In Kenya, for example, gender-sensitization workshops for education officials have been undertaken and have resulted in a marked improvement in gender awareness of teachers and education officials. Some countries promote linguistic research to introduce gender-sensitivity in the written and spoken language. Spain published a book on "Lo femenino y lo masculino en el Diccionario de la Lengua de la Real Academia Española". Some other countries, such as Luxembourg, for example, commissioned studies to better understand the existing bias, starting with studies of playing habits of young children in pre-school and the impact of use of non-sexist language on the development off girls and boys. To create an enabling environment for non-discriminative education, media campaigns and conferences also targeted parents.

In many countries, research was conducted on bias in teachers' attitudes and gender sensitivity. New insights were gained into the considerable gender difference between the male and female teachers in respect of the choice of subjects and teaching methods. Pre-service and in-service training was improved. In Greece, the national machinery together with the Ministry of Education planned and implemented a programme for educators on gender awareness. Colombia, for example, established a committee for non-sexist education and produced a guide on co-education. Training sessions on gender and non-sexist themes, as well as campaigns, were organized for special target groups such as educators, editors, communication professionals and social partners. In Haiti, gender-sensitization workshops were conducted in schools at all levels.

Many countries undertook a gender assessment of school curricula starting at the primary level, including educational philosophies, teaching methods and textbooks. Many established committees or task forces to elaborate recommendations on the removal of bias from curricula and textbooks and in some cases proceeded to revisions in textbooks and curricula. A government task force on the review of the educational curriculum for primary schools is in place in Trinidad and Tobago. In Italy, a self-regulated code of conduct for publishers of textbooks was formulated and a handbook produced for authors of new textbooks, teaching aids and guidelines for teachers. Changes to the school curriculum included the adding of new subjects in primary and secondary schools, such as, for example, home economics and technical studies in Singapore and family life education in Cameroon and Fiji.

Women's equal access to sport activities has been recognized as an educational tool for the empowerment of women. The National Policy on Education (1992) and Sports Policy in India incorporate the promotion of gender equality. The Islamic Republic of Iran made a commitment to the allocation of public expenditures to women's sports activities. The International Olympic Committee established a policy to enhance the role of women in sports at all levels, providing various training and scholarships programmes for athletes, coaches, officials, sports journalists and sports doctors as well as administrators. The Second World Conference on Women in Sports, organized every four years, took place in Windhoek, Namibia (1998).

The number of universities and colleges offering women's and gender studies has increased considerably all over the world. In particular since the Fourth World Conference on Women in 1995, the number of teachers involved, and of books and articles published has been impressive. China, for example, reports that 2,000 books and 23,000 articles have been published on women's studies and social gender studies. In Cyprus, the Islamic Republic of Iran, Italy, Kyrgyz Republic, Palestine, Papua New Guinea, Romania, the Slovak Republic and Turkey among others, for example, women's studies or gender studies programmes were created at university level. In addition, a gender and public policy module has been included in the post-university programme at the National School for Political and Administrative Studies. A link is often established between women or gender studies, and teaching and curriculum. In the Philippines, the Women's Studies Association has 50 member schools and over 300 teacher advocates all over the country who undertake teacher training and curriculum development.

(h) Women in decision-making positions at all levels of education

Some progress has been achieved with regard to the number of women in decision-making positions in education and training. In some countries, women's participation in various professional areas at higher education levels has changed. Hungary, for example, reports that the proportion of women has risen in the area of technical and agricultural majors and in faculties that were traditionally the preserve of male professionals. Several countries have taken action to counteract the prevailing under-representation of women by creating special professorships for women or introducing quotas to ensure more equitable representation. Italy established a national observatory to monitor the numbers and positions of women in university and scientific research institutions, their training and career paths. The Netherlands adopted an act to improve the proportional representation of women in managerial positions in the field of education, to encourage educational establishments to review their personnel policies and to conduct a more structural policy aimed at improving the status of women.

3. Obstacles in the implementation of strategic objectives

Despite the reported progress in various fields of education, several Member States acknowledge the persisting gap between ideological discourse and actual practice. Some note that the targets established in the Platform for Action are greater than the national capacity for implementation. For others, the education system does not have the resources to bring about the desired changes as long as it does not receive adequate attention in national budgets.

The lack of resources has first of all an impact on the infrastructure of education in such areas as construction, modernization and maintenance of school buildings, provision of teaching materials, transport, and training and remuneration of teachers. Some countries state that structural adjustment policies hit the education sector hard when they resulted in low investment in education infrastructure. The incapability of the education system to cater for all children at the age of compulsory education and the specific impact of this on the schooling of girls are of concern. Although the lack of resources has an impact on the education of both boys and girls, the negative effect on the schooling of girls is well documented.

Owing to lack of resources, planned educational reform could not be carried out in many countries. Curriculum development and monitoring, evaluation and follow-up were also neglected. Low wages of teachers in primary and secondary school as well as at university level compromise educational outcome and are a disincentive for prospective and current teachers. Certain population groups, such as women and girls living in rural areas or belonging to indigenous communities, are affected in particular by lack of resources. At the household level, the direct and indirect costs of education remain too high for many families. The role of the private sector, which should fulfil its social responsibilities and support existing effort to improve the educational infrastructure, was also mentioned.

In some countries, a non-stable political and economic situation, as a result, for example, of armed conflict, brought with it destruction of equipment and contributed to the resignation of teachers, the lack of interest of parents and widespread low esteem for education.

The challenge of mainstreaming a gender perspective in the education sector was in general not met. Mainstreaming in the education sector involves policy changes and changes in institution so that they support gender equality. It would entail changes at all levels: conceptual changes having impact on educational philosophies; technical changes transforming the management level; and operational changes involving educational projects and programmes. Only a few Member States provided information on the cooperation between various ministries and efforts to mainstream gender in the education sector. Swaziland, for example, conducted gender-sensitization workshops for policy makers in the education sector, inspectors, curriculum designers and guidance counsellors. The difficulty in establishing an appropriate relationship between administrative and curriculum reforms at the national, departmental and municipal level is recognized. Deficient coordination between the different levels of government and between all local, regional and national activities on schooling of girls is of concern. The national machinery responsible for equal-opportunity policies, *inter alia*, including in the field of education, often has little impact on the education ministry and on the school system.

Despite progress achieved, overall figures of illiteracy among women aged 15 years or over remain alarmingly high in many countries, in particular among indigenous, poor and rural women. In many countries in Sub-Saharan Africa in particular, illiteracy rates among women reach more than 50 per cent and may be up to 90 per cent. Some countries complain about the lack of reliable and recent data on illiteracy. Obstacles to literacy are well known and include women's high workload, frequent pregnancies, lack of qualified and motivated trainers, poverty and a lack of global programmes including literacy training. Some countries acknowledge the dependence on external resources and lack of coherence in the approach to literacy training and post-literacy training. The weak literate environment and non-availability of newspapers and books are an additional obstacle to maintaining literacy levels, especially among women. Women's motivation and awareness of the importance and benefits of literacy are low if they are not stimulated through campaigns that make women aware of the benefits of education such as improved living conditions and income-generation.

With regard to equal access at all level of schooling, disparities continue to persist between urban and rural areas. Lack of schools and long distances to schools are an obstacle for girls in rural areas in particular. The unsafe community environment limits their physical mobility. Many girls have to assume a heavy workload at an early age. They are expected to respond to family needs, and are faced with social expectations regarding motherhood. Traditional attitudes still prevail and result in lack of motivation of parents to send girls to schools. Certain groups of girls—such as girls from indigenous or nomadic communities, ethnic minorities and abandoned and disabled girls— face particular disadvantages.

A large number of girls end schooling earlier than boys, mostly in rural or impoverished areas. Early marriage, including forced marriage, and teenage pregnancies are reasons for drop-out. Several countries, including Belize and Grenada, for example, reported that pregnant girls were still expelled from school, and often denied readmission. Other reasons reported are the need to provide assistance to the family or to learn practical skills useful for employment such as dressmaking. In many countries, the re-entry and retention of girls after drop-out or pregnancy are difficult or are not allowed. Lack of childcare facilities is an additional obstacle for teenage mothers. Several countries note the lack of data on drop-outs that are disaggregated by sex, which makes it difficult to determine the percentage of girls not attending school.

The number of women that attend vocational training programmes often remains very small. This is a direct result of the smaller percentage of girls compared with boys attending and completing secondary education in many developing countries. Gender stereotyping still prevails in the technical and professional fields. In many countries, only courses such as tailoring, home economics, cooking and caring are accessible to young women. Even where they have open access to all professions, young women opt for typical female jobs. In the United Kingdom, for example, over 90 per cent of women start work in traditionally "female" occupations and less than 2 per cent choose engineering, construction or plumbing. In many countries, there is also a lack of educational opportunities (including distance learning programmes) providing for women to go back to work after a break for family responsibilities.

Despite progress achieved in tertiary education, gender differences continue among different fields of study. Traditional gender-based subject choices still prevail. When women attain higher degrees of education they are often faced with a lack of employment opportunities. Job opportunities are scarce for the few women in technical fields such as science and engineering. The discrepancy between women's higher degrees and employment corresponding to their qualifications is increasing. In many countries, less- educated males attract higher wages than their better-educated female counterparts who outnumber them in years of tertiary education. Unemployment is high for the increased number of female university graduates in many countries. Another problem is the tendency among women graduates not to pursue a professional career despite the important public or private investment in their education and training. Singapore, for example, is searching for a solution so as to minimize this trend. Although the problem of employment of graduates affects both men and women, it will continue to affect women in particular as long as they prefer traditional fields of study or face obstacles in entering male-dominated fields of work when they have chosen nontraditional subjects. Women's increased enrolment in tertiary education, as is the case now in many countries, has an impact on family formation. When young women achieve higher educational levels than young men, this may cause marriage and family formation to be further delayed or to become difficult, in combination with the factors of the desired age gap between spouses and traditional attitudes that men should be senior to their spouses in age and education.

While many countries report on initiatives to eradicate gender bias in education, they also complain about the persistence of gender bias in textbooks, educational curricula and teacher training. It seems that many efforts are still at the exploratory stage. Even countries that have made progress in raising awareness on gender bias acknowledge blatant contradictions in the content of school curricula and in teaching methodologies, as well as the absence of non-discriminatory practices in school reform projects. They recognize that the incorporation of a gender perspective is complex, especially in curriculum materials. Researchers blame the traditional patriarchal treatment of gender in educational theory and practice which prevents students' participation and use of their ability in a changing society. If gender training is not closely related to everyday practices in school and in the personal and family life of teachers, it will have little success. Without continuous support for teachers and establishment of networks, long-term projects and investment in training and personal and professional development, such efforts can be only sporadic. In countries where difficulty regarding the procurement of school materials, lack of qualified teachers or low pay were a principal problem, the incorporation of a gender perspective has been a low priority.

The low percentage of women in decision-making positions in academia remains of particular concern in the majority of countries. Out of the small number of women in scientific and technical fields of study, very few are in decision-making positions, either in academia or in industry. Women are still overlooked for professorial appointments and management positions in higher education and men still obtain preferential treatment in research occupations. Women in academia are frequently obliged to accept part-time teaching appointments or abandon advanced degrees because of family pressure and hostile environments. Little effort is made to introduce family-friendly environments, in particular in research institutions, where the provision of childcare services would benefit both male and female employees.

4. Conclusions and further actions

The pace of implementation in the field of education and training of women varies among regions, subregions and countries, within countries and for certain population groups. Further efforts need to be made to identify the causes of lagging implementation and even deterioration of the status quo, in order to define effective and useful approaches to intervention and assistance.

With regard to illiteracy, the consistently high—and, in some countries, increasing—illiteracy rate of women calls for sustained, concerted and more focused action to reach the targets established in international conferences. More accurate data on illiteracy is needed since the definition of "literacy" has become more complex and includes also life skills. It is necessary to measure literacy levels and to identify national and regional levels of learning achievement and population groups that are under-served or disadvantaged because of language, ethnicity, age or gender. The first step is to prevent the non-schooling of girls, which results in illiteracy in adult women, by ensuring equal access of girls to basic education and completion of basic education. The second step is to reach out to adult illiterate women through massive literacy campaigns by all modern means available and to sustain acquired knowledge through post-literacy training.

The achievement of education for all remains a priority. Progress has been achieved, *inter alia*, through the introduction of compulsory education which benefits girls where they are disadvantaged. The completion of secondary education by all children remains a goal to be achieved. The decline in the enrolment ratio at the primary and secondary levels, which has been observed in the 1990s for boys and girls in several countries of all regions, is alarming. Gender differences need to be carefully examined, since in many countries the enrolment ratio for boys is declining more than that for girls. In order to take effective measures, efforts should be made to identify the various causes, such as lack of infrastructure in countries with high population growth, armed conflict, impact of the HIV/AIDS pandemic, absence of teachers and economic hardship.

The feminization of tertiary education in many parts of the world is a new development and deserves greater attention. In the long run, a balance in female and male enrolment in tertiary education has to be pursued. While increasingly more women than men successfully pursue a tertiary education, gender differences in choice of subjects and the gender gap in decision-making positions persist. In many countries, especially those in transition, women graduates cannot find positions in the labour market commensurate with their university degrees and lose out to their male counterparts, who are often less educated, in respect of economic returns. The higher qualifications of women have an impact also on family formation. Social returns to women's and girls' education have so far not been fully explored. Well-educated women know better how to use opportunities, have healthier families and become involved in public life, and will often create self-employment. They are better consumers, health providers, community leaders and voters. A new balance needs to be found with respect to men's and women's achieving a better and more equal transition to the world of work.

Stereotyped attitudes reinforced at every institutional level, from kindergarten to university, remain root causes of inequalities and discrimination at all levels in society. Parents, teachers and women and girls themselves are vehicles for these attitudes in the field of education. Efforts to remove gender bias from educational material, curricula and teacher training are vital to ensuring a more gender-balanced education and need to be further developed.

C. Women and health

1. Introduction

The Platform for Action defined five strategic objectives under critical area of concern C, "Women and health": increase women's access throughout the life cycle to appropriate, affordable and quality health care, information and related services; strengthen preventive programmes that promote women's health; undertake gender-sensitive initiatives that address sexually transmitted diseases, HIV/AIDS, and sexual and reproductive health issues; promote research and disseminate information on women's health; and increase resources and monitor follow-up for women's health. In doing so, it also emphasized the importance of a holistic, life-cycle approach to women's health. The Platform for Action reiterated the agreements reached at the International

Conference on Population and Development in 1994, in particular with regard to women's reproductive health and rights, and added new ones, addressing the right of women to control all aspects of their health, and the relationship between women and men in sexual relations.

In line with the Programme of Action of the International Conference on Population and Development, [35] the Platform for Action set targets for "Governments, in collaboration with non-governmental organizations and employers' and workers' organizations and with the support of international institutions" (PfA, para. 106). These include, in particular: universal access to quality health services for women and girls; reduction of maternal mortality, and infant and child mortality (PfA, para. 106 (l)); worldwide reduction of severe and moderate malnutrition among children under the age of five, while giving special attention to the gender gap in nutrition; and a reduction in iron deficiency anaemia in girls and women (PfA, para. 106 (w)).

The Commission on the Status of Women in its agreed conclusions on women and health[36] reinforced the commitments of the Platform for Action and introduced new recommendations on women and infectious diseases, mental health, and occupational and environmental health, areas that had received little attention at the Fourth World Conference on Women. The Commission established a link between violence against women and their HIV status and appealed to women and men affected with HIV/AIDS and sexually transmitted diseases to inform their partners. It also addressed health sector reform and development, suggesting the integration of gender analysis in the health sector and the reduction of occupational segregation in the health workforce.

The special session of the General Assembly on an overall review and appraisal of the implementation of the Programme of Action of the International Conference on Population and Development (1999) evaluated progress made since the Conference in achieving its goals and objectives.[37] It agreed on interim benchmarks for achieving Conference goals which included targets related to safe and effective family planning methods, obstetric care, prevention and management of reproductive tract infections including sexually transmitted diseases, and barrier methods that should be offered by primary health care and family planning centres. Other targets were established for the number of births assisted by skilled attendants; reduction of the gap between the number of individuals using contraceptives and those expressing a desire to space or limit their families; access to information, education and services to reduce vulnerability to HIV infection; and reduction of the HIV infection rates.[38]

At its twentieth session (1999), the Committee on the Elimination of Discrimination against Women adopted general recommendation 24 on article 12 of the Convention on the Elimination of All Forms of Discrimination against Women—women and health,[39] based on the results of the Committee's examination of the periodic reports of States parties, which offers a detailed interpretation of women's right to health and recommendations to States parties to the Convention in respect of complying with the articles of the Convention. The Committee noted that women's right to health could be achieved only when women's fundamental right to nutritional well-being throughout the lifespan had been met. Many other provisions of the Convention have implicit or indirect bearing on women's rights in relation to health and have been taken up in previous general recommendations of the Committee.

National action plans on the implementation of the Platform for Action consider women and health a priority; out of 116 national action plans filed with the United Nations Secretariat, 90 per cent dealt with this critical area of concern and established national benchmarks or set specific targets.[40] Responses to the questionnaire regarding implementing the Platform for Action show that several countries referred to these national action plans.

2. Achievements in the implementation of strategic objectives

(a) National health strategies

In the follow-up to Cairo and Beijing, many countries have formulated national strategies for women's health, sometimes focusing on the protection and promotion of safe motherhood. Many have established national committees on women's health to address women's health needs, that go beyond reproductive issues to include women's health throughout the life cycle. Others have revised existing policies to incorporate gender, reproductive health and other emerging concerns. Monitoring mechanisms were established to oversee implementation of the national plans, sometimes consisting of representatives and insurers from various organizations in the health-care sector, social services, and patients' and women's organizations.

The Platform for Action recognized that "lack of food and inequitable distribution of food for girls and women in the household, inadequate access to safe water, sanitation facilities and fuel supplies, particularly in rural and poor urban areas, and deficient housing conditions" had a negative effect on health (PfA, para. 92). Some Member States have taken action to supply safe water to rural communities and promote safe housing. Changes in the supply of drinking water and better sanitation have improved the quality of the environment and thus the living and health conditions of women. Another important action is the sensitization of the population and women in particular to the importance of a clean environment and hygiene and its impact on health.

Many women suffer from malnutrition, in particular iron deficiency anaemia. It is reported that 67 per cent of countries affected by iodine deficiency disorders have made progress towards achieving universal salt iodization, and 48 per cent have made substantial progress since the major conferences in the 1990s on food and nutrition recommended action to reduce poverty, food insecurity and undernutrition.[41] Several countries added micronutrients to foods commonly consumed and provided micronutrient supplementation and food fortification (vitamin A, iodine and iron), in particular for pregnant women. Burundi reports that iodine capsules are distributed to pregnant women and infants. Algeria, for example, reports that the inclusion of iron supplements reduced anaemia from 40 per cent (1980) to 17 per cent (1996). To achieve sustainable food production and consumption, some countries promoted research into the nutritional values of local products. In the Philippines, a home and community food production programme was introduced to ensure and improve family food security by providing seeds, seedlings and other planting material for kitchen gardens. Many countries offered nutrition counselling and education on desirable food and eating practices for mothers, sometimes targeting high-risk pregnant women. Community nutrition centres and prenatal nutrition programmes have been established, along with programmes to protect women consumers from the risk of consumption or the use of health-harming goods, mainly food and cosmetics. Media-based programmes with a gender perspective focus on the increase of awareness of good nutritional habits. Efforts are being made to establish programmes on nutrition and the management of chronic diseases and HIV/AIDS through nutrition, in some countries; in others, campaigns address bulimia and anorexia among adolescents.

Several Member States have introduced legal measures to ensure women's access to quality health care, in particular with regard to reproductive health. Some laws stipulate that health plans should cover prenatal and post-partum care, birthing and breastfeeding-related care, while others define duration of maternity leave and leave for lactating women, in order to ensure better reproductive health. In Cyprus, for example, the Maternity Protection Law (1997) and Social Insurance Amendment Law (1998) guarantee paid maternal leave of 16 weeks to both biological and adoptive mothers. In Ireland, the Parental Leave Act (1998) gives both parents a statutory entitlement to unpaid parental leave. Legislation in San Marino provides for mandatory maternity leave of 150 days. The Islamic Republic of Iran reported that it had increased maternity leave from three to four months and that one-hour leave is now mandated for lactating women.

The Commonwealth Secretariat has worked extensively on gender management systems (GMS) and has introduced them into the health sector through a series of regional workshops involving all stakeholders in health and health care worldwide. Some national health plans incorporate a gender perspective or include at least a partial gender planning approach, such as data collection disaggregated by sex or identification of options for gender mainstreaming. In Bolivia, for example, the new Strategic Health Plan (1997) includes mainstreaming of the gender approach in all components.

The integration of care for women into public-health and welfare policy was a goal in many countries, sometimes accompanied by efforts towards decentralization and prioritization of rural and marginalized zones. The Islamic Republic of Iran, for instance, established "rural health houses". New technologies have also been introduced. In Mexico, isolated populations are connected to health services through a telephone service called "Planificatel".

Bilateral and multilateral development assistance recognized the crucial linkage between health and the promotion of gender equality. The OECD/DAC issued a 21st Century Strategy recognizing equality and empowerment of women as a key goal and building on the Platform for Action and the Programme of Action of the International Conference on Population and Development.[42] The Canadian International Development Agency (CIDA), for instance, established specific objectives in its health strategy to improve women's health and targets programmes for the girl-child and to address trauma and violence. The implementation of gender-based analysis throughout government health policies and initiatives has proceeded very slowly in some countries as a result of attitudinal, operational and theoretical barriers.

The gender bias in health research has been addressed by several countries. In Canada, Centres of Excellence for the Women's Health Programme, a partnership between academic and community-based groups, have been established. For clinical drugs trials, the Canadian Government stipulated that manufacturers applying for market approval of drugs had to include at least the same proportion of women in their clinical trials as would use the drug. Iceland reported that it had passed regulations on pharmaceutical research and its effects on women and men.

(b) Access to health care
Several countries have maintained efforts to provide guaranteed preventive primary health care in the form of free health services, family planning and sex education provided free of charge. Chile, for example, established a link between the decrease in the maternal mortality rate, the universal coverage of professional care at birth and the extension of primary health coverage. Others, for example, Armenia and Belgium, make access to health insurance easier by extending coverage to target groups for preferential treatment or providing a payment waiver for women from socially vulnerable groups. In Ireland, where medical insurance is still tied to employment, maternity and adoptive benefits were extended to the self-employed in 1997.

Many countries report the establishment of solidarity and community pharmacies and the provision of subsidized essential drugs. A few have established national centres for the procurement of essential medication to ensure access to generic medication at low costs. A few African States, for example, Cameroon, undertake research into traditional pharmacy and advance cooperation between traditional medicine and modern medicine in the treatment of women and children. Angola is offering training for traditional healers. In the Philippines, modules on self-care of women throughout the life cycle including the use of herbal medicines have been developed. Some countries with a high number of indigenous populations pay greater attention to programmes for traditional medicine and healing.

(c) Reproductive health

After the International Conference on Population and Development (1994) and the Fourth World Conference on Women (1995), several Member States introduced major changes in their reproductive health policy, shifting from mother and child health to reproductive health services and strengthening primary health-care services to include reproductive health. In India, the target-driven approach to population control has been replaced by an approach that is empowering women and improving overall health, especially reproductive health through informed choices. In Mexico, efforts have been made to improve maternal and infant mortality statistics through more accurate registry and information on the death certificate regarding whether the death was related to pregnancy.

Many countries improved access to and availability of reproductive health services. Cuba, for example, reported that its maternal and child health programmes contributed to decreases in the infant mortality, perinatal mortality and under-five mortality rates. In many countries, the number of assisted childbirths increased and continuing training was offered for doctors and birth attendants. Health services, in particular prenatal services, were extended to rural areas. Mobile teams, such as "solidarity caravans" and health workers travelling house to house, provide reproductive health care, including prenatal and postnatal care, family planning and gynaecology. Among the special measures taken was the introduction of new midwifery and elimination of tetanus infection among newborn babies. Some countries report that a significant number of traditional birth attendants and traditional healers had been trained in safe motherhood skills and infection control.

Strategies for safe motherhood such as the identification of risks for mothers and newborn have been developed. High-risk, vulnerable areas receive technical guidance for monitoring of maternal and perinatal mortality. In Peru, for example, weak points in the health system are identified in the pilot programme "10 steps for a healthy birth". Other countries provide basic packages of medications for immediate treatment of pregnancy complications, to be distributed to hospitals and health centres with large numbers of maternal deaths due to complications. Several countries mention the provision of emergency obstetric care. In Indonesia, the Mother-Friendly Movement developed mother-friendly areas and hospitals and succeeded in mobilizing community and intersectoral resources for safe maternity, including provision of village ambulances, and village maternity homes, and introduction of maternity saving programmes, as a means of achieving funding by local communities for expenses linked to maternity. It was noted that a transformed maternal and perinatal health programme with a gender perspective had to be less purely biomedical in nature.

Support for breastfeeding has increased. Some States have adopted national policies on breastfeeding. In South Africa, for example, the Labour Relations Act was amended in 1996 to include a national breastfeeding code. In Trinidad and Tobago, the national breastfeeding policy recommends that babies should be breastfed within one hour of birth. Some countries, primarily those in Africa, have undertaken awareness-raising campaigns for mothers about the benefits of breastfeeding and have revised the commercialization code of milk substitutes. Turkmenistan carried out public education campaigns on breastfeeding in different regions, while Ireland launched a Baby Friendly Hospital Initiative to encourage breastfeeding.

Several countries report inappropriate and excessive medication given to women during pregnancy and childbirth, noting particularly the medication and dehumanization of birthing. In Italy, three regions have passed legislation to modify the patterns of assistance in delivery, so as to reduce the excessive number of Caesarean sections. In Mexico, some hospitals established a programme called "Protocolo de Segunda Opinión" asking for a second opinion in order to reduce Caesarean sections from the current 30 per cent. Awareness-raising activities and information on women's health are considered important steps towards preventing excessive medicalization of health care.

Many Member States report an increase in use of modern contraceptives. Training was provided to private physicians and medical personnel on updated techniques of family planning. To provide information and create greater response to contraceptives, awareness campaigns and health education sessions were carried out, sometimes targeting specific groups such as couples registered for marriage, pregnant women and women's organizations. New Zealand provides two varieties of oral contraceptive free of charge. In Fiji, contraceptives and family planning counselling is provided free of charge in all medical centers and nursing stations. In France, two emergency contraceptives, otherwise known as morning-after pills, were introduced in 1999 and are available based on medical prescription.

The Platform for Action recommends that laws containing punitive measures against women who have undergone illegal abortions be revised (PfA, para. 106 (k)). In replies received from Member States, no reference is made to revisions of abortion laws related to this specific recommendation. A few countries have liberalized their abortion laws since the Fourth World Conference on Women. For example, Burkina Faso (1996), South Africa (1996) and Cambodia (1997) amended their existing legislation or enacted new legislation to improve women's access to safe and legal abortion. Others such as Guyana (1995), the Russian Federation (1996) and Portugal (1997) further defined the indications for the performance of abortions on social or medical grounds or extended the time-frame within which abortion was allowed. The Russian Federation indicated that it had reduced the number of abortions as a result of policies taken, including the increased availability of means of contraception. Others investigated the frequency of abortions as well as knowledge and attitudes of young women on family planning issues. Measures to raise awareness about the dangers of induced abortions have been introduced in Benin. Peru adopted a law on appropriate measures, coordinated by the Ministry of Health, to help women avoid abortion.

Infertility represents an emotional and financial burden for many couples and affects women in a particular way. With the development of infertility and reproductive technology becoming more widespread, especially in developing countries, the physical, psychological and social effects of medically assisted reproduction technology become an area of concern. Long-term effects include the psychological costs of failed treatment cycles, the employment costs of work absenteeism for treatment, and the health costs of multiple pregnancies to women, children and families. There is also a high rate of low birth weight infants, premature births and related harms and disabilities that require perinatal intensive care. Hormonal treatment might increase the risk of ovarian and breast cancer. A number of countries address the issue of infertility and its causes, acknowledging that prevention, in particular of sexually transmitted diseases, is the most important first step. Benin has elaborated a pilot project integrating treatment for sexually transmitted diseases, genital cancer and infertility into family planning. Information sessions, conferences and counselling on infertility, artificial insemination and assisted reproduction techniques have been organized in some countries.

Since the International Conference on Population and Development (1994), there has been general recognition that men have their own reproductive health needs and that their behaviour has an impact on the health of women. Voluntary and appropriate male methods of contraception are being promoted and tested, including new condoms, new hormonal methods of male contraception and reversible methods of male sterilization. In some countries, there is also a greater willingness of men to take part in clinical trials for male contraceptive methods.[43] Several countries have launched programmes to increase male involvement in reproductive health and increase women's attendance and better understanding of antenatal services. Efforts are made in India, for example, to involve men in growth monitoring sessions for children and provide information on childcare.

The Platform for Action recommends that girls have continuing access to information and services as they mature and recognizes the specific needs of adolescents with regard to education and information on sexual and reproductive health issues and on sexually transmitted diseases, including HIV/AIDS (PfA, paras. 106 (m) and 107 (g)). A first step is to gain knowledge of the reproductive needs and attitudes of young people. A project in Greece, for example, is investigating the extent of the knowledge and the attitudes of young women about family planning issues. Argentina is examining effects of institutional intervention on adolescent mothers. Many countries have developed strategies for the prevention of teenage pregnancy and sexually transmitted infections including measures for the promotion of better health for pre-teen and adolescent females. In the Russian Federation, for example, the first sanatorium or health resort division was established for the rehabilitation of reproductive disorders in teenage girls. Uganda introduced a Programme for the Enhancement of Adolescent Reproductive Health (PEARL) to raise awareness of adolescent girls' health. In Estonia, web sites for youth about reproductive health were opened in 1998.

The importance of campaigns, educational activities and training is recognized in many of the responses. Frequently these activities are carried out by non-governmental organizations or agreements have been established between health services and non-governmental organizations to create pedagogic material on sexual education for adolescents, parents and teachers. Youth organizations are also becoming involved in addressing family life education and conducting lectures, teacher training, peer counselling and parent team workshops.

(d) Sexually transmitted diseases (STDs), human
immunodeficiency virus (HIV) and acquired
immunodeficiency syndrome (AIDS)

The high incidence of sexually transmitted diseases (STDs) presents a great risk to reproductive health, through the risk of greater susceptibility to HIV infection and later infertility. Many countries have recognized the dangers linked to the spread of STDs and have taken steps to increase awareness and prevention and offer treatment. To improve accessibility and acceptability, treatment of STDs was integrated into family planning services in some countries. In Djibouti, a prevention centre for STDs was established. Special efforts were made in Rwanda, for example, to provide medicines for STDs.

Campaigns, workshops and clinics on STDs and their prevention have been conducted in many countries. Training courses on systematic management of STDs targeted general practitioners, medical officers, obstetricians, midwives and other basic health personnel in many countries. France carried out information campaigns for prostitutes so as to make them aware of STDs and HIV/AIDS infection. Public discussions on genital and urinary tract infections and diseases have been organized to create greater awareness of the problem. Saint Lucia, for example, produced a booklet on "sexual offences and the law" to familiarize women with problems such as STDs and measures for protection. The introduction of the female condom as a method of protection is reported in the Congo.

Little progress is reported with regard to HIV/AIDS, with the number of HIV infections among women rising steadily. In many developing countries, where 95 per cent of people with HIV live, the situation is deteriorating, especially in Africa. In Africa, the prevalence of HIV infection among females is now higher than among men, with young women under age 25 constituting the age group most at risk. Fifty-five per cent of HIV-positive adults in sub-Saharan Africa, 35 per cent in the Caribbean and 30 per cent in South and South-East Asia, are women, whereas the corresponding percentage in all other subregions is lower than 20 per cent. Many countries have developed national programmes or strategies to combat HIV/AIDS and incorporated gender-specific aspects. Increased attention has been given to HIV/AIDS infection among women of reproductive age and to mother-to-child transmission. Specific training programmes on HIV infection and pregnancy have been launched for midwives and obstetricians. In Burkina

Faso, for example, the training on HIV/AIDS of multipliers such as health workers, market women, students and young illiterate girls is one strategy being pursued. South Africa has set up a school health promotion programme with an emphasis on HIV/AIDS. Several countries give support to non-governmental organizations, in particular women's associations in AIDS education and prevention. Myanmar reports the production of information on HIV/AIDS prevention in different ethnic languages. Some national HIV/AIDS programmes include special measures for the protection of prostitutes such as regular testing. Others report positive results for treatment. Greece attributes a downward trend in the number of women suffering from AIDS in 1997 to free anti-retroviral treatment administered anonymously to all seropositive patients.

(e) Non-communicable diseases
With the increase in female life expectancy and changes of lifestyle, certain non-communicable diseases and disabilities become more common, in particular in older women. Women spend a greater proportion of their lives in the post-reproductive, post-menopausal years and become more vulnerable to non-communicable diseases such as cancer, cardiovascular diseases and other chronic diseases. A few countries report on initiatives taken. Hungary, for instance, introduced a "heart-friendly" programme for reducing heart and circulatory disease and promotion of good nutrition.

Early detection and screening are important, especially with respect to cancer. Many countries provide free cancer screening for all women aged 40-70 years, often through mobile screening units. Control programmes for breast and cervical cancers are considered a priority. Pap smears, early detection and treatment management are encouraged, and also, increasingly, in developing countries. As a result of greater awareness and screening services, the percentage of women over age 50 receiving mammograms has increased in the United States of America. Canada reports the lowest breast cancer mortality rates in the two provinces having the most extensive screening programmes and being among the highest utilizers of mammography. Several countries introduced new legislation and education programmes related to breast cancer detection and prevention. Belize, for example, produced a handbook on breast and cervical cancer to educate women and to offer encouragement to persons living with cancer.

Diabetes is affecting a larger number of women than men in developed countries (141 million women versus 31 million men), whereas the proportions are equal in developing countries (42 million in each case).[44] Several developing countries address chronic diseases, such as asthma, diabetes and hypertension, among women and have carried out campaigns or specific programmes such as screening.

(f) Other aspects of women's health
Given the increase in life expectancy, the number of older women has increased since 1995, in both developed and developing countries. In some developed countries, it is estimated that the proportion of older women will be as high as 23 per cent of the total female population in 2000. The age group of women aged 80 years or over is growing, with women outnumbering men 2.5 to 1 in Eastern Europe, Eastern Asia and Southern Africa. Several countries have carried out studies in gerontology to better understand ageing and its gender dimension. They address the health needs of elderly women and have established programmes to improve older women's access to quality health care. Most efforts focus on the prevention and treatment of chronic and degenerative disease, in particular osteoporosis. Hungary developed a national osteoporosis programme and established the Hungarian menopause society while San Marino set up a Centre for the Protection of Women in Menopause at the state hospital.

Many Member States have taken steps to ensure the effective integration of women with disabilities into society and their rehabilitation. In many countries, efforts are being made to increase the visibility of women with disabilities. In Ireland, for example, a 1996 Commission on the Status of People with Disabilities recognized disabled women as "double disadvantaged." In Ghana, the Ministry of Youth and Sports organizes annual games for people with disabilities, including women, and is providing facilities.

As more women enter the formal and informal labour market, approaches to occupational health and sexual harassment at the workplace have become part of national health strategies. The Finnish Institute for Occupational Health has conducted studies on how a gender perspective has been integrated into occupational health and safety and established a cross-disciplinary working party for the follow-up of women's occupational health and development. Norway is improving statistics on gender and work-related accidents and diseases. In Spain, a law for the prevention of occupational risks and promotion of safety and health of pregnant and lactating workers has been adopted. Romania set up an Action Programme on women's right to be healthy at work, focused on the promotion of reproductive health among female employees, which will be implemented by trade unions.

The number of women smokers is increasing, in particular among the young and very young age groups. Several countries report an increase of drug abuse by minors, including young women. Few countries have taken steps to counteract this trend by introducing specific tobacco prevention and rehabilitation programmes targeted at young women. The United States of America developed a comprehensive plan to reduce smoking among children and adolescents by 50 per cent. Interventions focus on strengthening smoking regulations, offering assistance and advice to those wishing to stop and preventing young people from taking up smoking. Efforts to limit smoking and alcohol consumption among pregnant women are increasing.

Some countries, such as Germany, have undertaken studies on psychotropic substance use in women to determine the gender aspects of addiction, prevention and treatment. Counselling and support for addicted women have been provided. In several countries, anti-smoking, -drinking and -drug campaigns in schools and communities are targeting particularly young women and parenting adolescents. Few countries offer specific rehabilitation programmes for female substance abusers who often drop out of mixed programmes. Rehabilitation therapies for women address the traumatic experiences of sexual and other abuse experienced by female drug users and provide childcare and vocational training.

There is growing recognition that women represent a large proportion of the estimated 400 million people with anxiety disorders and the 340 million with mood disorders worldwide.[45] Poverty, domestic isolation and overwork, powerlessness resulting from low levels of education and economic dependence, and violence in all its forms have an impact on the mental health and general well-being of the majority of women. Several countries have taken steps to improve the mental health of women. In Argentina, the first national meeting on psychological diagnosis addressed women's mental health. The Mental Health Foundation in the Netherlands carried out a study on the situation of HIV-positive women. Chad reported that it has established five centres for mental health for women, while San Marino announced the establishment of counselling services for women who have had mastectomies.

(g) Education and prevention

Many developed countries promoted education campaigns for healthy lifestyles which included physical exercise, balanced nutrition and no alcohol and no tobacco. Some countries highlight the importance of a healthy lifestyle in their national heath plans, in particular the fundamental role of sports and physical exercise along with diet and healthy habits. Some have developed national health plans along those lines. In the Islamic Republic of Iran, for example, the establishment of female sports clubs has been promoted, even in rural areas. In Italy, the Decree for the Reform of the Italian National Olympic Committee deals with equal representation of men and women in the elective offices of the national sports federations.

In many countries, comprehensive resource books on women's health have been published so as to make women aware of their health and body needs, enhance prevention and offer support in case of disease. These handbooks explain body functions, including reproductive health, and inform about diseases in an easily understandable way. Radio programmes are a popular way to educate a large female audience, for example, in the Congo.

Progress has been made in incorporating women's health and reproductive health in undergraduate and postgraduate curricula, in hospitals and universities. A few countries have introduced gender training in health services or a gender perspective into the training of health workers. In some countries, the medical curriculum for the medical midwifery and nursing schools has been revised, introducing violence against women as a topic.

To upgrade the training of health professionals, midwives and nurses, and improve the health provider-client relationship, workshops were held on specific topics such as updated techniques on family planning, cervical cancer and sexually transmitted diseases. Several countries offered retraining for health personnel to improve the health provider-client relationship, in particular through training in counselling and interpersonal communication. The development of ethical codes of conduct for the medical professions has been pursued.

3. Obstacles in the implementation of strategic objectives

The gap between policy and implementation persists. This is most visible in the field of reproductive health, where some programmes are still geared towards population control. The existing backlog in the adjustment of programmes and laws to meet international standards is of concern.

Many Governments state the difficulty in financial and human resources to ensure reliable provision of health care for women. The absence of infrastructure, information and qualitative services, in particular in rural areas, is the main obstacle. Lack of equipment and specialization as well as large requirements for infrastructure has an impact on basic services, including hygienic conditions, and affects, in particular, preventive medicine and the initiation of innovative programmes. Staff shortages, the high turnover rate of medical personnel and the brain drain of qualified staff are further impediments. Some countries recognize administrative deficiencies such as the malfunctioning of health committees, lack of strong management and failure to create a structural link between quality care and policy. Poor standards of health services are deplored in emergency situation conditions such as those in refugee camps. Poverty, illness and ignorance continue to cause malnutrition and anaemia. The recent economic crisis is also reported to contribute to serious nutritional disorders such as anaemia and toxaemia among poor pregnant women.

The increasing privatization of health and medical sectors in all parts of the world has an impact on ensuring equal access to health care, and affects, in particular, the early detection of diseases. User fees or co-payments, which have been introduced in public-health establishments by some countries, represent a burden for poor families in urban and rural areas. Weaknesses in the prevention and primary care services have an impact on the health of women. The separation between public and private health care and decentralization make circulation of information and knowledge as well as training for the implementation of new methods more difficult. In countries with inadequate health coverage and social security systems, women are particularly hard hit, especially women of childbearing age who spend more on out-of-pocket health-care costs than men do. Households with incomes below the poverty line and women belonging to vulnerable groups such as indigenous populations are especially affected.

Several developing countries report a lack of personnel, in particular female personnel, in health services. This is compounded by a lack of training institutions for nursing and paramedical staff, insufficient training of health providers in general and absence of specialized training such as training in the health of older people and HIV/AIDS. The lack of gender awareness among health professionals remains of concern everywhere. The participation of women in management of health, *inter alia*, in health committees, has not significantly improved and is very low.

The lack of gender-sensitive health research and technology remains of concern. Several countries report a lack of data disaggregated by sex and the persisting gap in systematic and continuous data-collection systems. Little progress has been achieved in the development of gender-sensitive, relevant and user-friendly programme indicators.

The persistence of sociocultural barriers and a weak response of the community to programmes are noted in many of the responses by Member States. Developing countries and countries in transition complain about the lack of health education and awareness of its importance. They recognize that women's lack of education hinders their access to health services and would ultimately require specific health campaigns designed to reach out to illiterate and less educated women. Mass media and other forms of education and information are still insufficiently used. Sexual education is often not included in qualitative education about health and healthy ways of life and no emphasis is put on reaching out to young people.

In reproductive health, cultural taboos and women's lack of knowledge about their bodies remain major obstacles, in particular among rural women and teenagers. Reproductive services may be inaccessible or little used when traditional attitudes prevail, as reflected, for example, in men's preventing their wives from using these services. Another obstacle is the unavailability of reproductive health services in regular health care, as well as lack of trained personnel and appropriate premises for family planning centres.

Although more women than ever before know of modern contraceptive methods, a huge gap persists in respect of availability and usage. In some developed countries, condoms and coitus interruptus continue to be the most prevalent method of contraception. In developing countries, the shortage of reliable, safe contraceptives and dependency on foreign supply or government services are of concern. The shortage is alarming in countries with high numbers of sexually transmitted diseases and HIV/AIDS. In many countries, particularly countries in transition, abortion is still considered as the accepted and even the primary birth control method. More needs to be done to increase men's involvement on a larger scale. The misperception that reproductive health and family planning are merely women's problems persists and is still leading to inadequate participation of males in women's health issues. The lack of information on the causes of infertility remains of concern. A financial, medical or psychosocial assessment of the impact that assisted reproduction techniques may have on the health of women and their children and society as a whole is not being made.

Women in rural areas and from indigenous communities are seldom reached by medical services and special efforts need to be made to expand them to hinterland areas. Some countries acknowledge that adequate attention is not given to menopausal and elderly women. The absence of a holistic approach to the needs of women and girls throughout the life cycle along with the lack of a gender approach in caring for the elderly has a negative impact. A lack of funds and specialized staff trained in dealing with drug-dependent women and ignorance about gender aspects of drug addiction are acknowledged. Tropical diseases and tuberculosis deserve greater attention.

4. Conclusions and further actions

Reproductive health, in particular the high rate of maternal and infant mortality, remains a concern in the majority of countries as well as a challenge for the international community. Efforts need to be made to implement the targets established in the Platform for Action, *inter alia*, through existing initiatives, such as the Safe Motherhood Initiative, the Baby-Friendly Hospital Initiative and the International Code of Marketing of Breast-milk Substitutes.

There is a growing demand for reproductive health services and for access to a wide range of contraceptive methods. Men's involvement in reproductive health and integration of a gender perspective in all programmes and initiatives need to be promoted more consistently. The causes of infertility, the burden it puts on couples and the effects of medically assisted reproduction technology on the health of women deserve increased attention.

HIV/AIDS infection rates among women have reached alarming numbers, in particular among the young. All methods of prevention including female-controlled methods need to be secured as well as access to treatment for those infected. HIV transmission from mother to child, including the dilemma centred around breastfeeding, deserves greater attention and ethically sound strategies.

Longer life expectancy of women and changes in lifestyle and diet bring with them increased lifestyle-related diseases and disabilities. Further efforts should go into research to explore gender differences over the whole lifespan in the prevention and treatment of non-communicable diseases. Education and public campaigns are instrumental in raising awareness on healthy lifestyles. Tropical diseases and tuberculosis place great limitations on the life of many women in developing countries. Mental disorders in women are often caused by social problems and need to be recognized and treated as such. With more women in the labour force, occupational and environmental health has gained in importance. Gender-sensitive work environments need to be safe and ergonomically designed to prevent occupational hazards.

The question of privatization of basic social services raises important financial and ethical questions on how to ensure access for all, including poor households and women belonging to vulnerable groups such as indigenous populations. Health sector reform and development efforts need to ensure the promotion of women's health in all its aspects, as expressed at national level in health budgets and through international cooperation.

D. Violence against women

1. Introduction

The Platform for Action identifies violence against women as one of the priority concerns of the international community and one particularly deserving of an urgent response. Critical area D, "Violence against women", categorizes such violence as an obstacle to the achievement of the objectives of equality, development and peace. This area is interlinked with critical area of concern I, "Human rights of women." These critical areas classify violence against women as conduct that both violates and impairs or nullifies the enjoyment by women of their human rights and fundamental freedoms. The Platform for Action points out that, in all societies, to a greater or lesser degree, women and girls are subjected to physical, sexual and psychological abuse that cuts across lines of income, class and culture.

Consistent with the Declaration on the Elimination of Violence against Women,[46] the Platform for Action defines "violence against women" to mean any act of gender-based violence that results, or is likely to result, in physical, sexual or psychological harm or suffering to women, including threats of such acts, coercion or arbitrary deprivation of liberty, whether occurring in public or in private life (PfA, para. 113).

Particular forms of violence against women not specifically mentioned in the Declaration are also specified in the Platform for Action. These include violations of the rights of women in situations of armed conflict, in particular murder, systematic rape, sexual slavery and forced pregnancy; forced sterilization and forced abortion; coercive/forced use of contraceptives; female infanticide; and prenatal sex selection.

Although noting that women in all countries, irrespective of culture, class and income, are at risk for all or some of these forms of violence, the Platform for Action indicates that some groups of women are especially vulnerable. These include women belonging to minority groups, indigenous women, refugee women, women migrants, including women migrant workers, women living in poverty in rural or remote communities, destitute women, women in institutions or in detention, female children, women with disabilities, elderly women, displaced women, repatriated women, women living in poverty and women in situations of armed conflict, foreign occupation, wars of aggression, civil wars and terrorism, including hostage-taking.

The issue of violence against women has been on the international agenda for over 20 years, and knowledge about its causes and consequences, as well as its incidence and measures to combat it, has developed greatly. Since the Fourth World Conference on Women, resolutions relating to the various forms of violence to which women are subjected in diverse settings have been adopted by the Commission on the Status of Women, the Commission on Human Rights, the Commission on Crime Prevention and Criminal Justice, the Economic and Social Council and the General Assembly. The agreed conclusions of the Commission on the Status of Women, particularly those adopted at its forty-second session in 1998 on violence against women,[47] also recommend ways to eliminate its occurrence. Particular manifestations of violence against women, including trafficking in women and traditional practices affecting the health of women and girls, such as female genital mutilation, have been the focus of the Subcommission on the Promotion and Protection of Human Rights. The problem has also remained a concern of the specialized agencies, funds and programmes of the United Nations, including the Office of the United Nations High Commissioner for Refugees (UNHCR), the United Nations Children's Fund (UNICEF), the United Nations Development Fund for Women (UNIFEM), the United Nations Population Fund (UNFPA) and the World Health Organization (WHO).

United Nations human rights treaty bodies have continued to pay close attention to the various forms of violence against women in their concluding comments/observations and general recommendations/ comments. In particular, the Committee on the Elimination of Discrimination against Women has examined developments in this context in its review of implementation of its general recommendations 12[48] and 19[49] on violence against women and 14 on female circumcision.[50] Since the Fourth World Conference on Women, the Special Rapporteur on violence against women, its causes and consequences, first appointed by the Commission on Human Rights in 1994,[51] has continued to report on and make recommendations relating to various forms of violence against women, including violence against women within the family, violence related to traditions and customs, such as female genital mutilation, dowry violence and widowhood rites, and violence in the community, including rape, trafficking in women and violence against migrant women workers. She has also considered violence against women in the context of armed conflict, and in prisons, and has reviewed States' compliance with their international obligations with regard to the elimination of domestic violence, and with regard to reproductive rights. In pursuing her mandate, the Special Rapporteur has embarked on missions to Member States of the United Nations, and made recommendations with regard to measures to eliminate violence against women. The various forms of violence against women have also been examined by other country-specific and thematic rapporteurs, including the Special Rapporteur on the sale of children, child prostitution and child pornography.

The Platform for Action establishes three strategic objectives relating to the elimination of violence against women: to take integrated measures to prevent and eliminate violence against women; to study the causes and consequences of violence against women and the effectiveness of preventive measures; and to eliminate trafficking in women and assist victims of violence due to prostitution and trafficking. Recommendations for the achievement of these strategic objectives essentially call for government condemnation of violence against women; due diligence in the prevention, investigation and punishment of acts of such violence; implementation of existing international standards with respect to violence against women and the support of international mechanisms in that regard; adoption or effective implementation of legal measures to confront all forms of gender-based violence against women; introduction or strengthening of awareness-raising in respect of the various forms of violence against women, their causes and consequences, in all sectors, *inter alia*, through an active and visible policy of mainstreaming a gender perspective in all policies and programmes related to violence against women, research and training and education for specific groups; and provision of services for those affected by violence. Specific recommendations also address the elimination of trafficking in women and the assistance of victims, particularly young women and children, of violence due to prostitution and trafficking.

Significant steps have been taken in the last ten years to address violence against women, with many strategies having been adopted since the adoption of the Platform for Action to translate its recommendations into action. In addition to information supplied by Member States in response to the questionnaire on the implementation of the Beijing Platform for Action, national action plans on the implementation of the Platform for Action address strategies that are planned or have been introduced to confront this critical area. The national action plans and the responses of Member States to the questionnaire indicate that in some countries initiatives to address the various forms of violence against women pre-dated the adoption of the Platform for Action, but have been improved or developed since September 1995. In other Member States, initiatives have been introduced in response to the Platform for Action.

2. Achievements in the implementation of the strategic objectives

(a) International level

Since the adoption of the Platform for Action, international activity relating to violence has included further development of legal measures and strategies to address gender-based violence against women; identification of specific settings in which women are especially vulnerable to the risk of gender-based violence; and continued emphasis on the mainstreaming of a gender perspective in all policies and programmes of the United Nations of relevance in this regard.[52] The mainstreaming directive has sought to ensure that relevant policies, programme formulation and delivery, for example, in the context of human rights, refugee protection, humanitarian relief and health, hitherto developed with little attention to their differential impact on women and men, take account of these differentials to promote the interests of women on a basis of equality with men.

On 6 October 1999, in its resolution 54/4, the General Assembly adopted an Optional Protocol to the Convention on the Elimination of All Forms of Discrimination against Women which allows women the right to seek redress for violations of their human rights, *inter alia*, with regard to gender-based violence. On 10 December 1999, the Optional Protocol was opened for signature, ratification and accession. On 22 December 2000, upon ratification by ten States parties, the Optional Protocol went into force. The Rome Statute of the International Criminal Court[53] adopted in July 1998 builds on provisions governing the International Tribunal for the Prosecution of Persons Responsible for Serious Violations of International Humanitarian Law in the Territory of the Former Yugoslavia since 1991 and the International Criminal Tribunal for the Prosecution of Persons Responsible for Genocide and Other Serious Violations of International Humanitarian Law Committed in the Territory of Rwanda and Rwandan Citizens Responsible for Genocide and Other Such Violations Committed in the Territory of Neighbouring States between 1 January and 31 December 1994, and the practices of those Tribunals, and specifically addresses gender-based international crimes relating to bodily integrity.

On 12 December 1997, at its fifty-second session, the General Assembly, in its resolution 52/86, adopted Model Strategies and Practical Measures on the Elimination of Violence against Women in the Field of

Crime Prevention and Criminal Justice, contained in the annex thereto. These Model Strategies are put forward as guidelines to be used by Governments in their efforts to address, within the criminal justice system, the various manifestations of violence against women. They outline detailed proposals with respect to criminal law and procedure; police practice; sentencing and corrections; victim support and assistance; health and social services; training for police, criminal justice officials, practitioners and professionals involved in the criminal justice system; research and evaluation; measures of prevention; and international co-operation. Specific recommendations are also made with regard to activities to follow-up the Model Strategies. Progress in the implementation of the Model Strategies based on information provided by 26 Member States was outlined in the report of the Secretary-General on the elimination of violence against women[54] submitted to the Economic and Social Council at its substantive session of 1999 and to the Assembly at its fifty-fourth session.

Monitoring of the implementation of the Plan of Action for the Elimination of Harmful Traditional Practices affecting the Health of Women and Children, adopted by the Subcommission on the Promotion and Protection of Human Rights[55] which recommends strategies to eliminate practices, including female genital mutilation, has continued within the Subcommission. The General Assembly addressed the issue of traditional or customary practices affecting the health of women and children in resolutions 52/99 and 53/117, and reports on the implementation of those resolutions, reflecting action taken at international, regional and national levels towards the eradication of these practices, were submitted at its fifty-third and fifty-fourth sessions in 1998 and 1999, respectively. UNFPA, UNICEF and WHO issued a joint statement on female genital mutilation in April 1997, offering collaborative support for government and community efforts in this regard. As part of an international advocacy campaign, UNFPA appointed a Special Ambassador for the Elimination of Female Genital Mutilation in September 1997. In May 1999, a workshop for members of the West African Economic and Monetary Union (UEMOA) held in Ouagadougou, Burkina Faso, adopted the Ouagadougou Declaration[56] which called for the adoption of national legislation condemning female genital mutilation, as well as other measures, such as the establishment of special services to control the migratory flow of circumcisers, in order to eliminate this practice. The Organization of African Unity (OAU) First Ministerial Conference on Human Rights in Africa, held from 12 to 16

April 1999 at Grand Bay, Mauritius, also urged all African States to work assiduously towards the elimination of discrimination against women and the abolition of cultural practices that dehumanized or demeaned women and children.

The vulnerability of women migrant workers to violence has emerged as a concern of the international community, as have the trafficking in women and violence associated with prostitution, *inter alia*, in the context of sex tourism. The Commission on the Status of Women, the Commission on Human Rights and the General Assembly have considered the Secretary-General's reports on these issues and have adopted resolutions that suggested strategies relevant to these settings. Pursuant to Assembly resolutions 53/111 and 53/114 of 9 December 1998, the *Ad hoc* Committee on the Elaboration of a Convention against Transnational Organized Crime formally began its work in early 1999. Significant progress has been made in drafting the convention and the three additional protocols to the convention, including those relating to the illegal transporting of and trafficking in migrants, and trafficking in human beings, especially women and children. At the regional level, The Hague Ministerial Declaration on the European Guidelines for Effective Measures to Prevent and Combat Trafficking in Women for the Purposes of Sexual Exploitation was adopted by the European Union Ministers for Equality and Justice in 1997. A second Communication to the Council and the European Parliament on Trafficking in women was issued in December 1998.[57] At the subregional level, the South Asian Association for Regional Cooperation is continuing to develop a convention against trafficking in women and girls.

(b) National level

Approaches at national level to gender-based violence against women emphasize policy and law reform; the provision of services and assistance; sector-specific and public education and programmes; training; and advocacy campaigns to address values, attitudes and actions related to violence against women.

Many Member States indicate that the eradication of violence against women is a national priority. Most countries that responded to the questionnaire identify violence against women as one of the critical areas in which action is necessary. Several, including Belize, Colombia, Finland, Germany, Mexico and Norway, have introduced or plan to introduce in the near future national action plans or programmes on violence against women, or on some forms of violence against women. Ministerial-level and other coordination committees across ministries and protocols for various agencies have also been introduced by some Member States including Chile, Japan and Peru. In 1997, a National Domestic Violence Summit was convened by the Australian Prime Minister, while in 1999 an inter-ministerial circular on violence against women signed by four government ministers was published in France. Since 1997, the Polish Government has executed a programme entitled "Counteracting Violence—Equalizing Chances" in cooperation with the UNDP. Several Member States, including Australia and Sweden, have earmarked significant resources for strategies to address gender-based violence against women. In some Member States, national programmes on forms of violence against women have incorporated specific projects on particular groups of women, including indigenous women, minority and immigrant women, older women, rural women and women with disabilities and children (Australia, Ireland).

The major focus of activity has been on law reform, with many Member States seeking to provide women with comprehensive legal protection from various forms of violence. Twenty-nine Member States in Latin America and the Caribbean have now ratified the Inter-American Convention on the Prevention, Punishment and Eradication of Violence against Women (the Convention of Belém do Pará),[58] which imposes on States parties immediate and progressive obligations to eliminate violence against women, and also provides for individual communications on the issue of violence. Thirteen of these have deposited their instrument of ratification since the adoption of the Platform for Action, and most of the States parties to this Convention have elaborated legislation and other measures with regard to various forms of violence against women (Argentina, Belize, Bolivia, Brazil, Canada, Chile, Colombia, Costa Rica, Ecuador, El Salvador, Guatemala, Guyana, Mexico, Panama, Peru and Uruguay). Measures taken by Member States of the Organization of American States (OAS) in this context are described in the report of the Inter-American Commission on Human Rights on the status of women in the Americas.[59]

Criminal and civil provisions to address violence against women in the family have been adopted, with many States recognizing that violence perpetrated by a husband should be treated in the same way as violence perpetrated by a stranger. In at least one country (Sweden), criminal acts directed by men towards women with whom they have a close relationship are defined as gross violations of a woman's integrity and attract more severe punishment than cases of the same acts directed against strangers. Sexual violence against women by their husbands has been criminalized in several States, including Austria, Belarus, Bhutan, Cyprus, Hungary, Mexico, Portugal and Seychelles where previously this conduct did not amount to criminal activity.

A number of States have introduced legislation on specific forms of violence against women. At least nine countries in Africa, for example, have introduced legislation to address female genital mutilation, while other countries with immigrant populations that practise this ritual have passed similar statutes (Australia, Canada, New Zealand, the United Kingdom and the United States of America). Legal provisions in this context have often been bolstered by public information and sensitization campaigns on the practice (Niger and Nigeria).

Innovative measures to combat stalking and harassment have been introduced in several States (for example United Kingdom). A number of States, including Belize, Bolivia, Iceland, Ireland, Israel, South Africa and Thailand, have introduced sexual harassment legislation pertinent to the workplace and educational institutions, while others, including the Netherlands and Sweden, have strengthened such legislation or widened it to address specific sectors, such as sports.

"Sex tourism" provisions that allow for the prosecution of acts of sexual abuse committed abroad have been introduced in several States (Belgium and Canada) and campaigns to increase public awareness of sex tourism offences, *inter alia*, on international aircraft, have also been adopted (Canada, Finland and Germany). In several countries, the criminal code has been reviewed to make offences of sex tourism, and corruption of minors, serious crimes (Belgium, Canada, Ethiopia and Mexico); a few also require all diplomatic and consular posts to report on sexual crimes committed by their nationals abroad (Belgium).

Evidentiary and procedural reforms, which seek to ameliorate court proceedings, have also been introduced with the aim of encouraging victims of abuse to come forward, with some countries allowing for the appointment of an assistant prosecutor to act on the complainant's behalf (Finland). Civil orders, such as restraining provisions and exclusion injunctions specifically applicable to cases of domestic violence, have been introduced in a number of States (Antigua and Barbuda, Austria, Italy and Turkey) or are under active consideration (Chile).

Several countries that already provided such orders have added innovative conditions to these orders, for example, with regard to firearms or alcohol (Australia and Canada). Since the adoption of the Platform for Action, for example, Israel's law on prevention of violence in the family has been amended to require a court that does not include weapons' prohibitions in injunctions to justify its decision in writing. Australia has also introduced gun control legislation and a national gun buy-back scheme under which 643,000 firearms have been surrendered since 1996. Access to firearms is also denied to those who have been the subject of a domestic violence injunction.

At least one country (Iceland) has adopted new legislation providing for State compensation of criminal activity, including violence against women. A number of countries have also sought to ensure that legal provisions that impact on the situation of women subjected to violence, such as immigration laws, do not lead to further victimization (Germany, for example, gives independent residence rights to women migrants).

Governments have continued to recognize the value of shelters, refuges and hotlines which offer support and assist survivors of forms of violence against women and also provide a focus for social services, such as counselling, public education and outreach services, and numerous States have sought to introduce such services (Belarus, Cyprus, Estonia, Haiti, Poland, the Russian Federation and Zimbabwe). Sierra Leone now provides free legal aid to battered and sexually abused women while in Mauritius a legal unit was set up within the Ministry of Women to provide free legal assistance to such victims. Several countries, including Israel, have sought to ensure that such services are available to minority and immigrant women. A number of countries have acknowledged the critical contribution of women's non-governmental organizations in the development of measures to address violence against women (Chile and Croatia), particularly shelters (Algeria and Pakistan) and legal services. Some have assured these services financial support and involved them in the development of government measures to address the problem. The European Union (EU) has adopted a community action programme (Daphne) which began January 2000 to support and promote non-profit organizations working in the field of violence against women.

Acknowledging the important role of the criminal justice system, and particularly of the police in the context of gender-based violence against women, Governments have encouraged the development of units within the police to address various forms of violence. Domestic violence units (Algeria, Brunei Darussalam, Mauritius), police victim support sections, and other specialized services, including anti-dowry cells, have been introduced in many countries, with officers working in these units seeking to develop specific expertise in the management of various forms of violence against women. Japan has introduced a sexual crimes investigation unit that is established in the headquarters of each prefectural police force. Policewomen are also appointed to conduct investigations and to provide support for victims. Guidelines and protocols, often with accountability procedures, have also been introduced in some countries, as have been kits, to ensure that victims are treated with sensitivity and to provide the best opportunity for a successful outcome in any legal proceedings. In Malaysia, for example, a standardized investigation kit is used in cases of sexual assault so that medical and legal evidence can be gathered effectively. Countries, particularly in the Latin American region, have also provided conditions for the development of dedicated women's police stations (Bolivia, Brazil, and Ecuador).[60]

Education and training for various sectors have also been priorities. Sweden has amended its Higher Education Ordinance to add gender-based violence issues to the examination requirements for members of several professions, including the police force, lawyers, medical practitioners, social workers and secondary school teachers. Many Member States (Australia, Guyana, and Sweden) have introduced or supported education and training for police (India and Kyrgyz Republic), criminal justice workers and others, such as prison and immigration officers (Germany and Venezuela). Comprehensive gender awareness education, incorporating modules relating to gender-based violence against women, has been introduced for the judiciary and other judicial officers (Argentina, Australia, Canada, Mexico and Senegal).

Other sectors whose education and training needs have been addressed in this context include health-care providers (Belgium, Portugal and the Republic of Moldova) including traditional birth attendants, welfare workers (the Republic of Moldova) and teachers. Focused education and training measures to address specific forms of gender-based violence, for example, relating to traditional practices, have also been introduced (Australia, Cameroon and Italy). Education materials, including guidelines and protocols and interdisciplinary curriculum guides, have been developed and in several Member States measures of accountability have been built into education and training strategies so as to ensure that lessons learned are implemented. A number have also prepared resources guides to encourage the sharing of best practices and good ideas that can be adapted for use in other settings or jurisdictions (Canada).

Several States have also developed specific education materials for migrant and aboriginal populations that address particular forms of violence against women (Australia and Canada). Others have introduced programmes aimed at violent men. For example, Iceland has introduced a two-year experimental project for such men entitled "Men of Responsibility". The project is monitored on a day-to-day basis by the Icelandic Red Cross and will be evaluated on its completion. Israel has established a shelter providing group and individual treatment for abusive men who have been removed from their homes by court injunction. Education and counselling programmes for perpetrators have also been introduced in Australia, and a national audit of the effectiveness of such programmes has been undertaken.

There is growing appreciation of the importance of public education, awareness and advocacy campaigns to foster a recognition of women's human rights, an atmosphere of public disapproval of violence against women and community responsibility for such violence. Local and national campaigns, often conducted with the cooperation of national women's councils or other non-governmental organizations, using various media, such as drama, press and print, including posters, radio, television and film, have been initiated in many countries, by Governments, non-governmental organizations and other parts of civil society, including the private sector (Namibia, Nigeria, Slovak Republic and Tunisia). Campaigns have ranged from general campaigns with regard to women's human rights to very specific campaigns relating to particular forms of violence, such as female genital mutilation, sexual harassment and trafficking. Some countries have introduced information campaigns directed at victims of violence (Pakistan and Switzerland). In several countries, comprehensive innovative multimedia "zero tolerance" campaigns have been initiated (Canada, Indonesia, Italy, Malta and the United Kingdom). These campaigns seek to create a community consensus that violence against women is unacceptable. Evaluations of these campaigns have suggested that they have had an important impact on public perceptions of, and tolerance for, the forms of violence against women that they have addressed. Specific measures aimed at sensitizing men to the impact of violent behaviour have also been introduced.

Countries in Africa and in Latin America and the Caribbean, such as Jamaica, have also participated in the United Nations inter-agency campaigns to eliminate violence against women which have been spearheaded by the UNIFEM and UNDP. Some cite the United Nations inter-agency teleconference held on 8 March 1999 as a focus of their strategies for anti-violence consciousness-raising (Cameroon and Ghana). As part of its attempts to stimulate increased knowledge and debate relating to gender-based violence, Sweden has established a web site on issues relating to violence against women. At least one country (Australia) has introduced measures to address portrayal of violence in the electronic media, *inter alia*, through the introduction of arrangements that would make it an offence to possess films, videos or computer games that have been or would have been refused classification because of violent content.

A number of States have introduced measures in relation to trafficking in women and girls and the exploitation of prostitution, with several States identifying trafficking, in particular, as a phenomenon requiring a coordinated response, *inter alia*, through education campaigns (Albania, Bulgaria and the Russian Federation) which in some countries are directed at potential victims. In Myanmar, for example, eight vocational centres for women and girls have been created in border areas in order to stop trafficking. Trafficking is perceived as a serious issue by a number of countries, including Lithuania, where a Division to Combat Trafficking has been established in the Organized Crime Investigation of the Police Department. A number of countries noted that there was a lack of statistical data on the issue and the development of strategies to confront it was complicated by its international character and the inadequacy of existing national legal provisions (for example Lithuania).

Several States have inaugurated strategies to address trafficking, including via arranged marriages and promises of employment, *inter alia*, through the introduction of amendments to their criminal codes, in particular in relation to abduction of women and children and forced prostitution (Cambodia and China). Some States have introduced specific legislation on trafficking in human beings, *inter alia*, for the purposes of sexual exploitation, forced labour, involuntary service and other forms of enslavement (Belgium, Costa Rica, Italy and Ukraine). In

1999, Australia introduced legislation that criminalizes and harshly punishes international recruitment of persons through deception or in order to have them function as sex workers under conditions of sexual servitude. States have established special agencies to address abduction of and trafficking in women and children, establishing cooperation between relevant government departments and, in some cases, non-governmental organizations or women's organizations.

In several countries, national committees or task forces on trafficking in women have been created, often with the cooperation of non-governmental organizations, to assess the extent of the problem and recommend solutions. In some countries, national plans of action on trafficking and commercial exploitation have been introduced and implemented. The effectiveness of measures to address trafficking, and to assist victims of violence resulting through prostitution or trafficking, *inter alia*, by examining the experiences of other countries, especially neighbouring ones, has been assessed by countries including Ethiopia. Efforts to combat trafficking have also included support for regional and global meetings that have sought to introduce a common strategy in this context. The Philippines has launched an initiative in cooperation with civil society and other Governments that includes, components for training of front-line agencies on how to address trafficking in women and children and develop procedures in this context. Campaigns aimed at potential victims of trafficking have also been introduced by some countries, along with projects on counselling, guidance and support of women affected by trafficking (for example Germany).

In accordance with the Hague Ministerial Declaration on the European Guidelines for Effective Measures to Prevent and Combat Trafficking in Women for the Purposes of Sexual Exploitation adopted in 1997, the Netherlands has appointed a national rapporteur to provide a comprehensive overview of data on trafficking in women and methods of prevention. The effectiveness of this institution will be reviewed two and four years after the establishment of the post of national rapporteur. As part of its strategy to eliminate trafficking in women, the Netherlands has also decriminalized prostitution, established a licensing system for brothel operators and raised the working conditions for sex workers. In order to make the sex industry more transparent and allow the police to monitor the situation effectively, the number and type of brothels are now controlled by a licensing policy, and regulations on the design and construction of brothels have been introduced, as well as on the way they are operated, that protect the mental and physical well-being of prostitutes and prohibit the employment of minors or illegal aliens. Intensive interdepartment and inter-municipality discussions, and the establishment of an Abolition of the Ban on Brothels Supplementary Policy Group under the auspices of the Ministry of Justice, took place prior to decriminalization and regulation.

Also pursuant to the Hague Ministerial Declaration, Sweden has assigned the task of national rapporteur to the National Police Board. Hungary has legalized prostitution in designated "tolerance zones" in order to allow for the provision of health care for prostitutes and more effective action against persons who abuse them. In 1998, in an effort to combat trafficking, and reduce prostitution Thailand introduced the Prostitution Prevention and Supression Act, decriminalizing prostitution, treating "sex workers" as victims of poverty and organized crime and penalizing brothel owners and those who seek sexual services. In 1999, Sweden also introduced legislation that penalizes those who seek to obtain sexual services.

Several countries have also amended their legislation to grant victims of trafficking the possibility of limited residence permits for humanitarian reasons so that they can be available as witnesses in criminal prosecution of traffickers and their accomplices and also file civil claims for compensation against perpetrators (Austria, Germany and Italy).

Protective measures, including repatriation and airport assistance, for nationals working abroad have been introduced by the Philippines. Pre-deployment programmes for those seeking to migrate to work, especially in vulnerable occupations, have also been introduced. Other preventive measures that have been introduced in this context include the prescription of a minimum age of 21 years for household workers, except for the cases of certain pre-identified countries, in which the minimum the age is 18 years, or of receiving countries where the age requirement is higher. Mandatory orientation programmes on migration have also been included in elementary and secondary curricula and a data bank and computerized programme including a serial sponsors watch-list to identify foreigners seeking more than one fiancée have also been developed. Inquiries into the phenomenon of mail-order brides have been launched in Finland. Countries with a significant number of overseas domestic workers provide for enhanced penalties for offences, including assault, wrongful confinement and insulting the modesty of household workers (Singapore), while others have passed specific legislation on domestic workers (Bolivia and Costa Rica).

3. Obstacles in the implementation of strategic objectives

Despite the clear progress in the achievement of its objectives, there remain important obstacles hindering full implementation of the Platform for Action directives with regard to gender-based violence against women. Several factors serve to limit the impact of strategies that have been introduced or are proposed in this context. First, there remains a continued lack of understanding of violence against women and its root causes, with efforts to address the issue being very often reactive—focusing on symptoms and consequences, not causes. Second, strategies tend to be fragmented, rather than integrated. Third, sufficient resources have yet to be allocated to measures to address the problem; and competing values and beliefs about women, and their place in the family, the community and society serve to undermine the measures and their implementation.

In addition, legal responses in some countries remain inadequate, with a significant number still failing to sanction activity such as rape in marriage. In some countries, domestic violence crimes, unlike other violent crimes, must be brought to the courts by victims of such abuse (Lithuania), while in others legislation does not provide law enforcement officials with the authority to address such crimes (the Gambia). Even where improved legal responses and reforms have been introduced, these may be flawed, as they tend to remain based on a model of gender-neutrality and rarely take into account the systemic inequalities in the legal system that are based on outdated sexual stereotypes. Furthermore, legal reforms have usually been piecemeal; hence, although important legal changes may have been introduced in one area, their effectiveness could be undermined by other laws and practices. The interaction of laws has sometimes inadvertently resulted in conditions that lead to imbalances in power relations between men and women and increase women's economic and social vulnerability to violence. For example, some countries have introduced increased penalties for trafficking in women and better implementation of controls against trafficking, but they have not introduced complementary reforms to protect victims of trafficking, especially from deportation. Again, the intersection of laws relating to female genital mutilation in some countries with immigration legislation has increased the vulnerabilities of victims of female genital mutilation and of their families.

The dearth of data and statistics on the various forms of gender-based violence against women also serves as an obstacle to full implementation of the Platform for Action. Many States, including Botswana and Burkina Faso, indicate that violence against women is an under-reported area. Several States point to the lack of sex-disaggregated statistics, or indicate that the disaggregation of statistics by sex has been a recent phenomenon. Others indicate that women fail to report incidents of abuse, because of shame or because of a mistaken view that such treatment is acceptable or is a private matter that should not be discussed publicly (Lithuania and Zimbabwe). Domestic violence is still considered to be a family matter in many States, and in a majority of countries sexual activity forced by a husband on his wife is not considered a criminal offence. In some States, including Zimbabwe, obstacles are created by men who resent programmes related to violence against women. In many countries, also, victims of sexual assault are stigmatized and frequently fail to report this violence. In others, victims may report violence but may then withdraw their allegations as a result of embarrassment or sometimes because of the threats of the perpetrators or of their families (for example Lithuania).

Traditional attitudes also impede full implementation of the Platform for Action in this context, with several States, including Burkina Faso, China, Cuba, Kenya and the Congo, indicating that violence against women is a deeply rooted pattern in their societies, or that the perception of male superiority and stereotypic roles for women and men remain powerful factors. Patriarchal attitudes are reflected in customs, such as bride price, in several States, for example, Vanuatu, while in others the general view that men have the right to chastise their wives, which was established in legal provisions, serves to perpetuate gender-based violence. In some countries, legal provisions are not adequate for addressing the issue, or are vague, imprecise or lack effective protocols relating to reporting or prosecuting violence. This is particularly the case for forms of violence such as trafficking in women in regard to which countries report that there is insufficient protection for witnesses. In some countries, such as Benin and Kenya, legal pluralism, including the coexistence of customary and general law, creates problems in addressing violence against women, while in others difficulties exist because of remaining discriminatory laws, and failure to recognize forms of violence such as rape in marriage.

A gender-insensitive legal system, which responds to myths relating to violence against women, creates difficulties in a number of States, with police, criminal justice personnel and judicial officers failing to act appropriately. The fact that court procedures are complex and slow in several States, and that there are no dedicated family or juvenile courts, may result in victims' withdrawing cases through embarrassment. Victims and others, including legal personnel, lack knowledge of the functioning of the legal system and are unaware of the legal provisions that promote their rights. Personnel trained in issues relating to violence against women remain limited, and resources to assist victims, including support and rehabilitation care, are insufficient. One of the most important obstacles to implementation is lack of awareness among the general public, including women, as well as relevant professional groups, that violence against women requires effective response. In addition, attitudes persist that trivialize the issue. This remains the case despite the awareness-raising campaigns and training and education strategies that have been introduced in many States.

The problem of gender bias in the legal system is made more serious by the ways in which it intersects with racial and ethnic biases in different countries. Particularly with regard to trafficking, it is clear that racial discrimination not only constitutes a risk factor for certain groups of women but also influences the way they are treated by immigration and law enforcement authorities in the countries of destination.

4. Conclusions and further actions

While much has been achieved in the context of the elimination of violence against women, there remains much to be done. While many countries have introduced legal provisions, others have yet to introduce effective legal provisions and procedures to address the various forms of violence against women. In still others, legislation that has been introduced requires amendment and steps are required to ensure that provisions in other sectors do not inadvertently revictimize those who have been affected by violence.

Consistent effort is required, moreover, to ensure that sectors that come in contact with violent behaviour are equipped to act effectively and sensitively. Most importantly, work is still required to ensure that the overarching attitudes towards women that are entrenched in stereotypic notions of their inferiority to men are addressed, so that violence, the most obvious manifestation of these attitudes, can be eliminated. In this regard, innovative programmes that raise the consciousness of all members of society, in particular children, with respect to the importance of non-violent conflict resolution should be priorities.

E. Women and armed conflict

1. Introduction

The Platform for Action, under critical area of concern E, "Women and armed conflict", addresses the effect of armed and other kinds of conflict on women, including those living under foreign occupation. It emphasizes that peace is inextricably linked to equality between women and men, but that aggression, foreign occupation and ethnic and other types of conflict are an ongoing reality affecting women and men in nearly every region. Noting that international humanitarian law, which prohibits attacks on civilians, is at times systematically ignored, and that human rights are often violated in armed conflict, thereby affecting the civilian population, especially women, children, the elderly and the disabled, the Platform for Action points out that, although entire communities suffer the consequences of armed conflict and terrorism, women and girls are particularly affected because of their status in society and their sex.

The Platform for Action draws attention to the fact that civilian victims, mostly women and children, outnumber casualties among combatants, and indicates that, although the abuses women and girls may suffer may take different forms, parties to conflict often engage in the rape of women with impunity, sometimes using systematic rape as a tactic of war and terrorism. The fear of these and other violations has created a mass flow of refugees and other displaced persons in need of international protection, as well as internally displaced persons, the majority of whom are women, adolescent girls and children who remain vulnerable to violence and exploitation while in flight, in countries of asylum and resettlement and during and after repatriation. Complex issues are also raised in this context in regard to repatriation.

Building on a number of the actions identified in the Nairobi Forward-looking Strategies for the Advancement of Women under the theme "Peace",[61] the Vienna Declaration and Programme of Action[62] and the 1993 Declaration on the Elimination of Violence against Women,[63] part E of the Platform for Action compiles concrete actions required from Governments, international and regional organizations, and civil society, including non-governmental organizations and the private sector, in order to achieve six strategic objectives to alleviate the effects of armed conflict on women, namely, (a) to increase the participation of women in conflict resolution at decision-making levels and protect women living in situations of armed and other conflicts or under foreign occupation; (b) to reduce excessive military expenditures and control the availability of armaments; (c) to promote non-violent forms of conflict resolution and reduce the incidence of human rights abuse in conflict situations; (d) to promote women's contribution to fostering a culture of peace; (e) to provide protection, assistance and training to refugee women, other displaced women in need of international protection and internally displaced women; and (f) to provide assistance to the women of the colonies and non-self-governing territories.

Since the adoption of the Platform for Action, there has been a growth in the number of conflicts and an increase in the abuse of the human rights of women and girls by both State and non-State actors, including privately financed militias.[64] One of the results of these conflicts and the violations associated with them has been an increase in forced internal displacement and refugee flows. At the same time, there has been a growing appreciation, at the international, regional and national levels, of the different impact that conflict can have on women and children, including an increasing awareness of the need to address the rights and needs of women and girls in the context of conflict and also in post-conflict reconstruction and the rehabilitation of war-torn societies.[65] In addition, there has been growing understanding of the role of women in conflict prevention, peacekeeping, peace-building and societal reconstruction.

2. Achievements in the implementation of the strategic objectives

(a) Addressing impunity

Since the Beijing Conference, there have been important developments in the treatment of harm experienced by women in situations of conflict, arising both as a means to end impunity for crimes against women, and as a way to ensure that abuses are redressed. International human rights law, international humanitarian law, particularly the four Geneva Conventions of 12 August 1949 for the protection of victims of war[66] and their two Additional Protocols of 8 June 1977,[67] and international refugee law provide a comprehensive framework in which to address the harm women experience in situations of armed conflict. Discriminatory interpretation and application of these areas of international law, as well as failure to recognize forms of harm to which women are especially vulnerable, have meant that this framework did not provide the protection and response such harm required. In particular, although recognized explicitly and implicitly in the international framework and prosecuted at national and international level, gender-based harm, including rape during conflict, have been viewed historically as less serious transgressions than their non-gender-based equivalents.

During this decade, and particularly since the Beijing Conference, steps have been taken to address the culture of impunity for these crimes. The statutes of the Tribunals created to address crimes committed in the former Yugoslavia and Rwanda both explicitly incorporate rape as a crime against humanity. The Statute of the International Tribunal for Rwanda[68] expressly includes rape, enforced prostitution and any form of indecent assault as a violation of article 3 common to the Geneva Conventions and of Additional Protocol II. As a result of gender-sensitive prosecutorial policies, sexual violence has been charged under the Statute of the International Tribunal for the former Yugoslavia[69] as a grave breach of the fourth Geneva Convention relative to the Protection of Civilian Persons in Time of War, as have enslavement, torture and crimes against humanity. In addition, the Rules of Procedure and Evidence of both the International Tribunal for Rwanda and the International Tribunal for the former Yugoslavia recognize the need for particular evidentiary exclusions in cases of rape and sexual assault. The Statutes and the Rules of Procedure and Evidence of the Tribunals provide for a range of protective measures for witnesses testifying in court. The Rules of Procedure and Evidence of the International Tribunal for the former Yugoslavia[70] also provide for the establishment of a Victims and Witnesses Unit to recommend protective measures for victims and witnesses, and to provide counselling and support. This Unit became operative in 1995.

Both Tribunals have issued several indictments relating to sexual violence.[71] In September 1998, the International Tribunal for Rwanda convicted the Mayor of Taba commune in Rwanda of crimes against humanity and genocide, *inter alia*, through acts of sexual violence. In the absence of a commonly accepted definition of rape in international law, the International Tribunal for Rwanda defined rape as a "physical invasion of a sexual nature, committed on a person under circumstances that are coercive". It also stated that it considered "sexual violence, which includes rape, as any act of a sexual nature that is committed on a person under circumstances that are coercive. Sexual violence is not limited to a physical invasion of the human body and may include acts that do not involve penetration or even physical contact". Notably, the International Tribunal for Rwanda concluded that rape and sexual violence committed with the specific intent of destroying in whole or in part, a particular group, constituted acts of genocide.

At the regional level, the Inter-American and European human rights bodies have also found sexual violence and rape in conflict situations to constitute violations of the human rights obligation of States under their respective human rights conventions. A few countries have translated the provisions of the Geneva Conventions and their Additional Protocols into domestic law, as required by those instruments, and criminal and civil proceedings have been initiated against individuals alleged to have perpetrated gender-based violence against women in conflict situations.

In July 1998, the United Nations Diplomatic Conference of Plenipotentiaries on the Establishment of an International Criminal Court, held in Rome, adopted the Rome Statute of the International Criminal Court.[72] The Court will be a permanent institution with power to exercise its jurisdiction over individuals responsible for the most serious crimes of concern to the international community. Its jurisdiction will be complementary to national criminal jurisdiction, and the crimes includes genocide, crimes against humanity, war crimes and crimes of aggression. Definitions of these crimes take gender concerns into account: genocide is defined to include measures intended to prevent births within a national, ethnical, racial or religious group;[73] and crimes against humanity—including rape, sexual slavery, enforced prostitution, forced pregnancy, enforced sterilization, or any other form of sexual violence of comparable gravity,[74] and persecution against any identifiable group or collectivity on grounds including gender—are defined as acts committed as part of a widespread or systematic attack directed against any civilian population. Gender is understood as referring "to the two sexes, male and female, within the context of society."[75] War crimes, which can occur in international or civil war, are defined to include rape, sexual slavery, enforced prostitution, forced pregnancy, enforced sterilization, and any other form of sexual violence constituting a grave breach of the Geneva Conventions.[76]

In addition to its explicit recognition of gender-based crimes, the Rome Statute makes provision for the application of gender-sensitive justice by providing that in the selection of judges, States parties shall take into account the need within the membership of the Court of, *inter alia*, a fair representation of female and male judges[77] and the need to include judges with legal expertise on specific issues, including violence against women and children.[78] The Registrar of the Court is also required to set up a Victims and Witnesses Unit within the Registry that shall provide, in consultation with the Office of the Prosecutor, protective measures and security arrangements, counselling and other appropriate assistance for witnesses, victims who appear before the Court, and others who are at risk on account of testimony given by such witnesses. The Unit is mandated to include staff with expertise in trauma, including trauma related to crimes of sexual violence.[79]

The Rome Statute also contains provision for protection of victims and witnesses, directing the Court to take appropriate measures to protect the safety, physical and psychological well-being, dignity and privacy of victims and witnesses. In so doing, the Court is required to have regard to all relevant factors, including age, gender and health, and the nature of the crime, in particular where the crimes involve sexual or gender violence or violence against children.[80] The Victims and Witnesses Unit may advise the Prosecutor and the Court on appropriate protective measures, security arrangements, counselling and assistance.[81]

The Preparatory Commission for the International Criminal Court, established by resolution F adopted by the United Nations Diplomatic

Conference of Plenipotentiaries on the Establishment of an International Criminal Court done at Rome on 17 July 1998[82] is preparing proposals for practical arrangements for the establishment of the Court, *inter alia*, with regard to rules of procedure and evidence and the elements of crimes. Proposals before the Commission have sought to incorporate a gender perspective.[83]

(b) Displaced and refugee women

Significant developments have occurred in regard to the protection of and assistance to, refugee women. Since the beginning of this decade, the Office of the UNHCR has issued Guidelines on the Protection of Refugee Women, as well as more specific guidelines on the prevention of and response to sexual violence against refugee women,[84] and proposed measures to prevent its occurrence. UNHCR has also sought to ensure that refugee women obtain adequate protection in international law, particularly in circumstances where they experience gender-based persecution, such as sexual violence in conflict situations and severe discrimination as a result of transgressing social mores.[85]

Some States have formulated guidelines for decision makers with regard to gender-related asylum claims. In a growing number of countries, refugee status has been granted on the basis of persecution on gender grounds, *inter alia*, through fear of female genital mutilation, forced marriage, forced abortion, or domestic violence.

Member States have increasingly recognized the importance of the provision of physical and psychological support for refugee women, particularly those who have suffered gender-specific abuses. Several have established units that offer such support. Others have addressed the needs of refugee women, who are frequently heads of households, with respect to basic health care and education and economic opportunities. In addition, some Governments have provided support for grass-roots empowerment and economic security projects for women affected by conflict, including widows and the displaced. Programmes have also been introduced that provide identity papers to undocumented populations allowing individuals, and particularly women, to attain the full exercise of their rights and the prerogatives of citizenship that have been lost, *inter alia*, as a result of forced displacement.

(c) Controlling armaments availability

Steps have been taken by a number of countries to reduce the availability of arms, particularly small arms and anti-personnel landmines. As of 31 December 2000, 109 States had ratified or acceded to the 1997 Convention on the Prohibition of the Use, Stockpiling, Production and Transfer of Anti-personnel Mines and on their Destruction, while a further 24 are signatories to the Convention. Several States are closely involved with the International Campaign to Ban Landmines and a number of these have begun programmes to destroy landmines in accordance with the Convention. Programmes that seek to alert national populations to the dangers presented by landmines and thereby reduce the number of mine incidents have been introduced in several countries, often in partnership with the International Committee of the Red Cross. In light of evidence from mine-affected States that women and girl survivors of anti-personnel landmine accidents are often financially and socially marginalized, several countries have established programmes that seek to ensure that there are no barriers to the participation of women and girls in mine education, nor in their access to trauma care, rehabilitation and reintegration. Amended Protocol II (on Prohibitions or Restrictions on the Use of Mines, Booby-Traps and Other Devices)[86] to the Convention on Prohibitions or Restrictions on the Use of Certain Conventional Weapons Which May Be Deemed To Be Excessively Injurious or to Have Indiscriminate Effects,[87] which restricts the use of anti-personnel landmines, as well as anti-vehicle and anti-tank mines, entered into force on 3 December 1998, and several countries including Australia have introduced legislation that create offences relating to the placement, possession, development and production of anti-personnel landmines by their citizens. Australia has also appointed a woman as its Special Representative on Demining.

Countries have ratified or acceded to the Comprehensive Nuclear Test-ban Treaty,[88] and others are seeking to ensure compliance with article VI of the Treaty on the Non-Proliferation of Nuclear Weapons[89] which requires negotiation of a Nuclear Weapons Convention prohibiting the production, use and threat of use of nuclear weapons and would provide for verification and enforcement of their destruction.

At the regional level, the twenty-fourth special session of the General Assembly of the OAS adopted the Inter-American Convention against the Illicit Manufacturing of and Trafficking in Firearms, Ammunition, Explosives, and Other Related Materials[90] directed at the elimination of small arms. The Convention entered into force on 1 July 1998. Forty OAU member States attended the First Continental Conference of African Experts on Landmines in Kempton Park, South Africa, in May 1997 and adopted a Plan of Action on Landmines.

(d) Participation of women in decision-making, and in the armed forces

Some progress has been made in promoting the participation of women in peace processes and peace-building, *inter alia*, through the strengthening of women's peace organizations. Progress has also been made in increasing women's participation in conflict resolution at decision-making levels, as well as during post-conflict, rehabilitation and reconciliation within their societies.

Several Member States, including Belgium, Ecuador, the Netherlands, Nigeria and the United Kingdom, have recognized the particular contribution women can make to the prevention of conflict and in post-conflict peace processes. *Women and Armed Conflicts*, a study carried out by Anita Helland and others for the Norwegian Ministry of Foreign Affairs, and published in 1999, outlines recent developments in this context, *inter alia*, in regard to United Nations and North Atlantic Treaty Organization (NATO) operations.[91] Financial support has been provided for a United Nations study on mainstreaming gender in multi-dimensional peacekeeping operations and several States have responded to the request of the Special Adviser to the Secretary-General of the United Nations on Gender Issues and Advancement of Women in collaboration with the Department of Peacekeeping Operations of the United Nations Secretariat to provide more women military personnel and civilian police for peacekeeping operations. Sweden financed a seminar in the Department of Peace and Conflict Resolution of the University of Uppsala where the Ministry of Defence outlined its experiences in this context. Georgia's Plan of Action for Improving Women's Conditions includes a requirement that women be involved actively in decision-making with regard to armed conflict, particularly peace-building, and special legal mechanisms are to be developed to ensure their participation in this process. While their role is to be general, these women are specifically tasked to develop strategies to protect women's rights during and after conflict, *inter alia*, with regard to strategies for separated families, provide for return of personal property lost during conflict, restore the right to free movement, design rehabilitation programmes for victims and involve non-governmental organizations in conflict settlement processes. The United Kingdom has ensured that women are included in the peace process in regard to the situation in Northern Ireland, while Greece has encouraged and supported the activities of non-governmental organizations in regard to armed conflict.

Women from several Member States and from the United Nations system participate in peacekeeping and election monitoring, while other States have cleared the way for female civil servants to be involved in consulting and teaching functions in conflict zones. Australia has provided civilian personnel for the regional group monitoring the ceasefire agreement in Bougainville, Papua New Guinea, and has strongly encouraged women to take part in these missions. The African region developed a "First Ladies for Peace Initiative" in early 1997 in order to assist in conflict prevention. Included in this initiative has been a summit on peace and humanitarian issues, the resolutions of which were presented to African Heads of States and Government at the thirty-third ordinary session of the OAU Assembly. Also held were the Pan-African Women's Conference on the Culture of Peace, Zanzibar, 17 to 20 May 1999, and the launching of the OAU/ECA Women's Committee on Peace and Development in the same year. In several Member States, including the United Kingdom and the United States of America, women occupy high-level decision-making posts that have important implications for conflict prevention and peace processes. These women include Secretaries of State and departmental heads with oversight for United Nations affairs and peacekeeping and conflict prevention.

Projects to support the role of women in peacemaking and reconciliation have also been initiated by non-governmental organizations in a number of Member States, including Australia, often with the support of Government. Peace-building research initiatives focused on the gendered experiences, accounts, impacts and perspectives of armed conflict and seeking to integrate a gender perspective into national policy development and peace implementation programming have also been introduced.

Several Member States have sought to reinforce women's positive role in peace-building in their cooperation efforts. Belgium, for example, has initiated a joint project with the UNICEF through which a women's non-governmental organization identifies detained children and negotiates their release from rebel soldiers. Belgium has also supported the use of women mediators in conflict and developed an initiative for peace-building between the women of two parties in conflict. The Netherlands has introduced a development action programme entitled "Engendering the Peace Process" which, *inter alia*, supports activities to encourage Israel and Palestine to appoint more women to negotiating teams and to political decision-making posts in respect of the ongoing peace process.

A number of countries have taken steps to increase the numbers of women in the armed forces, and in Denmark, women have reached high levels in the military. This Member State has also enacted legislation to allow women to be recruited under the same conditions as men, and is making efforts to ensure that more women are promoted. Female personnel attend the same armed forces' management development programmes as male personnel and are also entitled to be enrolled in special programmes to increase the appointment of women to higher ranks. Norway has introduced specific targets with the objective of recruiting and keeping women in the armed forces and the military, namely, 7 per cent female officers and enlisted personnel by the year 2005; 13 per cent women, civilian and military, in leading positions by the year 2001; and 40 per cent civilian women among certain groups of defence force personnel. Norway also completed an armed forces personnel policy in June 1999 along with an action plan to achieve the objectives of the policy. In Israel, where conscription of women is compulsory but service in the military is differentiated by gender, the Government has reviewed its admission procedures with regard to the airforce in response to a decision of the Supreme Court of Justice. Women who meet initial requirements are now entitled to take the entrance examination for pilot training. The military has also increased the number of positions open to women, while the importance of the elimination of sexual violence and harassment has been emphasized in awareness-raising and empowerment programmes. Reviews of the cultural and social barriers to women's career progression and retention in the defence forces have been undertaken twice in Australia since the Fourth World Conference on Women.

Further strategies introduced to increase the number of women in the armed forces include a civilian mentoring programme, where women officers participate as mentors, and the allocation of earmarked resources for gender equality in the Ministry of Defence budget. The

United States of America has established a Working Group chaired by an Assistant Secretary of the Navy to address this issue.

(e) Sensitization and education
Strategies to ensure that the gendered impact of armed conflict is understood by the military have been introduced in a number of Member States in several countries, such as Belgium and the Philippines, and training in international human rights and humanitarian law, including their gender dimensions, is provided to the armed forces. The Philippines has reaffirmed its adherence to international human rights and humanitarian law in the conduct of military and police operations by its Armed Forces and National Police. With regard to the gender dimensions of peace operations for military and civilian participants in peace operations, Canada and the United Kingdom have introduced a joint gender awareness training initiative in this context that aims to enhance awareness of the gender dimensions of peace operations and provide participants with the ability to employ gender analysis in the field. In response to the activities of its personnel deployed in one United Nations peacekeeping mission. Belgium's Defence Department commissioned its Centre to Combat Racism to recommend a series of measures concerning peacekeeping, including the prevention of racism, and to propose specific criteria for mission selection. As a result, its army is developing a new code of conduct to address issues, including those related to gender, arising in the context of peacekeeping.

Several Member States have also sought to raise the consciousness of their general populations, particularly certain groups, with regard to the gendered impact of armed conflict and the importance of women in encouraging a culture of peace. The Minister for Women of Burundi has organized a peace campaign, and several States have hosted or supported meetings or seminars on the theme of women and armed conflict (Belgium, Canada, the Congo, Italy, Nigeria, the Philippines, Senegal and Tunisia). Burundi and Tunisia have initiated televised civics campaigns that include coverage of human rights, while other States have integrated conflict resolution and peacemaking issues into the school curriculum, and still others have disseminated human rights information to law enforcement personnel, academics and educators and integrated these issues into information and election campaigns. Innovative strategies have been introduced in several States, including a chain letter for peace in the Philippines. Peru has also developed programmes aimed specifically at border populations that encourage a culture of peace and seek to root out gender-based violence. A publication documenting best practices in peace-building and non-violent conflict resolution in Africa was issued by six United Nations entities in 1997.

3. Obstacles to the implementation of the strategic objectives

Despite the progress that has been made, much more remains to be done to reach the objectives outlined in the Platform for Action with regard to this critical area. In its agreed conclusions on women and armed conflict decided at its forty-second session,[92] the Commission on the Status of Women proposed various steps to accelerate implementation of the strategic objectives in regard to this area, specifically in relation to ensuring gender-sensitive justice, addressing the specific needs of women affected by armed conflict, increasing the participation of women in peacekeeping, peace-building, pre- and post-conflict decision-making, conflict prevention, post-conflict resolution and reconstruction, preventing conflict and promoting a culture of peace, and disarmament measures.

Achievement of the strategic objectives of this critical area of concern is affected by several important obstacles. Important among these is the relative absence of women from decision-making positions with regard to conflict, both at the pre-conflict stage, and during hostilities, as well as at the point of peacekeeping, peace-building, reconciliation and reconstruction. Few women are Ministers of Defence or Ministers of Foreign Affairs and even fewer women head their countries' delegations in the Security Council of the United Nations. In addition, the representation of women in the armed forces, particularly at their highest levels, is small. Barriers to women's participation in these contexts include stereotypic attitudes, competing work and family responsibilities, and women's lack of access to such careers, *inter alia*, as a result of lack of access to appropriate education. In addition to the absence of women from decision-making positions, there is a failure to value the contribution women can make to conflict prevention and the achievement of a culture of peace.

Perhaps the most crucial obstacle to the achievement of the Platform for Action's objectives in this context has been the changed pattern of conflict since the end of the cold war and the collapse of the former Union of Soviet Socialist Republics. The Platform for Action pointed to the fact that, although the threat of a global armed conflict has been reduced as result of the end of the cold war, wars of aggression, armed conflicts, civil war and terrorism continue to plague many parts of the world. Since the adoption of the Platform for Action, this trend has escalated, with a large number of actors, including non-State actors, private militias and children, now having access to weapons that range from anti-personnel mines to assault rifles and surface-to-air missiles. Access has been facilitated by the opening of borders, a proliferation of arms, particularly small arms, and the rapid expansion of free trade.

Many of the actors currently involved in conflict situations disregard the rules of international human rights, international humanitarian law and international refugee law that provide minimum protections for individuals who are caught in such situations. In particular, many of these actors in conflicts target civilians, including women and children, often in gender-specific ways.[93]

4. Conclusions and further actions

Acceleration of implementation of the strategic objectives of the Platform for Action in the area of armed conflict will be achieved only through implementation of the existing legal standards enshrined in international human rights and humanitarian law. In particular, support for the work of the existing *ad hoc* war crimes tribunals and ratification of the Rome Statute of the International Criminal Court are required to end impunity for all crimes committed in armed conflict, including those affecting women and girls. Increased support for gender-sensitive justice in the work of these bodies is also required. Steps must also be taken to reduce the availability of weapons, particularly light and small arms, which has facilitated the involvement of non-State actors in conflict and, ultimately, the prevalence of conflicts in all regions of the world.

Energetic measures must also be taken to ensure that women are involved in decision-making at all levels, including as special envoys and special representatives, particularly in regard to conflict, both at the pre-conflict stage, and during hostilities, as well as in the process of peacekeeping, peace-building, reconciliation and reconstruction. In this regard, special emphasis should be placed on ensuring that women are encouraged to enter and remain in the armed forces, as well as to take up non-stereotypic functions in this context.

F. Women and the economy

1. Introduction

The Platform for Action under critical area of concern F, "Women and the economy", addresses the effects of gender inequality in women's access to economic opportunities. The Platform for Action points out that, in most parts of the world, women's control of, and participation in, decision-making concerning capital, credit, property, technology, education and information are seldom present, despite the fact that their participation in remunerated work has grown steadily everywhere in the world. The Platform for Action highlights the barriers to women's economic empowerment and entrepreneurship, which are mainly related to unfavourable working conditions, discrimination in education, training and hiring, domestic responsibilities, and lower levels of pay and promotion than men for equal work. This situation reinforces pressures on women's unemployment and underemployment as well as on the unequal allocation of time between workplace and home, and is especially prevalent during economic downturns. Thus, women end up unemployed and/or carrying a large burden of unpaid work, especially those who work in agriculture, while recognition of their actual contribution to economic development is underestimated or unrecognized. The Platform for Action stresses the paramount importance of research and gender analysis with respect to revealing and improving the understanding of economic disparities between men and women, so as to enable Governments to design a gender-sensitive system of social accounting and sounder and fairer economic policies.

Building on a number of actions identified in the United Nations conferences and summits at Cairo, Rio de Janeiro, Vienna and Copenhagen during the 1990s, section F of chapter IV of the Platform for Action calls for concrete actions from Governments, central banks, multilateral business organizations, international and regional development organizations and civil society, including non-governmental organizations and the private sector, in order to achieve six strategic objectives to eliminate gender inequality in this critical area. These objectives are: to promote women's economic rights and independence, including access to employment, appropriate working conditions and control over economic resources; to facilitate women's access to resources, employment, markets and trade; to provide business services, training and access to markets, information and technology, particularly to low-income women; to strengthen women's economic capacity and commercial networks; to eliminate occupational segregation and all forms of employment discrimination; and to promote harmonization of work and family responsibilities for women and men.

Since the adoption of the Platform for Action, there has been a greater reliance on market-led development and increased deregulation in the global economy. As a consequence, although the female share of employment has steadily increased, existing gender inequalities in the labour market with respect to quality, conditions and pay for work have intensified. This has particularly negatively affected the living conditions of poor women around the world, especially in the agricultural sector. Women's capabilities continue to be undervalued as they increasingly work in the services sector and perform more part-time and unpaid work than men. At the same time, there has been a growing recognition, at the international, regional and national levels, of women's contribution to economic development as well as an increasing awareness of the need to address women's economic rights in the context of control and management of economic resources. In addition, countries in all regions have adopted measures designed to promote women's entrepreneurship, professional opportunities and rewards, and equalize the gender responsibilities of family caregiving.

A body of international standards has already established equal access to employment, elimination of occupational segregation, prohibition of sexual harassment, right to equal pay and reduction of child labour, while ensuring that abuses are redressed. These include International Labour Organization (ILO) Conventions on worker rights and labour standards that affirm the rights of freedom of association, fair wages and compensation, and adequate conditions of work; and the 1993 Standard Rules on the Equalization of Opportunities for Persons with Disabilities[94] which state that individuals with disabilities have the same rights as other human beings, including the right to economic security, rehabilitation and training, and full development of their human potential. The States parties to the 1989 Convention on the Rights of the Child[95] recognize the right of children to be protected from economic exploitation, harmful work, and sexual exploitation as well as their obligation to take appropriate measures to ensure the implementation of these agreements (article 32). These international conventions and rules provide a comprehensive framework for ensuring women's equal participation in the economy. Particularly important are the ILO Convention No. 100 (Equal Remuneration Convention, 1951), which elaborates on the principle of equal remuneration for women and men for work of equal value; ILO Convention No. 103 (Maternity Protection Convention (Revised), 1952), which elaborates on maternity leave for women employed in industrial undertakings and in non-industrial and agricultural occupations including wage earners working at home; ILO Convention No. 111 (Discrimination (Employment and Occupation) Convention, 1958), which elaborates on equality of opportunity and treatment of women and men in respect of employment and occupation (non-discrimination); ILO Convention No. 156 (Workers with Family Responsibilities Convention, 1981), which elaborates on equal opportunity and treatment for women and men workers with family responsibilities; and ILO Convention No. 177 (Home Work, 1996) which entitles home-based workers the same rights as wage-earners regarding wages and working conditions, including the right to form associations and engage in collective bargaining. [96]

Deficiency of enforcement and implementation, as well as failure to recognize forms of gender discrimination to which women are especially subject, has meant that the international standards framework has not been sufficient. In particular, although recognized both nationally and internationally, gender-based inequalities, *inter alia*, in access to resources, remuneration for equal work, and distribution of work within the household, have not been given the same priority as their non-gender-based equivalents. In the midst of economic downturns in some developing countries, this situation has meant unemployment, underemployment, insufficient number of posts at the decision-making level and, especially for women, being overburdened with household work.

2. Achievements in the implementation of strategic objectives

(a) Promoting women's economic rights and
equal access to economic resources

Some Member States have taken steps to bring their laws and policies into accord with international conventions, particularly since the Beijing Conference (Albania, Armenia, Chile, the Dominican Republic, Finland, Ghana, Italy, Japan and Poland). For example, Japan ratified ILO Convention No. 156, which became effective as of June 1996. In the same spirit, on 18 June 1997, Japan also amended the Equal Employment Opportunity Law, the Labour Standards Law and the Child Care and Family Care Leave Law, which together prohibit employers from discriminating against women in recruitment, hiring, assignment and promotion, while abolishing restrictions on overtime, holiday work or night work by women aged 18 years or over. In 1997, Indonesia ratified ILO Conventions Nos. 100 and 111. In 1995, Chile ratified ILO Conventions Nos. 103 and 156, and in 1998 modified its Labour Code to prohibit employers from discriminating against women, based on women's reproductive role, in their access to employment and promotion. Brazil passed legislation prohibiting employers from terminating employment for refusal to comply with demands for certification or examination regarding pregnancy or sterilization.

Some Member States have adopted additional legislation to enforce international labour conventions. China, for instance, has introduced legislation monitoring and enforcement mechanisms such as the labour administrative departments in order to provide labour protection and guarantee women's right to employment. Germany amended its Civil Code and the Labour Courts Act in 1998, thereby redefining the liability of the employer for gender-specific discrimination. Under this edict, the employer must compensate the person discriminated against, regardless of the degree of responsibility in the violation of the ban on discrimination. Ireland's 1998 Employment Equality Act prohibits discrimination based on disability, sexual orientation and age. Canada revised its Employment Insurance System in 1996 and 1997 to mandate that those who found it difficult to re-enter the labour force, such as those who had left the labour market for maternal or parental leave, did not lose social security. Uruguay has established the Housewives and Consumer Protection League to train women to defend and fully exercise their rights as citizens. Many Arab countries have included poor women under the protection of the

Social Security Law, while Algeria has added a provision where house-wives and part-time women workers contribute to a pension fund and receive benefits after 60 years of age.

A few Member States have passed legislation that recognizes women's equal rights to land ownership, thus planting the seeds for equal access and distribution of land between the sexes. While all women in these countries have been considered, this type of legislation is particularly important for women living in rural areas. The new laws seek to correct customary practices and traditions favouring men's patrimony in re-spect of owning land, by establishing the same rights for women. Countries such as Bolivia, the Dominican Republic, Eritrea, Malaysia, Nepal, Uganda, the United Republic of Tanzania and Zimbabwe count among those that enacted land laws favouring women's ownership. More to the point, the 1999 Civil and Family Laws of Mongolia recog-nize women's equal rights to inheritance, land use, and ownership of livestock and other properties. Armenia has also established equal ownership rights for women and men in real estate and other property, while its Family and Marriage Code guarantees equal rights of spouses to jointly owned property.

Several countries have adopted legislation to prevent abusive behaviour against women in the labour market. Belize, for instance, in 1996 passed the Sexual Harassment Act to protect women in the workplace, institutions and places of accommodation. The Canadian Human Rights Commission developed a model of anti-harassment policies in 1998 and made it available to employers. Sweden amended its Equal Op-portunities Act in 1998 to increase employer obligations to prevent sexual harassment at the workplace. Similarly, the 1999 budget of the United States of America has expanded the Equal Employment Op-portunity Commission's alternative dispute resolution programme, thus reducing the backlog of private sector discrimination complaints, which include sexual discrimination.

Several countries and regions have sanctioned the right to equality in employment and promoted equal opportunities in the workplace. Ar-gentina, for example, adopted the Plan of Equal Opportunities between Women and Men in Employment, which establishes an agreement be-tween the National Council of Women and the Ministry of Labour and Social Security on actions to promote equal opportunities. In 1998, the Ministry of Labour in Argentina created the Tripartite Commission for Equal Treatment and Opportunities for Men and Women in the Workplace, through which the Government, the private sector and labour unions should establish mechanisms to promote equal opportunities. Albania's new Constitution, adopted in 1998, sanctioned the principle of equality, and so all Albanian legislation including the Labour Code has reflected this principle. Finland enacted the 1995 Amendment to Equality Act, which establishes a 40/60-quota system for female representation in government service. Also, Canada, in 1996, approved the new Employment Equity Act, which requires companies doing business with the federal Government to achieve and maintain a gender balance in the workforce.

(b) Supporting women's economic empowerment
Many States have taken steps to strengthen women's executive and professional abilities, increase women's access to traditionally male-dominated occupations, and promote women's management of their own businesses. Most activities were in support of women's enterprises. Governments have applied policies and developed specific projects that use local, national and international networks to facilitate information, technology, credit and training for women entrepreneurs as well as programmes to enhance women's education.

Member States have increasingly recognized the importance of specific legislation with respect to establishing a propitious framework in which to promote women's economic activities. For example, the Republic of Korea enacted the Women's Entrepreneurs Support Act in 1999, which stipulates the establishment of the Women Entrepreneurs Association of the Republic of Korea and encourages central and local governments to provide support for women who start new businesses as well as those who are already doing business. Likewise, considering that the current labour market offers great potential for women's self-employment and their setting up of new businesses, Italy enacted a law in 1992 that provides funds for start-up and development of women's entrepreneurial activities, training, information, and technical and managerial assistance. The United States of America has strengthened the financial capacity of women-owned small businesses by granting microcredits and loans via the Small Business Administration Programme (SBA) and the Community Development Financial Institutions Fund (CDFI). Croatia is also implementing a programme for granting loans with favourable credit conditions to small enterprises, in particular to women entrepreneurs in deficit professions.

Many Member States in collaboration with multilateral organizations have funded projects that promote women's entrepreneurship in rural and/or urban areas (Algeria, Benin, Bolivia, Côte d'Ivoire, the Dominican Republic, India, the Islamic Republic of Iran, Namibia, the Niger, Pakistan, the Republic of Korea, Rwanda, Senegal, Thailand, the United Republic of Tanzania and Yemen). For example, the Benin Government supports credit programmes for the development of microenterprises (PADME) and for the development of the agricultural sector (PADSA). By May 1999, about 80 per cent of PADME's credit benefited women, and PADSA has planned to allocate 500 million francs in credits. Algeria supports programmes for the creation of microenterprises for people 19-35 years of age, and for infrastructure and credit to rural female production cooperatives. Other Arab countries (Bahrain, Egypt, Kuwait, Qatar and Yemen) also encourage women to undertake business activities by carrying out small enterprise projects that provide loans for income-generating activities. In the United Republic of Tanzania, the Women Development Fund (WDF), established in the Ministry of Community Development, Women Affairs and Children, provides funds on credit terms and small interest to small groups of women and private individuals in both urban and rural areas. Interestingly, the Government of India has accumulated a rich know-how in respect of supporting women's entrepreneurial activities by ensuring, for instance, that no less than 30 per cent of the budgetary allocations for development sectors reaches women, and that a 30-40 per cent reserve of funds/benefits in almost all wage employment and asset creation programmes of the Government is channelled to women. In Bolivia, the Inter-American Development Bank is financing the project entitled "Strengthening of Business Management and Technology of Small and Medium Enterprises Focusing on Women," in which main cities and small towns would become involved in this special kind of funding. The Dominican Republic has also established a cooperative of production for women, in which funding is part of a comprehensive programme for women's enterprises. Some Governments' funding has focused on helping some of the most disadvantaged women to become involved in income-generating activities. For instance, the Islamic Republic of Iran has facilitated free-interest credit for rural disadvantaged women and female-headed households in order to support their productive activities; and the Agricultural Cooperative Credit Bank in Yemen in 1996 gave loans to rural women to improve their income and food intake.

Many Member States have sought to improve women's entrepreneurial activities with technological support, training and seminars to upgrade their business skills (Benin, Bhutan, Bolivia, Estonia, Grenada, Italy, Jamaica, Jordan, Mali, Mexico, Nigeria, the Russian Federation, Senegal, South Africa, Swaziland and Tunisia). Some examples follow: in South Africa, the Technology for Women in Business (TWIB) programme, launched in 1998, facilitates access to technology of women in small business. This programme emerged from the realization that small, micro and medium-sized firms, in particular those owned by women, were at risk from the impacts of globalization.[97] Within the Deputy Prime Minister's office in Swaziland, the Women in Development Programme provides training and seed money to women so that they may start their own businesses. Likewise, Tunisia, with significant participation of women, has put into practice the programme for Professional Initiation and Employment Assistance, including high school centres in the countryside, and seminars for using the Internet and other communication technologies. Bolivia reported that, within the framework of supporting small enterprises and microenterprises, programmes to improve women's technical skills are under way. The Governments of Mexico and Italy have funded programmes as well for the entrepreneurial activities and training of women, especially women who live in less developed areas of their country.

Some Member States have sought to improve women's employment outlook and upward mobility with training models directed towards upgrading their professional and management skills. For instance, China has launched the programme Women's Action to Assist Laid-Off Workers in being Re-employed, in which 480,000 women found re-employment and one million laid-off women workers received training in 1996-1997. Under the programme Women's Action to Help Women Become Competent and Talented Persons, China has also set up training programmes to increase women's capability to participate in the Government and a women's talent bank to recommend women cadres to relevant government departments. The Russian Federation has embarked on a wide training and retraining programme 1998-2000 directed towards improving women's employment prospects. Denmark has been applying affirmative action policies that mandate employment of men in social support sectors and employment of women in traditionally male- dominated sectors. In Australia, the Women in Small Business Mentoring Project has developed a mentoring network linking new starters with experienced business owners to promote sharing of knowledge and experience. The Republic of Korea has made remarkable progress in the recruitment of public servants and in respect of incentive awards encouraging State-run companies to employ women.

(c) Developing gender analysis and research
Member States have supported policies that promote studies on gender and the identification of the barriers to economic empowerment that women face (Angola, Australia, Benin, China, Cuba, France, Guinea, the Islamic Republic of Iran, Malaysia, Sweden and Turkey). For instance, the Australian Government has funded research projects for identifying barriers to education, training and employment for girls and boys as well as to women's access to information technologies. Among these, the Schools Work Towards Gender Equity programme has developed resource material to assist principals and school staff in investigating their school gender equity needs and determining action to bring about gender equity reform. France, from 1996 onwards, has conducted questionnaires on the situation of women in rural areas, while the Service for Women's Rights has funded a study about violence against women at their job centres, based on the archives collected by the European Association. Benin has published statistical reports to raise awareness on the persistence of poverty among women. The Government of China has encouraged the admission of women's and gender studies into the scientific research and teaching of social science, while also providing financial support for this. In Turkey, sex-disaggregated data have been compiled, produced and disseminated to assess the performance of Government in specific gender development fields and hold Government accountable. Egypt, Jordan and Oman have also developed database systems disaggregated by sex as a foundation for planning and women's development. In Sweden, the Commission on the Distribution of Economic Power and Financial Resources between Women and Men presented a report on how economic policy affects the situation of women and men, highlighting differences in economic and financial conditions between them, while also proposing measures in this field.

Some Member States have focused on finding ways in which information systems and communication technologies could improve the lives of women. In Argentina, the National Women's Council is establishing a national information system that will develop a system of indicators with a gender perspective. Similarly in Germany, on behalf of the Former Ministry for the Equal Opportunities of Women and

Men of North Rhine-Westphalia, a study on the effects of information and communication technologies on the employment situation of women was presented in 1997. Kenya has established a database in the Planning Department with comprehensive and easily accessible sex-disaggregated data.

(d) Harmonization of family and work
   responsibilities

Some Member States have adopted policies to improve the relationship between parents' work and home life. Austria has created a flexible system of sharing maternity leave for both parents, flexible reporting periods and an original claim for maternity leave by fathers. This Member State has also stimulated the creation of more day-care centres and new regulations for their opening hours. In 1997, Denmark amended the Act on Equal Opportunities for Women and Men with regard to Access to Employment and Maternity Leave, entitling fathers to be absent for two additional weeks for parental leave. In 1999, the Italian Parliament approved a law that banned assigning women to night-time shifts during pregnancy and up to one year of age of the child; and indicated that male and female workers would not be obligated to accept night-time shifts if they had a child under age 3, if they were a single parent of a child under age 12, or if they lived with a disabled person.

Several Member States have adopted comprehensive policies regarding childcare and family care leave. Japan, for instance, has revised its Child Care Leave Law, establishing childcare and family care leave benefits. In effect since April 1999, the new Child Care and Family Care Leave Law establishes rights in respect of the family care leave scheme, shortening of working hours and support of parents taking care of children or family members. Poland's Labour Code and Family Welfare Code guarantee equal rights for women and men concerning family care, while entitling women to special protection on grounds of motherhood.

3. Obstacles in the implementation of strategic objectives

The gains and losses of today's global economy have been asymmetrically distributed, as reflected by the complexity of wider economic disparities and persistent gender inequality. Although there have been gains for women in labour-market participation, intensification of international flows of capital and labour, and also the weakening of State regulations have put further pressures on women's discrimination. The fact that migrant/rural women in particular have become more vulnerable to the flexibility of labour markets hampers their possibilities for earning a decent income, for receiving equal pay for equal value of work and/or for reducing work at home.

Only a few countries have enacted legislation favouring women's ownership of land and other kinds of property. Customary traditions, institutions and gender-biased laws hamper the process of giving women equal access to, and use of, land and other fixed assets. Obstacles to equal access of women and men to the means of production ultimately prevent the synergetic interaction that would otherwise occur between a more participatory society and an effective and sustainable use of countries' resources.

Women's income levels and career advancement have persistently lagged behind those of men with similar comparative skills, while their reproductive role continues to be perceived as a stigma. This trend has persisted regardless of boom and crisis periods of the economy, with poor women taking a larger share of oppressive inequalities. Indeed, recent economic and financial crises in Latin America, South Asia and Eastern Europe have hit the most vulnerable social groups hardest, and women in particular have ended up with bigger burdens of unpaid work and/or their pursuit of senior-level posts halted. This situation has also undervalued countries' actual productive capacities. Put in another way, women's needs to earn an income and develop a career have clashed with their conventionally ascribed role in child-rearing and care for older family members, and this has resulted in women's undergoing more stress and performing more unpaid work.

Many women work in the informal economy, where subsistence labour predominates and income flows and social security are rather irregular. This situation is further aggravated when women working in these areas have children or family members to take care of. Even countries with well-developed programmes to support women's economic activities find this a very pervasive problem.

Two common themes run through many of the responses to the questionnaire with regard to constraints on government efforts to support women's economic rights and empowerment: insufficient State resources and persistent gender discrimination. Although most Member States have promoted women's entrepreneurship, lack of sufficient financial, human and material resources has prevented them from tackling more effectively the issues of information needs, credit opportunities, access to economic resources, unpaid household work, lack of sex-disaggregated statistics, and illiteracy among women which limits their knowledge of their economic rights. In this respect, policy neglect coupled with the downside aspect of economic globalization has especially affected rural women. On the other hand, the persistence of traditional and gender-bias mentalities in the public sector, private sector and civil society jeopardize women's empowerment and career development. Indeed, one of the main barriers to women's employment stems from the challenge of balancing work and family responsibilities. Laws and institutions often reinforce and perpetuate cultural and traditional gender biases by limiting their attention to less broad and less effective gender-biased policies. Thus, institutions such as schools and religious organizations continue to reflect gender-biased career programmes and creeds, while the private sector encourages and reinforces occupational segregation and wage inequalities. For instance, some beliefs and cultural traditions relegate family responsibilities to women; furthermore, although the number of women in traditionally male areas of study (medicine, engineering and business) is increasing in some countries, women are still concentrated in the social sciences—their choices reinforced by textbooks, teachers and the factor of job opportunities.

4. Conclusions and further actions

Many Member States have made progress in enacting legislative, institutional and/or economic policies to eliminate gender inequality and discrimination. Member States have favoured new legislation to amend ownership laws and labour laws, prevent abuse in the workplace, guarantee economic rights of women and family, and promote equal access to economic resources and opportunities. Some Member States have supported institutional change and economic, technological and social programmes to stimulate women's entrepreneurship, employment, career advancement, and involvement in income-generating activities. These actions have often been taken in collaboration with non-governmental organizations, which have grown numerically since Beijing. All Member States should ensure that these kinds of policies and their implementation gain broader support in civil society owing to their potential in respect of creating much more productive and democratic societies, albeit Governments might still face constraints in tradition, funding and/or institutional bases.

Several Member States have promoted the creation and implementation of programmes to empower women working in agriculture. For most Member States, the task ahead is both complex and challenging given the endemic situation of illiteracy, poverty and traditional patriarchy in which most rural women live. In spite of its gravity, rural women's situation is still seldom present in the design of macroeconomic policies of many countries, while that situation becomes even more precarious during economic downturns. Moreover, the economic fragility of rural women becomes acute when, as is the case more often than not, they have children and/or family to support. Paradoxically, however, rural women play a central role in both the productive and reproductive spheres, as demonstrated by their involvement in agricultural production and caregiving. Member States need to renew their efforts to implement holistic projects for the agricultural sector emphasizing the advancement of rural women, with a long-term view and substantial resources committed for literacy, credit, and technical assistance programmes.

Differences between countries in respect of recent data on labour markets show more variation for women than for men, suggesting that women's situation may be more responsive to changes in State policies and cultural traditions.[98] Thus Governments need to take an active part in implementing development policies at the regional level in order to influence, rather than merely react to, unpredictable market dynamics.

Many Member States have supported the collection of data and information and gender studies, many of which have been produced in the last decade and particularly since Beijing. Initiatives have ranged from developing local questionnaires to setting up centres for gender research. Positive results of this type of project will encourage Governments to continue in this direction and, for instance, change their social monitoring and accounting systems to include gender-sensitive indicators. At the same time, there is a need for country comparison and in-depth research on informal sector work, unpaid work, occupational segregation and wage differences by sex and time-use surveys in rural areas. Research on these issues should help to reveal women's time devoted to unpaid household work, childcare and subsistence labour as well as further our knowledge of gender inequality in the world.

G. Women in power and decision-making

1. Introduction

The Platform for Action made it explicit that women's lives should be viewed within the social, economic and political framework of the society, and not outside of it. Critical area of concern G, "Women in power and decision-making", reaffirmed that "women's equal participation in decision-making is not only a demand for simple justice or democracy but can also be seen as a necessary condition for women's interests to be taken into account. Without the active participation of women and the incorporation of women's perspectives at all levels of decision-making, the goals of equality, development and peace cannot be achieved" (PfA, para. 181). Therefore, any attempts to advance the status of women and to achieve the goals of gender equality need to encompass all efforts aimed at increasing women's participation in decision-making in all walks of life.

The Beijing Platform for Action also affirms that women have the equal right to participate in governance and, through that participation, to contribute to the redefining of political priorities, placing new questions on the political agenda and providing new perspectives on mainstream political issues (PfA, para. 182).

The Platform for Action defined two strategic objectives under this critical area (Women in power and decision-making): to ensure women's equal access to and full participation in power structures and decision-making; and to increase women's capacity to participate in decision-making and leadership. The following measures were recommended for implementation of the first strategic objective: to establish an affirmative action policy; to integrate women into elective positions in political parties; to promote and protect women's political rights; and to reconcile work and family responsibilities for both men and women. With regard to the second objective, the Platform for Action recommended the following: to organize leadership and self-esteem training; to develop transparent criteria for decision-making positions; and to achieve gender-balanced composition in selecting bodies and to provide gender-awareness training to promote non-discriminatory working relations and respect for diversity in work and management styles.

To accelerate the implementation of action in the critical area of concern of women in power and decision-making, the Commission on the Status of Women, at its forty-first session in 1997, adopted agreed Conclusions 1997/2[99] wherein it was further emphasized that achieving the goal of equal participation of men and women in decision-making would provide the balance needed to strengthen democracy. The Commission reaffirmed the need to identify and implement the measures that would redress the under-representation of women in decision-making. The removal of discriminatory practices and the introduction of positive action programmes were identified as effective policy instruments to that end.

The Convention on the Elimination of All Forms of Discrimination against Women in its article 7 called upon States parties "to take all appropriate measures to eliminate discrimination against women in the political and public life of the country" and in article 8 "to ensure to women, on equal terms with men and without any discrimination, the opportunity to represent their Governments at the international level and to participate in the work of international organizations".

At its sixteenth session (January 1997), the Committee on the Elimination of Discrimination against Women adopted general recommendation 23[100] regarding the participation of women in political and public life (articles 7 and 8 of the Convention) which underscores the importance of equal representation of women in decision-making at national and international levels and calls on the State parties to comply with these articles of the Convention. The Committee emphasized that State parties should ensure that their constitutions and legislation complied with the principles of the Convention and that they were under obligation to take all appropriate measures, including temporary special measures, to achieve the equal representation of women in political and public life.

By mid-1999, when the Division for the Advancement of Women had received 116 national action plans, more than 80 identified the issues regarding women's participation in power and decision-making as a priority. Most plans focused on establishing institutional mechanisms and procedures to ensure women's equal access to, and full participation in, decision-making at all levels. Many countries were planning to establish targets and quotas for increasing the number of women elected and appointed to public office and in political parties at the highest levels.

2. Current trends in women's participation in power and decision-making

Despite almost universal *de jure* equality between women and men in the area of political participation and the attention that this issue has been receiving in the governmental dialogue and in numerous non-governmental meetings in all parts of the world, women's actual representation at the highest levels of national and international decision-making has not changed since the Beijing Conference. In general, the available figures show only a symbolic increase and indicate that the goal of gender balance is still far from being reached.

According to data generated by the Inter-Parliamentary Union, given in the tables below, women continue to be in the minority in national parliaments, with an average proportion of membership of 12.7 per cent worldwide in 1999 (in both houses of parliament), despite the fact that women constitute the majority of the electorate in almost all countries. More detailed information is provided in tables 1 and 2.

Table 1 indicates an increase in women's representation in parliaments from 11.7 per cent in 1997 to 12.7 per cent in 1999. Table 2 shows that the highest proportion of women in parliament, 38.9 per cent, were found in the parliaments of the Nordic countries and the lowest, 3.4 per cent in those of the Arab States.

The Nordic countries continued to lead in the proportion of women in parliaments: they have managed to sustain a critical mass, averaging 36.4 per cent (33.7 per cent in 1993). Sweden had the highest share of women in the lower or single house—40.4 per cent. The success of Nordic countries can be explained by many factors such as the equality of educational opportunity, the recognition by women of the importance of voting and of helping to determine election results, and the establishment of comprehensive State policies aimed at reconciling family and professional responsibilities for women and men.

A reverse process has occurred in Eastern Europe, where the percentage of women in parliament has seriously declined with the transformation directed towards democracy and free parliamentary elections. The abolition of the 25-33 per cent quotas for women that had existed under the old regimes drastically reduced the number of women in parliaments. Although the situation has been gradually improving, at least in some countries, it proves that the establishment of a pluralist parliamentary democracy does not in itself guarantee equal representation of women and men in political decision-making.

Moreover, no major changes in data or trends regarding women's participation in governments have been identified since the Beijing Conference. As at 31 December 2000, there were only ten women heads of State and Government, namely, those in Bangladesh, Bermuda, Finland, Ireland, Latvia, Netherlands Antilles, New Zealand, Panama, San Marino and Sri Lanka.

Women's representation in government decision-making positions at the cabinet (ministerial) level and sub-ministerial levels (minister, deputy minister, permanent secretary and head of department) shows very slow progress. In 1996, women made up 6.8 per cent of cabinet ministers worldwide, 7 per cent in 1997, and 7.4 per cent in 1998. The majority of women ministers are still concentrated in social sectors such as education, health and women and family affairs.[101] At sub-ministerial levels of decision-making, women's representation was 11 per cent in 1998, representing an increase from 7.1 per cent in 1994 and 5.7 per cent in 1987.[102]

At the international level, while certain progress has been made in improving the representation of women in the United Nations Secretariat at the senior and policy-making levels, the goal of reaching 50/50 gender distribution by the year 2000 has not been achieved. As of October 1999, women constituted 30.1 per cent compared with 17.5 per cent in June 1995, of geographical appointments at the D-1 level and above.[103] There was an increase in representation of women among Permanent Representatives to the United Nations in New York, the number of women having increased from 7 as of January 1994 to 11 as of December 1999.

Table 1
Women in national parliaments

	Single house or lower house		Upper house or senate		Both houses combined	
	1997	1999	1997	1999	1997	1999
Total members	34 839	35 190	5 914	6 630	40 753	41 820
Gender breakdown for	32 831	32 444	5 662	6 252	38 493	38 696
Men	28 875	28 189	5 106	5 594	33 981	33 783
Women	3 956	4 255	556	658	4 512	4 913
Percentage women	12.0	13.1	9.8	10.5	11.7	12.7

Source: Inter Parlamentary Union

Table 2
Percentage of women in national parliaments, by region[a]

	Single house or lower house		Upper house or senate		Both houses combined	
	1997	1999	1997	1999	1997	1999
Nordic countries	36.4	38.9	[b]	[b]	36.4	38.9
Americas	12.9	15.4	11.5	13.9	12.7	15.1
Europe: OSCE[c] member countries including Nordic countries	13.8	15.4	8.5	10.0	12.6	14.1
Asia	13.4	14.4	9.9	10.8	13.1	14.0
Europe: OSCE[c] member countries excluding Nordic countries	11.6	13.1	8.5	10.0	10.9	12.3
Pacific	9.8	12.2	21.8	22.1	11.6	13.7
Sub-Saharan Africa	10.1	10.0	13.6	12.2	10.4	10.2
Arab States	3.3	3.6	2.1	2.5	3.3	3.4

Source: Inter Parlamentary Union

[a] Regions are classified by descending order of percentage of women in the lower or single house.

[b] Not applicable.

[c] Organization for Security and Cooperation in Europe.

The data on women's participation in diplomacy have remained very fragmented and incomplete. Only a few countries reported on this issue and have emphasized that women's low representation did not match their contribution to disarmament, security, peace negotiation and conflict resolution at the non-governmental level. Jamaica, for example, like some other countries, constitutes an exception to the rule, with 38 per cent of women among the heads of diplomatic missions.

There is very little information regarding women's participation at the local level of government. In general, the proportion of women at the local level of government tends to reflect that at the national level. Almost everywhere in the world, women are not present at the local levels proportionately to their presence in the population. Even in those countries, for example, Australia and Germany, where women are significantly represented in the local government, their functions are often merely a continuation or extension of their traditional responsibilities in the private sphere. They are mostly represented in matters related to social affairs, education and the arts, whereas decision-making concerning such issues as land use, construction and the economy is dominated by men.

All countries exhibit to a varying degree a "deficit of democracy" in terms of gender. It has been emphasized that, because of inequality, women's interests, experiences and concerns are not represented adequately at decision-making levels, and women cannot influence key decisions that affect their lives and the future of society. Therefore, it is important to identify and take into account the benefits of "the difference" that women's participation might bring to the political process, in terms of its content and outcome, and the costs for ignoring their valuable contribution. The current status quo in world affairs will not be changed for the better without gender-balanced participation in power and decision-making.

3. Achievements in the implementation of strategic objectives

The Beijing Conference has created a new momentum for addressing the issue of women's participation in power and decision-making bodies. During the Beijing Conference, out of the 90 countries that made commitments to improving the status of women, only 21 gave the highest priority to the issue of increasing women's participation at all levels of decision-making. Responses to the questionnaire show that almost all countries reported on having undertaken activities to improve the status of women in this area.

As a result of these efforts, one third of the countries responding, in-cluding Canada, Namibia, New Zealand, Papua New Guinea, San Marino, the United Republic of Tanzania and Viet Nam reported an increase in women's participation in power and decision-making since 1995. Nearly two thirds reported little change, while several countries, including Hungary and Jamaica, reported a decrease in women's par-ticipation in power and decision-making since 1995.

The review of Governments' replies to the questionnaire showed that, in many countries, a certain progress has been achieved to varying de-grees in the following areas:

• Participation of women in the electoral process and political parties;

• Implementation of affirmative action policies and programmes and the introduction of targets and quotas;

• Reconciliation of family and professional responsibilities;

• Increase in women's capacity to participate in decision-making and leadership, including the expansion of leadership and self-esteem training and public awareness campaigns;

• Research on women's participation in decision-making.

(a) Women in the electoral process and
political parties

The Beijing Platform for Action committed Governments to "review the differential impact of electoral systems on the political representa-tion of women in elected bodies and consider, where appropriate, the adjustment or reform of those systems (PfA, para. 190 (d))". Although very few countries provided information in that respect, some at-tempted to introduce changes within the existing systems. El Salvador, for example, established the Central Consultative Gender Board in the Municipality of San Salvador. Brazil passed legislation in 1995 estab-lishing a minimum share of 20 per cent for women in party candidate lists. In Albania, a number of laws and amendments were enacted to guarantee a gender balance in electoral lists. Yemen amended its elec-tion law in 1998 to enhance women's participation in elections and created a women and statistics unit.

At the end of the twentieth century, one of the obvious manifestations of the democratization process can be seen in the expansion of the po-litical pluralism that is taking place in more and more countries. The political parties are playing increasingly important roles in defining policies and making key decisions in a large number of countries. In view of this development, it is very important that women take active roles in political parties and acquire leadership positions within them.

The participation of women in political parties is also important because it provides a path to power and political decision-making. It leads to participation in parliaments and other elected bodies, as well as nominations to positions in the cabinet or other political and judicial offices. Part of the solution to the problem of increasing the low representation of women in parliaments should be sought within political parties, especially in their hierarchy and electoral practices.

Country responses to the questionnaire provide some positive information about a small number of countries. Women's participation on party ballots is under 20 per cent in Paraguay and over 30 per cent in Bolivia and Venezuela. The Republic of Moldova reported an increase of women's participation in political parties: in 1995, women had made up 1 per cent of the membership in political parties; in 1999, 43-45 per cent. Canada reported that the political participation of women had increased 50 per cent between 1995 and 1997. Spain also reported that women's participation in political life had progressively increased. In terms of women's political participation, it ranks seventh among the 15 States of the EU.

Several countries such as Cameroon, El Salvador, Nigeria, Paraguay and Seychelles reported that women themselves have established political networks, building linkages among grass-roots organizations, women's movements and female politicians. Experience shows that, in countries where such networks exist, and where there are advanced studies and training courses on political leadership for women and well-developed social support services, women's mass participation in politics increases and their participation in decision-making is higher than the global average. For example, in 1997, both Botswana and Cameroon established the Caucus for Women in Politics.

As already stated, the Beijing Platform for Action committed Governments to review the differential impact of electoral systems on the political representation of women in elected bodies and consider, where appropriate, the adjustment or reform of those systems. Usually two factors are mentioned in this respect: the process of selection of candidates within the political parties and the nature of the electoral system.

According to research conducted by the Council of Europe in March 1997,[104] the parties that have established explicit rules standardizing the selection process, and in which this selection process is ultimately controlled by the central power of the party, give women a better chance of access to political office than those parties with more informal processes.

According to the Inter-Parliamentary Union (IPU) report 1997,[105] there is a strong correlation between the types of electoral systems and the number of women in parliaments. Various studies show that the majoritarian system is unfavourable to women because the party's electoral success depends on one candidate. Such a situation usually works against women's candidacy. It should be noted that all the countries in Western Europe with a high level of women's participation have adopted the proportional system. Finland, for example, has confirmed that the recent electoral success of Finnish women has been due to its system of direct proportional voting. In Latin America, Venezuela also drafted a law to reform the Voting Act so that women would have a proportional representation in the electoral process.

(b) Implementation of affirmative action policies
and programmes and introduction of targets
and quotas
Article 4 of the United Nations Convention on the Elimination of All Forms of Discrimination against Women permits the adoption of temporary special measures aimed at bringing about *de facto* equality between men and women. The Beijing Platform for Action commits both Governments and political parties to providing women with equal access to full participation in power and decision-making structures, including, *inter alia*, setting specific targets and, if necessary, through positive actions.

Whereas in many countries the strict concept of equality opposes the introduction of positive affirmative action, many countries have reported progress in carrying out positive action programmes. Ghana adopted an affirmative action proposal to reserve 40 per cent of positions in decision-making bodies for women; it has also established a Women's Desk on affirmative action in Parliament. Several countries incorporated the principle of affirmative action policy into their constitutions (Uganda), or submitted a draft law to reform the constitution so as to include affirmative actions in electoral laws (Italy). Uganda has

also established the Ministry of Gender, Labour and Social Development to implement its affirmative action policy. In Bangladesh, the
Government has introduced a lateral entry policy to increase the number of women in decision-making positions.

Based on the analysis of Governments' replies, 18 countries have reported on applying quota systems in decision-making including governmental bodies, national parliaments and political parties. Finland
established a female quota of 40/60 in governmental bodies; India successfully introduced a 33.3 per cent quota for women at the local level;
Ghana established a female quota of 40 per cent in Parliament; and
both Italy and Austria established a female quota of 20-40 per cent in
certain political parties. Quota systems were successfully implemented
in various areas in Argentina, Bolivia, Ecuador, Eritrea, Germany,
Haiti, Namibia, Norway, Turkey and the United Republic of Tanzania.
After the Beijing Conference, Senegal set a compulsory quota of 25 per
cent of seats in all of the 24 recognized parties, except for one party
that set a quota of 30 per cent. Elsewhere quota systems have been incorporated as a goal of national action plans. In Mauritius, for example,
the National Gender Action Plan proposes that 30 per cent of candida-
cies be reserved for women in all political parties.

In 1997, the Southern African Development Community (SADC)
Heads of State or Government signed the Declaration on Gender and
Development that commits them to ensuring the equal representation of
women and men and the achievement of a target of at least 30 per cent
of women in political decision-making structures by the year 2005.
Belize is considering the possibility of increasing the target for women
in public service from its current level of 30 per cent. The United
Kingdom is committed to the principle of 50/50 representation in public appointments. Targets have also been set for the representation of
women in the senior civil service. By 2004-2005, 35 per cent of the
senior civil service will be women and 25 per cent of the top 600 posts
will be also filled by women. In Peru, the Electoral Code requires that
25 per cent of candidates on the parliamentary list be women and a new
general law for municipal elections establishes a quota of 25 per cent
women candidates on the municipal election lists.

Despite this, the establishment of a quota system is still quite contro-
versial in some parts of the world, especially among the Eastern European countries, where existing quotas were largely abolished at the time
of the establishment of democracy. For this reason, Latvia rejected con-

stitutional amendments regarding a 33 per cent election list quota. The Republic of Moldova in 1998 adopted a law promoting the mainstreaming of a gender perspective into the work of political parties and other social-political organizations, but rejected a law ensuring at least 30 per cent of both men and women on the electoral lists.

The resistance to the establishment of quotas reflects the experience of the past, when women were appointed to fill quotas and held no real power. There is a tendency to believe that the quota system reduces voters' freedom to choose and that women politicians would be evaluated on the basis of their gender and not taken seriously. However, a certain progress is observed in the Eastern European region. In spite of the prevailing attitude that men are better suited to political roles, the women's movement in Central and Eastern European countries is now reopening the debate on the necessity of their representation, and pointing to the successful introduction of quotas in other parts of the world.

In the early years, the struggle for equality was mainly considered a women's issue. Now, with wider recognition of the importance of a gender approach to the resolution of social and economic problems, there is a demand for men to be more involved in the debate and to participate in all efforts aimed at redefining traditional roles for both sexes in family and professional life.

(c) Reconciliation of family and
   professional responsibilities
Replies to the questionnaire indicate the growing recognition that equal participation in public life implies that there should be equal sharing of tasks in the private sphere as well. While such recognition may eventually facilitate change in traditional attitudes and stereotypes, and enhance women's opportunities to participate in political life, the success of this approach depends on the adequate provision of resources, kindergartens, day care, flexible working hours, and parental leave available to both parents. In the Netherlands, new tax incentives have been established for employers who are providing childcare facilities. Denmark emphasized that the implementation of comprehensive policies in this area has resulted in a visible increase of women's participation in decision-making. In order to assist female politicians in performing their duties, such as taking business trips and attending late meetings, the Government is paying 10,000 kroner annually per child which can be used for babysitting services. The Government of Saint Vincent and

the Grenadines reported that, owing to the Equal Pay and Domestic Workers Act which allows for status recognition in shared parental responsibilities, there had been an increase of 40 per cent in men's participation in parenting programmes.

(d) Training for leadership and self-esteem
In most countries, women do not have the same experience in decision-making and leadership as men; the fact that girls are socialized differently from boys in families and schools negatively affects their self-confidence and the development of the necessary skills. In addition, in most countries, women have a higher level of illiteracy and sometimes fewer years of schooling.

Education and training are considered by many countries to be an important mechanism for improving women's participation in decision-making, and for improving their access to the higher levels of power. Furthermore, those countries have recognized that education is not only contributing to the reduction of traditional prejudices but also helping women to become active citizens. Many countries reported on the implementation of programmes in leadership education and training for women. In most cases, such programmes are complemented by gender-sensitive training for elected officials and awareness-raising campaigns. The initiatives that several countries cited as advances included gender training on leadership, publicizing the names of the leaders who did not support gender issues, and establishing networks to support those who were promoting gender equality.

Mexico, for example, has launched programmes for leadership training targeted at women civil servants at local and national levels, while Singapore and Italy have introduced a gender perspective into training programmes for public administrative officers. Uruguay and Chile established programmes for leadership training for women community leaders. Guyana established a Women's Institute for leadership; the Islamic Republic of Iran developed training courses to encourage women's participation in the electoral process and political activities, including training in public speaking and leadership. Finland started a project to promote education among indigenous women so as to increase their participation in decision-making. Several countries in Africa reported having introduced training programmes for female candidates during election campaigns (Cameroon, Côte d'Ivoire and Guinea).

*(e) Research on women's participation in
decision-making*

Following the Platform for Action's recommendations that emphasized the importance of quantitative and qualitative data on the roles of women and men in decision-making, many countries have undertaken research on women in political life and decision-making. The purpose was primarily to identify the factors preventing women from participating equally in decision-making at the local, national or regional level. Denmark established a committee to conduct research on the division of formal and informal power; Ghana produced a directory of women in decision-making and others with leadership qualities; and Belize has prepared an assessment survey on the political participation of women.

The findings of various studies have shown that nowhere are women present in decision-making structures in accordance with their numbers in the population, that men are almost always resistant to women's participation in decision-making, and that the issue of reconciling professional and family responsibilities is mostly regarded as a woman's problem. These findings were found to be very useful in defining future priorities for policy formulation and implementation.

*(f) Women in decision-making in the United
Nations and its system of organizations*

The Platform for Action called upon the United Nations to implement existing, and adopt new employment policies and measures in order to achieve overall gender equality of 50 per cent women, particularly at the Professional level and above, by the year 2000. In the United Nations Secretariat, the proportion of women with appointments of one year or more in the Professional and higher categories was 36.1 per cent as of 30 November 1999. In the smaller population of staff on geographical appointments, the proportion of women in the United Nations Secretariat had increased from 34.1 per cent in June 1995 to 38.6 per cent in November 1999, an increase of 4.5 percentage points. While overall progress in improving women's representation has been slow, notable progress has been made in increasing the percentage of women at the senior and policy-making levels. Since June 1995, the number of women at the D-1 level and above on geographical appointments has increased from 57 to 95, corresponding to an increase in women's representation at the senior and policy-making levels from 17.1 to 29.7 per cent. In the larger population of staff with appointments of one year or more, there are currently 104 women (24.5 per cent) at the D-1 level and above, compared with 321 men.

Although policies have been strengthened and initiatives taken within individual organizations to improve the status of women, the pace of progress in achieving the goal of gender balance within the United Nations system as a whole has been slow, with the increase in the representation of women averaging less than 1 per cent a year over the three-year period 1 January 1995 to 31 December 1997. As of 31 December 1997 (the most recent reference point for system-wide data), the proportion of women with appointments of one year or more at Headquarters and other established offices of the United Nations system of organizations was 31.8 per cent compared with 29.2 per cent in January 1995. Although greater progress has been made in improving women's representation at the senior and policy-making levels, the percentage of women at the D-1 level and above remains unacceptably low and well below the 50 per cent target, with women accounting for only 15.9 per cent of staff at these levels in the United Nations system as of 31 December 1997. Among organizations, UNFPA has the highest representation of women, having met the goal of 50/50 gender distribution in the staffing of Professional and higher-level posts in 1999.

To accelerate their progress in meeting gender equality goals, a number of organizations have adopted positive measures, including the establishment of targets for the recruitment of women, the strengthening of special measures governing the recruitment, promotion and placement of women, the development of action plans for the achievement of gender balance in individual departments, the evaluation of progress in meeting gender equality goals in performance appraisal reviews, and the institution of gender-sensitivity and gender mainstreaming training. The Secretary-General has also instituted quarterly reviews by the Senior Management Group of progress made in meeting gender equality goals in departments of the United Nations Secretariat and in United Nations funds and programmes. Increasing attention is also being paid to the review of quality of work/life issues including spouse employment, flexible work arrangements, childcare, and family-related leave arrangements. Other developments include the General Assembly's approval, in resolution 53/210 of 18 December 1998, of a number of positive amendments to the regulations of the United Nations Joint Staff Pension Fund that concern the position of spouses, in particular former spouses who were divorced from participants in the Fund and spouses who were married to participants following their retirement. On the issue of family support obligations, the Secretary-General announced, in his bulletin entitled "Family and child support obligations of staff members",[106] that the United Nations would voluntarily deduct the funds owed from the salaries of staff members in default of court-ordered family support payments and pay these funds to the spouse and/or children.

4. Obstacles in the implementation of strategic objectives

The unequal participation of women in power and decision-making structures at the local, national, regional and international levels reflects structural and attitudinal obstacles prevailing in all societies.

Reports from almost all countries emphasized the dominance of cultural patterns that assigned private and public spheres respectively to women and men. These cultural patterns are derived from a patriarchal system and are often enforced and perpetuated in future career choices by family, educational systems and the media.

In most countries, the political elite tends to be dominated by representatives from a small number of occupational groups such as lawyers, journalists, businessmen and academicians. In general, women are under-represented in these categories or occupy the lowest levels in each of these professional groups.

Many countries acknowledged that the media played an important role in supporting and maintaining the existing gender stereotypes. Despite certain positive changes in terms of presenting women not only as wives and mothers but also as successful professional and entrepreneurial women, the prevailing image of women conveyed by the media is still dominated by a patriarchal view.

Among the obstacles limiting women's access to power, it is worth mentioning the fact that often women who occupy positions of power fail to support other women and do not advocate in favour of women's issues. This observation was confirmed by an on-line discussion on women's participation in decision-making organized by WomenWatch in September to October 1999. A total of 862 members contributed approximately 105 messages. Some explanation might be found in the low representation of women in decision-making structures. For women, it is often difficult to take a strong stand on gender issues for fear of losing the support of their constituency.

The lack of accountability of elected officials with respect to promoting gender issues constitutes another obstacle, although one mentioned by only a few countries including Côte d'Ivoire and Australia.

Many countries identified the lack of human and financial resources as a serious obstacle to the implementation of the Platform for Action's recommendations.

Many countries have identified the low participation of women in power and decision-making as an obstacle that, by itself, impedes the advancement of women and gender equality in all other areas.

With regard to the situation in the United Nations and the United Nations system, low staff turnover, recruitment freezes and downsizing have had a major impact on the ability of organizations to meet the goal of gender balance. Other obstacles include the lack of specific targets for improving women's representation in individual departments and offices, the generally lower number of women applicants for posts and the smaller pool of qualified women in certain professions, and the absence of effective tools for monitoring managers' performance in meeting gender equality goals.

5. Conclusions and further actions

The principle of equal participation of men and women in power and decision-making is affirmed by the Charter of the United Nations (Preamble, Article 8), the Universal Declaration of Human Rights[107] and many other international instruments, including the Convention on the Elimination of All Forms of Discrimination against Women.

Despite the long-standing recognition, at the international and national levels, of the fundamental right of women and men to participate in political life, in practice the gap between *de jure* and *de facto* equality in the area of power and decision-making remains wide. As a result, women's interests and concerns are not represented at policy-making levels and women cannot influence key decisions in social, economic and political areas that affect society as a whole. There is an urgent need to promote gender balance in power and decision-making; otherwise, gender equality and development will remain an elusive goal.

Governments should intensify their efforts towards, and commit them-selves to, implementing comprehensive actions to ensure a critical mass of women leaders in all areas and at all levels of decision-making in the near future. It is important to integrate women into political parties, facilitate their participation in the electoral process and political activi-ties, and promote gender issues in political agendas. More attention should be given to measures allowing for the reconciliation of family and professional responsibilities for both men and women. It is equally important that women and girls have equal access to the same quality and type of education as men and boys.

However, these measures alone are not sufficient. It is crucially im-portant to address the institutional context of decision-making and create more people-friendly institutions and organizational cultures. Some countries have already started to move in that direction by in-troducing flexible time and career structures, providing childcare and parental leave.

It is also important that women in senior positions act as role models and mentors for other women and establish more informal networks that will support the career development and promotion of women.

The advancement of women requires not only active participation of women in power and decision-making but also their active involve-ment in defining the political, economic and social agenda. There is evidence that only when women entered the decision-making bodies in significant numbers were such issues as childcare, violence against women and unpaid labour considered by policy makers. Hence, the Nordic countries and Australia, for example, are promoting family-friendly employment policies more actively, are trying to incorporate the value of unpaid work and are fighting violence against women more efficiently.

The area of decision-making has long been defined and dominated by men and reflects mainly male values and norms which are often differ-ent from those of women. For this reason, it is important to facilitate gender-awareness campaigns and gender training among men. Women and men together should create a new institutional culture that will be responsive to both and facilitate women's equal participation.

H. Institutional mechanisms for the advancement of women

1. Introduction

The ability of Member States to implement the strategic objectives of the Beijing Platform for Action has been enhanced by the creation and successful functioning of national-level institutional mechanisms for the advancement of women. Whereas 11 critical areas of the Platform for Action explore issues of a substantive nature that are of concern to women and girls, and make specific recommendations, critical area of concern H, "Institutional mechanisms for the advancement of women", conceptualizes the roles and responsibilities of the mechanism established to implement the recommendations in these key areas.

Discussion of the role of national machineries had preceded the 1975 World Conference of the International Women's Year, followed by a recommendation emerging from the Conference that all Governments establish the machinery to promote the status of women. The Commission on the Status of Women designated "national machineries" as a primary theme at its sessions in 1988 and 1991, with the discussion centring on the function of national machineries in promoting women-specific issues. By the time of the 1995 Fourth World Conference on Women held in Beijing, the mandate of national machineries had evolved to encompass the mainstreaming of gender equality into all government legislation, policies, programmes and projects.

The Platform for Action identifies the main task of national machineries as being "to support government-wide mainstreaming of a gender-equality perspective in all policy areas" (PfA, para. 201). Gender mainstreaming is a strategy for making women's as well as men's concerns and experiences an integral dimension of the design, implementation, monitoring and evaluation of policies and programmes so that women and men benefit equally and inequality is not perpetuated. As stated in Economic and Social Council agreed conclusions 1997/2,[108] of 18 July 1997, it is important to emphasize that gender mainstreaming is a tool for effective policy-making at all levels and not a substitute for targeted, women-specific policies and programmes, legislation on gender equality, national machineries for the advancement for women and the establishment of gender focal points. At the governmental level, national machineries are catalysts for gender mainstreaming in all policies and programmes and not necessarily agents for policy implementation. Nonetheless, from time to time, as partners in policy formulation, national machineries can and do choose to become involved in the implementation of particular projects.[109]

The Beijing Conference called on all Governments to prepare national action plans for the implementation of the Platform for Action. As the central gender-related policy-coordinating units, national machineries played a leading part in both developing and operationalizing national action plans. Out of 116 national action plans submitted to the Division for the Advancement of Women by Member States and two observer States, well over 80 per cent of plans specifically refer to institutional mechanisms, including the creation of new national machineries or the strengthening of existing ones.[110] In fact, nearly three quarters of Member States had established some form of a national machinery for the advancement of women by October 1999.[111] A survey of national machineries among Member States conducted by the Division for the Advancement of Women revealed that while the Platform for Action had recommended that national machineries be located at the "highest possible level in the government", one third of the respondents indicated that their national machineries were placed in a non-governmental organization or a mixed structure. The diverse organizational structures and functions of national machineries reflect the national culture, local conditions and political systems of the countries within which they reside.

The Commission on the Status of Women, at its forty-third session, recognized that the effectiveness and sustainability of national machineries were highly dependent on their embeddedness in the national context, the political and socio-economic system and the needs of and accountability to women, including those with the least access to resources.[112] Given the contextual variety at the country level, a tension may exist between the potential benefits of locating the national machinery within the Government, in terms of authority and access to decision-making bodies, and those of locating it externally, in terms of greater flexibility, freedom from political constraints, and enhanced interaction with civil society. Findings from an Expert Group Meeting organized by the Division for the Advancement of Women and

ECLAC in September 1998, indicate that, in some cases, a national machinery located in the central planning or policy coordination area of government is better able to monitor all policies to ensure gender mainstreaming, while, in other cases, the existing political systems restrict the functioning of the machinery rather than facilitate its role in mainstreaming.

2. Achievements in the implementation of strategic objectives

(a) Strengthening national machineries
The majority of national machineries (over 60 per cent) were created or strengthened after the Fourth World Conference on Women. In fact, since the Beijing Conference, global progress has been achieved in the creation or strengthening of national machineries, including upgrades in status, increases in budgetary allocations and instances of budgetary oversight, extension into local government structures, improved coordination at the intergovernmental level, and enhanced staffing through training and other staff development mechanisms. The improvement in status has occurred in various ways depending on the country context. In Ghana, for example, the Government has enhanced the status of the national machinery by placing it at the highest possible level within the Government, under the Office of the President, with direct linkages to ministries, departments and agencies. Some Member States, including Cambodia, Costa Rica, Italy, Namibia, Panama and Saint Vincent and the Grenadines, among others, have created new Ministries to house the national machinery, upgraded the national machinery to a Commission under the leadership of a Cabinet Minister, or designated a new Minister to head the national machinery. Over the past five years, Albania has augmented the institutional framework of the national machinery, elevating it to the Council of Ministers level, with the Chairperson reporting directly to the Vice-Prime Minister, and the national machinery serving as the administrative arm of the Vice-Prime Minister for the coordination of equal opportunity policy. In Grenada, the staffing of the national machinery was increased from 7 to 26 employees in 1997, while in Jamaica, the acquisition of new premises with improved facilities and enhanced staffing demonstrated the Government's commitment to strengthening the national machinery.

Responses of Member States indicate that many national machineries have made progress in encouraging and providing know-how to line ministries and local governments in integrating gender mainstreaming. Some countries, including Argentina, the Fiji and the United Kingdom, among others, have created federal councils or cabinet subcommittees, under the national machinery, for the purpose of facilitating inter-agency cooperation. In the Kyrgyz Republic the National Council on Gender Policies was set up for this purpose within the Office of the President. Other countries, including Ethiopia, Indonesia, the Islamic Republic of Iran, Kenya, Mexico, Nigeria, Senegal and Zambia, among others, have established agencies for women's issues or gender units at the municipal, district, regional, provincial, ministry, departmental or specialized agency level. In Viet Nam, the Government assigned the Ministry of Planning to prepare the national action plan for the advancement of women, the Ministry of Finance to balance the budget, and the national machinery to monitor the plan's implementation. Each ministry, branch and provincial government is therefore responsible for developing its own plans and establishing internal machinery for the advancement of women. In Kuwait, the national machinery appointed women representatives to sit on the board of directors of cooperative societies and endowment committees engaged in local development activities, areas where women traditionally had not taken decision-making roles. In Mongolia, after the national machinery developed a national action plan for the advancement of women, each province designed its own subprogramme, to ensure the active involvement of a broad cross-section of women.

(b) Inclusion of gender concerns in development
plans and budgets

Many Member States reported that national machineries had been instrumental in shaping national development policies. For example, in Maldives, Kenya and Tunisia, as in other countries, the national machinery helped to ensure that the Government's commitment to gender mainstreaming was incorporated into the country's national development plan. In Swaziland, a Gender Sector Committee was one of eight sector-based committees established to prepare input for the National Development Strategy. The national machinery of Luxembourg has been consulted on the formulation of a national action plan on employment, and it is a member of a national watch on social development. An important role of national machineries involves advocating for the inclusion of gender concerns in all development plans, budgets and public statements indicating government priorities. Both South Africa and the Philippines, for example, have adapted Australia's model of a "gender budget". Gender budgeting entails that all government agencies and departments prepare a budget document that disaggregates outlays in terms of impact on both women and men. In the case of the Philippines, the Government has adopted a "gender and development" budget policy, whereby the annual General Appropriations Act directs all agencies of the Government to formulate a gender and development plan, at no less than 5 per cent of their total budget. The national machinery guides agencies in developing the plans, which are then reviewed by Congress and the national machinery. After plans are approved, each agency is required to report on the implementation of their budget to Congress. In 1997, 71 agencies complied with the gender and development budget policy, with 26 agencies meeting or exceeding the minimum budget. Other Member States incorporate gender concerns into their budget processes in more informal ways. For example, in the Islamic Republic of Iran, where the head of the national machinery is a member of the Cabinet, inclusion of women's issues in budgetary matters is facilitated in this way. In addition, the national machinery reviews national budget items and comments on the allocation to women's issues.

(c) Mechanisms to integrate gender perspectives
    into legislation, policy and programmes
While the Platform for Action specifies the functions of national machineries, it is less clear about the structures that are required to achieve gender mainstreaming. Accordingly, in addition to government bodies, national machineries might include external bodies, such as an ombudsperson or equal opportunity commission, charged with ensuring compliance with gender equality legislation. For example, following the Beijing Conference, India drafted the National Policy on Empowerment of Women, which outlines legal, institutional and programmatic responses to gender discrimination, established the Parliamentary Committee on Women to oversee government measures to empower women, and designated the National Commission for Women as an Ombudsperson for women. Similarly, in Georgia, the Institute of the Public Defender was established as an Ombudsperson to oversee the protection of human rights, including women's rights, and the Ministry of Justice evaluates all laws and bills from a gender perspective. In addition, many Member States have instituted mechanisms to institu-

tionalize gender equality within national legislation, including legal reform initiatives. For example, in the Dominican Republic, in 1995, the Senate named a Commission of Women in the Senate, composed of members of the national machinery, various political parties, legislators, jurists and activists, to recommend modifications to existing legislation and to promote new legislation in support of the advancement of women. In 1997, in the Russian Federation, the State Duma and the Federal Assembly adopted "guidelines for legislative activities to protect the right of men and women to equality of opportunity", which outline a strategy for the development of legislation to prevent gender discrimination. In Portugal, in 1995, a parliamentary commission was created to review all legislation from an equality perspective.

Since the Beijing Conference, national machineries have undertaken a variety of activities to support the mainstreaming of a gender perspective into all government policies and programmes. For example, since the adoption of a National Policy on Women in Development and a National Gender Programme Framework, Botswana has developed a comprehensive advocacy and social mobilization strategy, which will incorporate consensus-building, resource mobilization and methods for fostering a sustained commitment to the Programme, including identifying key institutions and organizations to embrace gender mainstreaming. In the Congo, the national machinery has developed a policy document on integrating women into the development process. In 1998, the Belize Equity and Equality Strategic Plan was developed with a goal of integrating a gender-sensitive approach into government and civil policies and programmes. In addition, a gender and equity task force was given the mandate of facilitating and monitoring the implementation of a national gender management system within the public and private sector. In Colombia, a Standing Advisory Team in the field of gender equality was created within the National Planning Department, with a broad mandate to ensure gender mainstreaming within national policies. In the French-speaking regions of Belgium, an advisory committee was created to review equal opportunity matters, with nine members appointed by the Executive of Legislative Council for the duration of a political term.

(d) Mechanisms for monitoring and
accountability

National machineries are critical to the implementation of the Platform for Action, as they provide the institutional base and accountability structure for efforts to achieve gender equality. Monitoring progress in implementing the Platform for Action and instituting mechanisms for accountability are chief among these commitments. In Belarus, for example, progress in implementing the national action plan for gender equality is monitored at local and national levels at regular intervals. Regional programmes are reviewed by executive committees of specialists in areas such as health care, law and education. At the national level, information is collected through the ministries and regional executive committees, and summarized progress reports are submitted to the Ministry of Social Welfare and then to the Council of Ministers. In addition, a biannual report on the situation of women in the country is submitted to the President of the republic. In Finland, the national machinery has coordinated an internal follow-up system that operates within each Ministry, and established a working party for follow-up, chaired by the General Secretary of the national machinery, with representatives from all ministries and experts on statistics and women's studies. In the United States of America, through the national machinery, and working groups set up under its jurisdiction, government agencies have assessed the progress of implementation of the Platform for Action, culminating in annual progress reports available to the public. In Rwanda, a committee composed of members of the national machinery, United Nations organizations, bilateral agencies, non-governmental organizations and civil society was established to monitor implementation of the Platform for Action. The national machinery of Malaysia monitors the implementation of programmes carried out by the various ministries through its liaison officers. In Jordan, where the national machinery is composed of high-level government and non-governmental organization representatives, each participating body is required to submit regular progress reports.

Civil society can also play an important role in monitoring and drawing attention to government accountability for gender mainstreaming. In fact, in order to hold Governments accountable, the general public needs to have access to data concerning government performance. In the Philippines, the Philippine Beijing Score Board, a network of non-governmental organizations, monitors the implementation of the Platform for Action by reviewing the Government's progress in operationalizing national laws and international instruments promoting the status of women. The Score Board also works in partnership with the Senate Committee on Women to create opportunities for government agencies to make public reports on their performance in relation to the implementation of the Platform for Action.

(e) Capacity-building and staff training
Some Member States have taken steps to implement the commitment to capacity-building and ensuring adequate staffing for national machineries. For example, staff of the national machinery in Mali received training in project planning, monitoring and evaluation, and database systems, as well as in a "gender approach". In Guinea, national machinery staff were trained in management, information and administration systems. After the gender mainstreaming concept was first incorporated within the standing rules of the Ministry where the German national machinery is located, Ministry staff received training in gender perspectives.

Many countries have made efforts to educate staff of government ministries and agencies, as important partners of the national machinery, about gender mainstreaming and other issues related to improving the status of women. For example, the Kenyan national machinery provided gender-sensitization seminars for personnel from Units of Gender Issues within ministries. The national machinery also carried out sector-specific training, including workshops for senior staff in the Ministries of Health and Agriculture, to create a deeper understanding of gender issues in policy formulation and programme planning, design and implementation. Likewise, the national machinery of Guyana implemented part of the Government's Poverty Alleviation Programme, through the training of government managers on gender consciousness, awareness and needs assessment, with a focus on gender and poverty, political leadership for women, and the role of gender analysis in policy and planning. In Mozambique, the national machinery first trained members of the Ministries' Gender Focal Points on gender issues and then offered training to other government employees.

The national machinery of Chile runs a training programme for government officials with respect to introducing a gender perspective into public policy, and maintains a network of information on gender for government employees. In Ecuador, the national machinery's training unit produces educational materials and conducts workshops on gender in municipal government offices. In the Gambia, as in other countries, the national machinery has found that seminars, workshops and conferences are effective for translating gender-sensitive research findings

into concrete actions for wider development goals. The national machinery has trained, among other groups, government ministers, legal
personnel, members of the media, fishery workers, police and immigration officers and non-governmental organization representatives.
The national machinery of Nepal held a workshop on a gender perspective in development planning for the heads of planning divisions
within the government. In 1998-1999, the national machinery of China
conducted over 54 courses at various levels of government on monitoring and appraisal of the implementation of the Platform for Action,
as well as four regional working conferences on this theme.

(f) Collaboration with
  non-governmental organizations

Because all institutions, including national machineries, are part of social networks, the support of civil society is critical to the sustainability
and legitimacy of national machineries. Partnerships between national
machineries and civil society can lead to social transformations in the
status of women. Support from civil society organizations enhances the
bargaining positions of national machineries within Governments,
while national machineries also act as important conduits between civil
society and other parts of the government. Since the Fourth World Conference on Women, many national machineries have established formal
and informal links with non-governmental organizations. At the same
time, many Member States have reported that the Beijing Conference
itself led to a proliferation of new non-governmental organizations with
women's issues central to their mission. For example, in the Islamic
Republic of Iran, since the Beijing Conference, the number of registered non-governmental organizations has increased by more than 50
per cent, and in the United Republic of Tanzania, a Women's Media
Association and a Women Lawyers Association have been established
since 1995.

In 1997, In recognition of the fact that civil society is an important
source of support and legitimacy, the national machinery of Turkey
established non-governmental organization commissions on health,
education, employment and law to assist in the follow-up to the implementation of the Platform for Action. In Botswana, the national machinery has actively sought partnership with non-governmental organizations to facilitate implementation of the country's national gender
programme, regularly hosting a women's non-governmental organization coalition forum for information-sharing. In Cameroon, where a

"women's watch" has been established to follow the progress of women, over 200 women's non-governmental organizations have registered as partners with the national machinery. An umbrella association of women's non-governmental organizations with over 3,000 members has recently formed in the Niger, and has begun to collaborate with the national machinery. While there is no formal mechanism through which non-governmental organizations may participate in the policy-making process in Albania, non-governmental organizations have been involved with the national machinery in drafting and amending legislation related to the status of women.

In the Russian Federation, where the emergence of social partnerships between the State structures and non-governmental organizations is a relatively new phenomenon, the Government and women's non-governmental organizations have participated in joint round tables; for example, a round table operates in the Ministry of Labour to work on improving the socio-economic situation of women. The Women's Council of Brunei Darussalam, an umbrella organization of women's organizations with over 2,000 members, has collaborated with the national machinery and other government bodies in the establishment of an HIV/AIDS foundation and a committee on social issues. In Cuba, where the national machinery itself is a non-governmental organization in special consultative status with the Economic and Social Council, non-governmental organizations are engaged in follow-up to the Beijing Conference, as well as to other international conferences. In Eritrea, the national machinery is also a non-governmental organization, with a network of over 200,000 members, and branches at the regional, subregional and community levels. Since members of the national machinery's central committee are also members of Parliament or in high-ranking government posts, this helps to consolidate the role of the national machinery within the Government.

(g) Linkages with national, regional and
international bodies

Some national machineries have been successful in drawing upon international agreements, such as the Convention on the Elimination of All Forms of Discrimination against Women, to bolster their gender mainstreaming efforts. For example, in 1996, the national machinery of Turkey was able to ensure that the Penal Code on Adultery was annulled, on the grounds that it violated the principle of equality before the law because it regulated the behaviour of men and women differently, thereby running counter to the provisions of the Convention. In another example, Croatia considers the Convention "a powerful instrument for the legal establishment of the status of women", and is amending domestic legislation accordingly. Similarly, in accordance with the Convention, which was ratified by Botswana in 1996, the country carried out a comprehensive review of all laws affecting the status of women and proposed strategies for redress. In Argentina, constitutional reform placed the Convention on a par with the country's Constitution, enshrining in law the right of every citizen to lodge a complaint with the Ombudsperson, or the appropriate agency, if equality of opportunity and treatment was violated on the basis of sex discrimination. The national machinery collaborates with the Ministry of Justice to promote affirmative action measures for women, and to bring legislation in line with international treaties to which Argentina is a signatory.

National machineries have also established links at the regional level to facilitate gender mainstreaming. For example, under the framework of the Southern Cone Common Market (MERCOSUR), member countries, including Argentina, Brazil, Paraguay and Uruguay, established an expert forum to consider the status of women under existing legislation, and the progress of equal opportunity policies and programmes in member countries. The first expert forum, held in Brazil, discussed strategies for incorporating a gender perspective at the regional level. In another instance, through its Presidency of the EU, Finland sought to strengthen the Union's gender mainstreaming policies, and also those of the Nordic Council of Ministers. In East Africa, Kenya, Uganda and the United Republic of Tanzania have strengthened subregional cooperation through the East African Cooperation Treaty, having advocated the inclusion of gender mainstreaming issues in the document.

(h) Public awareness and use of mass media
Heightening public understanding of the relevance of gender issues is an important function of national machineries. Accordingly, some national machineries have used mass media to raise awareness regarding gender equality, and to increase public support for women's issues. For example, in 1997, the Austrian national machinery set up a web site to provide the public with information on activities related to women's issues. Similarly, the national machinery of Japan has created a web site to provide information about women's issues and to engage in dialogue with non-governmental organizations within the country and abroad

about the status of gender equality issues. In another instance, one year after the Beijing Conference, the national machinery of the United States of America sponsored a national conference via satellite to report on progress, with many non-governmental organizations having organized local events to coincide with the broadcast, as a way of connecting partners across the country.

National machineries have also sought to transform deep-seated cultural perceptions and attitudes that inhibit the status of women through public outreach or media campaigns. For example, in Cuba, the national machinery has worked with the National Union of Cuban Writers and Artists, a non-governmental organization, to project a more balanced image of women in mass media, art and advertising, while in Spain, the national machinery created an "advertising monitoring unit" with a toll-free telephone number for reporting advertisements offensive to women and an "image evaluation council" to assess the image of women as portrayed by the media. The first Finnish "Gender Barometer", an extensive interview survey exploring the experiences and attitudes of "ordinary people" related to male-female equality, was published in 1998. According to the "Barometer", the general climate of opinion is in favour of equality, with approximately half of the respondents having indicated that they believed that there would be growing equality over the next decade. However, although respondents also affirmed that women were still primarily responsible for the family's well-being, both men and women believed nearly unanimously that men should take greater part in caring for and raising their children. The Government plans to conduct future "Gender Barometers" at regular intervals to reflect trends in male-female relations. Along similar lines, in Japan, the national action plan proposes a comprehensive examination of social systems and practices that affect lifestyle choices, in light of the fact that many such social systems reflect assumptions of fixed gender-based roles, even when no overt discrimination against women is apparent.

(i) Improvements in data collection, indicators,
   gender-related research

Many Member States have reported efforts to fulfil the commitment to generate and disseminate sex-disaggregated data and information for planning and evaluation. For example, in collaboration with the Central Bureau of Statistics, the national machinery of Kenya has established a sex-disaggregated database, with data on women's groups and statistical indicators on the status of women. Future plans include refinement of gender monitoring indicators and an evaluation framework. In Belarus, the Ministry of Statistics and Analysis and the Gender Information and Policy Centre are carrying out joint work on improving gender statistics, including training statisticians, broadening indicators, disaggregating data by sex and publishing a statistical collection entitled "Women and Men of Belarus". Likewise, in the Republic of Moldova, the first statistical yearbook on "Women and Men of Moldova" has recently been published. In Belgium, since the Beijing Conference, efforts have been made to improve data collection, including the disaggregation of data by sex. Universities have been in partnership with the national machinery, and various statistical compendia have been published, or are forthcoming. Similarly, in Hungary, the national machinery collaborates with the Central Office of Statistics to incorporate a gender perspective in the collection and analysis of data; and in Yemen, a "men and women statistics directorate" has been established within the Central Organization of Statistics to address gaps in the availability of sex-disaggregated data.

Countries have also made improvements in gender-related research and documentation, and the establishment of new research centres devoted to this area. Some examples include the recent completion of a study on understanding the gender dimensions of projects and programmes in the Niger, and the establishment of a national Centre for Information, Training and Action-Research on Women in Burkina Faso. With assistance from the national machinery, each sector Ministry in Iceland has agreed to conduct a gender-based analysis of Ministry staff, and to prepare plans for improvements, if warranted.

3. Obstacles in the implementation of strategic objectives

The most common obstacle to the smooth functioning of national machineries stems from a nearly universal lack of adequate financial and human resources to fulfil the commitments made at the Beijing Conference. Competing government priorities are at the heart of this chronic shortage of resources, sometimes complicated by a lack of acceptance or understanding of gender-related issues. Governments may marginalize the national machinery by deeming certain issues such as the economy, defence or privatization "not matters concerning women".

Conversely, issues considered to be "matters concerning women" often end up sidelined in the political process. Many Member States deplore the fact that the national machinery lacks the resources necessary to carry out its mandate fully. For example, one country pinpoints the weak commitment of decision makers to actions that promote women's development as a factor that has led to insufficient human and financial resources and the high turnover of officials. Another country identifies the sluggishness of the bureaucracy and the lack of political clout of the national machinery as contributing to the problem of insufficient resources. In yet another country, where the national machinery has had low status since its inception, this dearth of authority is compounded by the machinery's lack of adequate staff training and resources to carry out an important mandate.

Several Member States indicate that their Governments, in light of financial constraints, have prioritized other issues, such as economic and political situations, or transportation, health and education, over gender issues. An important concern of developing countries, particularly those countries perceived to be "less needy", is the withdrawal of foreign aid which threatens the financial sustainability of gender programmes. Financial constraints can also limit the ability of national machineries to conduct outreach and extend their mandate to encompass local governments. For example, one country comments that financial constraints have limited contact across geographical areas, including the hinterland, thus constricting the reach of the national machinery.

External factors, such as the dislocating effects of economic crises or austerity measures imposed by structural adjustment programmes (SAPs), natural disasters, armed conflict or large refugee flows, may inhibit the ability of the national machinery to carry out its scope of work. For example, one country reports that many of the goals set forth in the Platform for Action have yet to be realized owing to a host of external factors, including economic difficulties, increasing levels of poverty, high burden of foreign debt repayment, reduced access of the poor to social services caused by SAPs, severe drought following the El Niño weather pattern, and ethnic tensions in parts of the country resulting in a drop in tourism, among other problems. In The United Republic of Tanzania, the national machinery notes that globalization has had a more negative impact on women than on men, with women suffering from a disproportionate share of sudden lay-offs in the civil service. Foreign debt repayment consumes about 40 per cent of the country's annual budget, consequently disrupting social services, especially those targeted towards women. Venezuela reports that the effects of globalization and SAPs on women include: the deterioration of living conditions for heads of households, increased unemployment, widening wage disparities between men and women, and an increasing percentage of women working in the informal sector.

Other external obstacles include political instability that leads to frequent staffing changes in the national machinery. For example, in one country, political instability resulted in a high turnover of ministers appointed to head the national machinery (there were nine such ministers appointed between 1989 and 1999). In another, a high-level advisory committee that had been proposed as an inter-agency non-governmental organization forum to follow up progress of gender mainstreaming in the country did not meet owing to frequent changes in government. A third country reports that attempts to revise the Constitution in support of women's rights have been hampered by the shifting political structures of elected Governments and their changing social policies.

Most Member States reveal that entrenched social and cultural beliefs about prescribed gender roles for women and men hamper the progress of the national machinery. For example, Luxembourg identifies the hierarchical nature of its society, in terms of civil, political and economic life, as an obstacle to progress in gender mainstreaming. This country also remarks that changing traditional roles requires a profound questioning of personal attitudes and hence is a slow process. Swaziland indicates that certain cultural practices and traditions impede the advancement of women and reinforce male dominance, particularly cultural values that designate women as "minors" within the legal system, thereby denying them rights to inheritance of assets such as land and cattle. Cuba notes that stereotypes persist in a society struggling to keep pace with the recent economic, political and social changes in the status of women.

Some of the challenges faced by national machineries stem from structural or communication problems between or within the institutions that are designated to address women's issues and gender mainstreaming. For example, in some cases, where women's issues are still viewed as the exclusive responsibility of the national machinery, other government departments may consider such work "secondary". Thus, the fact that it can be difficult to reach agreement on the respective roles of each department ultimately hinders the work towards women's empowerment. Indeed, one country notes that all mechanisms and programmes (both government and non-governmental) concerned with women's affairs lack powers of decision-making because they are subordinated to sectors not completely committed to their mission. Botswana, for example, states that, in cases where the main role of the national machinery is one of coordination and policy formulation, efforts can be thwarted if the implementing agencies, including government departments and non-governmental organizations, lack the resources to carry out the programmes and policies as specified by the national machinery.

An additional challenge is empowering local government units and agencies to develop their own initiatives for implementation of the Platform for Action. Some countries identify a need to decentralize operations of the national machinery in order to sustain programmes at the district and community levels, while others cite as major impediments difficulty in coordinating inter-ministerial actions to promote women's development and duplication of effort among differing institutions. One country reports tensions regarding jurisdiction among various departments and actors, with the result being that most participating ministries have a perfunctory "add women" approach to their mainstream—so-called gender-neutral—programmes. Limited knowledge of, and appreciation for, gender mainstreaming among line ministries are a related problem. Therefore, many national machineries are conducting sensitization training for line ministries or planning future training sessions.

Some Member States with a federal structure have reflected on the challenges that this particular structure posed to the implementation of the Platform for Action. For example, as reported by Canada, under the distribution of powers, the jurisdiction over some areas affecting women falls to both federal and provincial governments, while in other cases it falls either under provincial control (as is the case for the provision of social services) or federal mandate (as is the case for criminal law). Accordingly, this structure requires coordinated partnership among all levels of government, which can be difficult to achieve.

Some countries address the inherent contradiction between progressive policies that exist on paper and the reality of policy implementation, which oftentimes can be inefficient or ineffective. For example, the

Russian Federation notes that, according to the Constitution, men and women have equal rights and freedoms and equal opportunities, but constitutional provisions are still "often declarative in nature, since the system of measures to ensure their implementation is not sufficiently developed or effective". Similarly, Italy remarks that the fact that a Ministry and Department for Equal Opportunities have been created does not in itself mean that a strong resistance within the public administration, even at the highest levels, towards women's empowerment policies, has been overcome. A third country, Malaysia, indicates that, while most laws are not discriminatory in intent, they are so in practice. Accordingly, the national machinery, in collaboration with the national university, conducted a study on the effectiveness of existing laws in providing protection to women. They found that the existing laws were sufficient but that the implementers of the laws were not fully sensitized to the needs of different groups of women. Based on this analysis, the national machinery is organizing gender awareness and legal literacy training courses.

The limited involvement of civil society in gender mainstreaming can be a hindrance to the work of national machineries. In cases where civil society is less developed, the national machinery may confront difficulties in forming partnerships with non-governmental organizations, as reported for example by Belarus, or the few non-governmental organizations devoted to women's issues may not coordinate efforts, thereby diminishing their impact on government institutions, as noted by Latvia. Even in cases where civil society is more vibrant, many countries, including Botswana, Burkina Faso, the Congo and Guinea, acknowledge that some women's non-governmental organizations lack skills in project management, budgeting and fund-raising and therefore more efforts must be made to provide skills-based training to enhance their abilities to act as partners in gender mainstreaming activities. For example, Panama reports that many women, both working class and professional, lack awareness of the Platform for Action and consequently their non-governmental organizations do not formulate their work plans within the Beijing framework.

Other factors may also hamper the efforts of the national machinery. For example Guyana reports on the lack of formal mechanisms for partnership with non-governmental organizations, while Goergia, Maldives and Mali, among others, report that the geographical isolation of some communities can make it even more difficult to reach rural women's groups. A generalized lack of advocacy with policy makers, planners and communities on the gender dimensions of development was mentioned as an obstacle to gender mainstreaming efforts by the Congo and Kenya. In addition, bringing a gender equality agenda to the grass roots is difficult when there is little representation of the national machinery at the field level.

Most national machineries confront challenges in conducting monitoring and evaluation activities, particularly in terms of assessing the impact of gender mainstreaming policies and programmes. For example, one country identifies the national machinery's insufficient means to monitor progress at the regional level as an ongoing challenge. Another acknowledges that impact evaluation of measures, programmes and policies is not yet standard procedure. While it is relatively easy to describe "actions" being undertaken (for example, the creation of a certain number of focal points), it is much more difficult to analyse how these actions result in tangible improvements in women's lives. An additional complication is that, in many cases, government actions are programme- or project-driven, and while beneficial to women in the short run, they may not be sustainable in the long run. Given these challenges, one country identifies a need to move beyond particular programmes or projects, to ensure that national policies and laws are put into place as mandates for future actions, with the concerns of the Platform for Action integrated into each agency's regular functions, rather than as "special initiatives for that agency's women constituents". In this way, programmes and projects would be in line with each agency's own priorities, appropriate staffing and resources would be assured, and regular monitoring and evaluation would occur based on the agency's work plan.

4. Conclusions and further actions

Despite the obstacles elaborated above, national machineries have devised various innovative approaches to their work. Of particular note are advances that have been made in integrating a gender perspective into budgeting, accountability and auditing functions, and in communications technology. Tying gender concerns to budgeting and auditing can be an effective tool for holding Governments accountable for mainstreaming gender. As Governments provide gender disaggregation of budgetary outlays when reporting to Parliament, the process raises awareness among officials of the differential impact of seemingly neutral budgetary decisions. National machineries can also play a part in ensuring that gender auditing is included in the Government's routine auditing function. Sustained commitment on the part of national machineries and the political will of Member States are essential to further progress in these areas.

The untapped potential of electronic communications, and other mass media, for generating awareness among the public about issues related to women's status and gender mainstreaming, is critical to the strengthening of national machineries. Countries that have utilized electronic communications, particularly the Internet, find that they can reach a wide audience and engage in dialogue with a range of actors about gender and other relevant issues. In the future, as more and more countries and individuals are able to expand their electronic communications capabilities, these forums for exchange of information will greatly facilitate the work of national machineries. Consequently, more efforts are needed to strengthen existing communication systems or to introduce them where they are not yet in place.

Efforts to work with men on changing attitudes and behaviours, as a fundamental component of ensuring gender equality, constitute an emerging strategy that merits greater attention. Topics such as reconciling work and family life and mainstreaming the principle of equality relate to men as well as to women. Accordingly, some national machineries have carried out a range of activities involving men, such as incorporating strategies to reinforce men's roles as fathers and grandfathers into their national action plans, or creating Men's Committees to carry out special projects related to men. The new focus on men should be complementary to, and not a substitute for, sustained efforts to promote the advancement of women, such as women-specific programmes and projects. Since the Beijing Conference, there has been a greater appreciation for the value of diversity, with the result being that the male norm is less often held up as the "yardstick" with which to measure women's progress. In the future, the role of men in working towards gender equality and mainstreaming will become increasingly important as national machineries become more advanced in their mission. Furthermore, innovative work with younger men on changing attitudes and values related to gender roles will be essential to any long-term strategies established to address deep-seated biases against women.

Depending on the level of development of the national machinery, Member States face special considerations for future work. Progress has been made in areas such as: creating gender focal points within government ministries and departments; expanding outreach at the provincial, district, community and village levels; developing national action plans; incorporating the goals of the Platform for Action into national development plans; and gender-sensitization training for a variety of constituencies. Where the national machinery is well established, new demands are placed on the machinery as equality policy becomes part of the mainstream. As the agendas of national machineries grow, Member States need to ensure adequate resources for creating additional bodies to keep pace with these new requirements.

Other issues that advanced national machineries contend with include a perception among members of the population, particularly young people, that equality has already been reached. Therefore, national machineries need to design and conduct public education campaigns to inform people about persistent areas of discrimination against women and future equality goals. Ironically, as activities are successfully "gender-mainstreamed" from the jurisdiction of the national machinery to within government as a regular function thereof, the public may erroneously perceive this as a diminution of commitment to women's issues. Again, public education can rectify these misperceptions. Even in societies where the overall status of women is relatively high, immigrant or minority women often experience severe discrimination based not only on gender but also on racial, religious, ethnic or cultural origin. Accordingly, the national machineries of immigrant or refugee recipient countries need to create policies and programmes to address the special needs, and to protect the rights, of women in these circumstances.

Where the national machinery is less developed, Member States face a different set of challenges, including garnering political will for the strengthening of the national machinery and other mechanisms for the advancement of women. The next critical phase involves creating new or reinforcing still fledgling structures so as to build a stronger foundation to sustain societal support for gender equality.

Ultimately, the goal of equality between women and men is contingent upon profound transformations in attitudes and behaviours at every level of society, from the grass roots, through the highest echelons of government. National machineries can play an instrumental part in stimulating and nurturing these transformations at every level.

I. Human rights of women

1. Introduction

Attention to the human rights of women has acquired a new dimension over the course of the last decade. Although the 1985 Nairobi Forward-looking Strategies for the Advancement of Women proposed various basic strategies for women's legal equality in its chapter I on equality, little attention was paid, in the chapters on development and peace (I and II), to international human rights law as a framework and obligation of Governments in respect of the realization of women's equality. Since then, the Vienna Declaration and Programme of Action and the Beijing Declaration and Platform for Action, as well as the outcomes of other global United Nations conferences and summits of the 1990s, have reaffirmed that enjoyment by women of their human rights is a priority for Governments and the United Nations and essential for the advancement of women (Vienna Declaration and Programme of Action, sect. II, para. 36; and Platform for Action, para. 213).

Rights are a matter not simply of policy choices for Governments but of the imposition of legally sanctioned duties to respect and ensure the rights in question. Moreover, the full recognition of rights requires the creation of effective channels of redress so as to hold States accountable for violations of those rights. Guaranteed rights are reinforced by international mechanisms of monitoring and supervision that ensure governmental accountability for their implementation and realization at the national level. Women's empowerment is advanced by establishing concrete standards and mechanisms of accountability for violations of human rights, encompassing civil and political rights, as well as economic, social and cultural rights. Thus, the rights approach is being increasingly pursued by those seeking to promote gender equality and women's empowerment.

The Beijing Declaration and Platform for Action provide a framework for translating human rights law into concrete actions for achieving gender equality. The Platform for Action's critical area of concern I, "Human rights of women", takes a comprehensive approach to women's human rights, calling for an active and visible policy of mainstreaming a gender perspective in all policies and programmes (PfA,

para. 229). It underlines the importance of gender analysis in addressing the systematic and systemic nature of discrimination against women
in order to achieve the full realization of human rights for all (PfA,
para. 222). Both the Fourth World Conference on Women and other
recent United Nations conferences have contributed to the understanding that women's equality and non-discrimination between women and
men, as well as women's equal enjoyment of human rights and fundamental freedoms, do not occur automatically as a result of the overall
protection and promotion of human rights (PfA, para. 215; and Vienna
Declaration and Programme of Action, sect. I, para. 18).

Attention to gender equality and the human rights of women is reflected
in the results of all recent United Nations conferences and summits.
Those results consider women's equality and empowerment an essential
means of achieving stated goals and objectives, but also include it as a
specific objective in itself. Through these clearly established linkages,
Governments have committed themselves to making gender equality an
integral part of all policy-making. Furthermore, global policy instruments are couched in terms of the Universal Declaration of Human
Rights and other international human rights instruments, and are directed towards the realization of human rights and fundamental freedoms, including civil, cultural, economic, political and social rights and
the right to development, for all. These global policy instruments are
therefore a further illustration of the rights contained in international
human rights instruments. Women's enjoyment of their human rights is
thus a firm basis from which to pursue such policy goals.

In this endeavour, the significance of the general prohibition of discrimination is paramount. It has two aspects that are both reflected in
the broad objectives of the Platform for Action and the Convention on
the Elimination of All Forms of Discrimination against Women: one, to
ensure that gender does not impair women's ability to exercise their
human rights; and two, to undertake specific efforts to change—and
transform—structures and processes that perpetuate women's inequality in all spheres of life. Through its recommended actions, the Platform for Action aims at eliminating discrimination on the one hand,
and at ensuring the achievement of equality for women on the other.
The human rights of women are also addressed, directly or indirectly, in
several other critical areas of concern, with women's enjoyment of human rights identified as instrumental for the achievement of the goal of
gender equality in these areas. Thus, critical areas D on violence

against women, E on women and armed conflict and L on the girl-child, consider the human rights of women and girls. Strategic objectives in other critical areas, such as A on women and poverty, B on education and training of women, F on women and the economy and G on women in power and decision-making also refer to human rights.

The Platform for Action's critical area of concern I identifies three strategic objectives, namely, to promote and protect the human rights of women, through the full implementation of all human rights instruments, especially the Convention on the Elimination of All Forms of Discrimination against Women (I.1); to ensure equality and non-discrimination under the law and in practice (I.2); and to achieve legal literacy (I.3). The actions recommended under critical area I and in other critical areas of concern are indicative of the continuing existence of obstacles to women's *de facto* enjoyment of rights. They are also indicative of the multifaceted actions necessary to eliminate discrimination in the enjoyment of rights by women.

The Platform for Action establishes that Governments have primary responsibility for its implementation. In the context of the human rights of women, this is reflected in recommended legislative and regulatory actions, in the full implementation of international human rights instruments, and the realization of equality and non-discrimination in law and practice. The centrality of the Convention on the Elimination of All Forms of Discrimination against Women to women's advancement and the achievement of gender equality is underlined, and universal ratification of the Convention by the year 2000 is envisaged. Actions directed at the development of an enabling policy environment, as well as specific programmes to facilitate realization of rights, and to prevent and combat abuses and violations of rights, are called for. Governments are also invited to establish institutional mechanisms, and to pursue women's enjoyment of human rights as a policy objective, as well as to ensure effective means of redress for violations.

In addition to Governments, the Platform for Action identifies non-governmental organizations, including women's groups and organizations of civil society, as actors responsible for implementation. Awareness-raising and sensitization efforts, the distribution of information and the provision of support services and legal aid, in respect of claiming protection from violations, are among the activities suggested. The United Nations, including specific bodies and entities of the United Nations system, are given a prominent role with regard to implementation of strategic objective I.1, with intergovernmental as well as expert bodies and special mechanisms called upon to ensure full attention to the human rights of women in all general human rights activities.

2. Current trends

Since the adoption of the Platform for Action, there has been increased emphasis on women's enjoyment of their human rights at the national and the international level. Some 90 national action plans of a total of 116 prepared by Governments following the adoption of the Platform for Action covered this critical area of concern. New and revised legislation, the establishment or strengthening of recourse mechanisms and the increasingly active and sympathetic role of courts, national machinery and non-governmental organizations in support of women's human rights attest to this growing awareness. The number of ratifications of the Convention on the Elimination of All Forms of Discrimination against Women, the adoption of a new international instrument on a right to petition, and the explicit reflection of gender in general human rights activities are indicative of progress in the implementation of the Platform for Action in this critical area of concern at the international level. At its forty-second session in 1998, the Commission on the Status of Women contributed to this accelerated implementation when, in agreed conclusions on the human rights of women, it proposed actions on creating and developing an environment conducive to women's enjoyment of their human rights and awareness-raising; on the legal and regulatory framework; and on policies, mechanisms and machineries.[113]

As they continue to promote actively the human rights of women at national level, many Governments also champion the human rights of women at the international level, especially in intergovernmental bodies. Concerns encountered at the national level are increasingly recognized as relevant to women in many parts of the world and consequently as legitimate concerns of the global community. Opportunities to address and support these concerns in international forums are sought, and international action to legitimize such concerns leads to instruments such as treaties, declarations, resolutions and agreed conclusions. These in turn provide expanded justification for the pursuit of these concerns at the national level, which inevitably accelerates implementation of the Platform for Action in the area of human rights of women. The attention to violence against women, and to gender-specific violations of women's human rights in situations of armed conflict, exemplifies this interaction between the national and international levels.

3. Achievements in the implementation of the strategic objectives

The prominence given to human rights of women in national action plans is reflected in the information provided by Governments on the implementation of action in this critical area of concern. Many replies to the questionnaire provide specific examples of steps taken and policies, programmes and projects implemented. A number of replies deal with human rights of women in conjunction with other areas, most notably, violence against women, or they deal with violence against women in a human rights context (the Netherlands and Germany). Some replies dealt with the human rights of women in general terms from a policy perspective. In this regard, several replies emphasized that the human rights of women were integrated into all Government policy and action, and guiding principles cutting across all critical areas of concern (Australia, Greece and Spain).

(a) International legal instruments
As of January 1995—the time of preparation of the second review and appraisal of the implementation of the Nairobi Forward-looking Strategies for the Advancement of Women—the Convention on the Elimination of All Forms of Discrimination against Women had 135 States parties thereto. As of 31 December 2000, there were 165 States parties to the Convention. Brunei Darussalam and the Islamic Republic of Iran were actively studying their adherence to the Convention, the United States of America hoped to honour its commitment made at Beijing to ratify the Convention by 2000 and Swaziland was advocating for ratification of the Convention.

Most of these States parties have accepted their obligations unconditionally, although several have entered substantive reservations, some based on religious law and cultural traditions. A number of States have withdrawn reservations, or have amended or modified them (Bangladesh, Belgium, Brazil, Jamaica, Liechtenstein, Maldives, Turkey, and the United Kingdom). A number of States, in light of ongoing legal reform, keep their reservations to the Convention under active review with a view to their withdrawal. A number of States have entered objections to reservations entered by other States parties on the basis of their incompatibility with the object and purpose of the Convention (Austria, Finland, France, Germany, the Netherlands, Norway, and Sweden). The Committee on the Elimination of Discrimination against Women adopted a statement on reservations to the Convention discussing, in particular, impermissible reservations thereto.[114]

In a further indication of progress achieved in the implementation of the Platform for Action, work on an optional protocol to the Convention on a right to petition procedure commenced in 1996. In 1999, the Commission on the Status of Women adopted the Optional Protocol to the Convention by consensus, and recommended it for adoption and opening for signature, ratification and accession by the General Assembly, through the Economic and Social Council. The Assembly took action on this draft resolution on 6 October 1999.[115] On 10 December 1999, the Optional Protocol was opened for signature, and 23 States signed that day.[116] The Optional Protocol entered into force on 22 December 2000, upon ratification by 10 States parties.

(b) International human rights machinery and
*   mechanisms*

The Platform for Action puts emphasis on the capacity of the Committee on the Elimination of Discrimination against Women to discharge all its functions under the Convention and the Platform for Action. In 1996, the General Assembly, in its resolution 51/68, authorized the Committee to meet annually for two three-week sessions, each proceeded by a one-week working group meeting, pending the entry into force of the amendment to article 20, paragraph 1, of the Convention, which would allow the Committee sufficient meeting time to fulfil its mandate under the Convention. As of 31 December 2000, 24 States had accepted this amendment. Since the Beijing Conference in 1995, the Committee had considered the reports of 68 States parties required under article 18 of the Convention. At 31 December 2000, there were 119 States parties whose reports under article 18 were overdue, of these, 49 States had not submitted initial reports.

Measures have been taken by human rights treaty bodies to assess enjoyment of rights by women under the terms of the respective convention or covenant. Findings contained in a study submitted to the tenth meeting of chairpersons of human rights treaty bodies[117] showed, *inter alia*, that attention to the situation of women in the framework of guarantees of equal enjoyment of rights and of non-discrimination was being broadly achieved. The study also noted, however, that, while human rights situations that were specific to women were now recognized and awareness of the gender nature of human rights was developing, there was still insufficient understanding in the work of treaty bodies that gender was an important dimension in defining the substantive nature of rights.

Studies of the work of special mechanisms of the Commission on Human Rights, such as those of thematic and country rapporteurs, also show significant progress towards broader and more consistent attention to, and analysis of, women's human rights, but they point out remaining gaps and inconsistencies as well. These gaps include limited and isolated references to women as victims of violations rather than systematic reflection of gender-specific information and gender analysis, inattention to women's human rights during on-site visits, and absence of gender-sensitivity in recommendations.[118]

The Commission on Human Rights is now according increasing attention to the human rights of women. It now includes in its agenda a regular item on the integration of the human rights of women and the gender perspective, while at the same time emphasizing the need to mainstream a gender perspective under all items in its agenda.

Many Governments actively promote the human rights of women in international forums, and through mechanisms established by such forums. They sponsor resolutions, mainly in the Commission on Human Rights, on human rights of women or particular aspects thereof, such as violence against women, and the integration of a gender perspective in the work of the general human rights activities. Governments have also worked to ensure that women's human rights are addressed in thematic and country-specific resolutions of the Commission on Human Rights (including, most recently, those on the situation of human rights in Afghanistan; in the Islamic Republic of Iran; in the Sudan; in Myanmar; in the Federal Republic of Yugoslavia (Serbia and Montenegro), the Republic of Croatia and Bosnia and Herzegovina; in Equatorial Guinea; in Rwanda; in the Democratic Republic of the Congo; in Somalia; in Cambodia; and in Haiti)[119] and that the mandates of Special Rapporteurs/Special Representatives direct them to mainstream a gender perspective in their analysis and recommendations. They cooperate with Special Rapporteurs of the Commission on Human Rights. Cuba, for example, invited the Special Rapporteur on violence against women to visit the country in 1999.

(c) International cooperation for the protection
and promotion of women's human rights
Several European and other Governments, including Denmark, Sweden, Finland and Australia, identified the human rights of women and the elimination of discrimination against women as an important area of focus and a cross-cutting theme in their development cooperation, as well as in cooperation with neighbouring countries. This has encompassed increased emphasis on the human rights of women in development cooperation and in the political dialogue with programme countries, *inter alia*, concerning ratification and implementation of the Convention on the Elimination of All Forms of Discrimination against Women by such countries. The Swedish International Development Cooperation Agency (SIDA) published a handbook on the Convention which has been widely disseminated for use in bilateral development dialogues. Several Governments, including Australia, Finland and Italy, highlighted their involvement in the negotiations of the Rome Statute of the International Criminal Court to include gender-specific provisions. Italy reported on its active participation in campaigns aimed at the protection of the human rights of women victims of fundamentalism and intolerance, while the Netherlands noted that it continues to call for a specific ban on discrimination and violence based on sexual orientation, both within the United Nations and EU.

Governments, through development cooperation, continue to support women's non-governmental organizations and academic and research programmes that focus on the Convention on the Elimination of All Forms of Discrimination against Women, or that work for legal change to benefit women in the development process. Such efforts increasingly focus on institutional change within countries' judicial systems, as legal reform alone is considered insufficient for achieving equality.

(d) Ensuring equality and non-discrimination
under the law and in practice
The Platform for Action directs Governments to take action to realize the strategic objective of ensuring equality and non-discrimination in law and practice. The replies to the questionnaire and other informa-

tion, especially reports of States parties submitted in accordance with the Convention on the Elimination of All Forms of Discrimination against Women, indicate progress in all regions in establishing, strengthening and refining the legal framework for equality, bringing it more closely in line with the requirements of the Convention. Governments have put in place incentive systems, as well as enforcement measures, to ensure adherence to legislation. Mechanisms to remedy violations of rights have become better established, with courts in a growing number of countries actively fostering compliance with women's human rights.

Provisions have been strengthened in several Constitutions, including those of Ethiopia, Eritrea, Morocco and Poland, guaranteeing equality between women and men and providing a constitutional basis for the protection of women's human rights. Canada added sexual orientation as constituting prohibited grounds for discrimination under its human rights act. In many countries, constitutional provisions of equality and non-discrimination are reinforced by legislation. Protective measures for women, however, remain in place in some countries, especially in conjunction with women's roles as mothers and within the family. These measures frequently prohibit night work, dangerous work or work that is considered bad for women's health. Regulations prohibiting women from working for periods before and after childbirth also exist in some countries.

Legislative changes have been adopted in a range of areas. Governments, especially in federal systems, have adopted, or revised, equal rights acts to ensure that equal rights and equal opportunities for women apply across the territory of States. While several countries have strengthened women's work-related rights through amendment of labour codes to establish equal rights of men and women in labour matters and equal opportunities and treatment of women in the area of work and employment, others now guarantee women equality of opportunity and treatment with men in public employment. Positive programmes and incentive systems continue to play an important role in achieving government goals of equal opportunities.

A few countries reported progress in women's enjoyment of political rights, including the introduction of quotas for elections to legislative bodies. For example, all women were granted the right to vote in Oman in 1997, and Nepal put in place a policy reserving 20 per cent of seats for women in elections for village development committees as well as municipalities. Argentina declared 23 September as the National Day of Women's Political Rights.

Several countries, including Monaco and the Republic of Korea, have revised their nationality laws to eliminate provisions that discriminated against women. Revised laws provide that citizenship may be granted to a child if either parent is a citizen at the time of the child's birth. Moreover, the Republic of Korea eliminated provisions that restricted a woman's right to select her nationality.

Civil and family codes have been revised in some countries, and such revisions are in progress in other countries, especially in Africa. New codes reflect the equal sharing of communal property between spouses, equality between women and men in marriage and divorce law, and standardization of inheritance to override customary rules that are discriminatory to women. Brunei Darussalam has drafted a new Islamic Family Law which has been submitted to the relevant authority for final approval. This law will cover divorced women, custody of children and marriages. A few replies, including those of the United Republic of Tanzania and Mongolia, noted progress in realizing women's equal rights with men in respect of inheritance, property, land and other ownership rights, by the repeal and replacement of discriminatory legislation. Nepal reported that a Property Rights Bill for women has been submitted to Parliament. Burkina Faso has eliminated a law on the interdiction of publicity about contraceptives.

Several African countries, including Ghana and Senegal where such practices continue to exist, have introduced legislation prohibiting and criminalizing harmful traditional practices, such as female genital mutilation, observance of harmful widowhood rites, kidnapping for marriage and ritual slavery. Similar measures have also been taken by some Western European and other States, including Canada and France, that have immigrant communities that employ such practices. Several countries drew attention to their preparation of national action plans to eliminate female genital mutilation, support for various projects to combat such practices, and the implementation of sensitization campaigns on the changed legal situation with regard to such practices. The issue of harmful traditional practices is assessed also in the section of this document on violence against women.

Changes in penal codes were accomplished. These included elimination of differential treatment of men and women with respect to adultery, as well as for the murder of a spouse, with both men and women now subject to the same punishment. New legislation also establishes that rape followed by marriage of the victim to the alleged rapist no longer eliminates the possibility of criminal prosecution of the perpetrator. Turkey reported that, in 1996, its Constitutional Court had annulled a provision of the penal code on adultery (husband's) on the grounds that the said article violated the principle of equality before the law, as the same article regulated adultery differently for women. The Court noted in particular that such differential treatment of adultery of husband and wife also ran counter to the Convention on the Elimination of All Forms of Discrimination again Women. Subsequently in 1998, the Court also annulled a provision on adultery (wife's) on similar grounds. As a consequence, adultery is no longer defined as a crime under the penal code. The Danish Parliament has amended the penal code with regard to prostitution. While prostitution is still not legal, prostitutes have been decriminalized. According to the new code, it is now illegal for clients to buy sex from prostitutes under 18 years of age.

Ongoing law reform efforts, *inter alia*, through the establishment or re-establishment of law reform commissions, were highlighted in the responses of many States. Some, such as Canada, highlighted efforts to improve the criminal justice system and to make it more accessible to vulnerable groups, including aboriginal women and women with disabilities. Several States, including the Islamic Republic of Iran and Nepal, have made progress in establishing special family courts, and women's offices in the judiciary. Examples of inter-ministerial cooperation between Women's Ministries or offices and other Ministries aimed at increasing gender-sensitivity and realizing the human rights of women were provided in a few cases, *inter alia*, by the Philippines and Uruguay.

Governments have recognized the need to complement legislation with other measures to ensure *de facto* realization of the human rights of women. Several Governments underlined the fact that the realization of equality of women and men goes beyond legislative action and also requires social reform. They have broadened the range of tools available in this regard, including better monitoring. For example, some countries have introduced enforcement measures against discrimination based on sex or marital status in the area of work, while others have added incentives and monitoring mechanisms to eliminate discriminatory labour practices, *inter alia*, in cooperation with labour inspectorates. Replies also drew attention to regulations protecting women from dismissal due to pregnancy and birth, and to the introduction of maternity leave. Paid maternity leave and related benefits have been made available in many countries. While women's retirement age continues to differ from men's in some countries, women's childbearing years are counted towards pension and retirement age in others. Belgium adopted a code of conduct for the evaluation of functions in the framework of equal pay for work of equal value, introduced reclassifications and developed a manual and training model for this purpose. Other countries revised employment regulations to establish women's equal right to training, social security, health and work safety.

Recognizing that the drafting of anti-harassment policy can be a daunting task, particularly for small employers, the Canadian Human Rights Commission developed model anti-sexual harassment policies for the workplace, with separate models for use by medium-sized and large employers, and by small employers. India reported that the national women's machinery had issued guidelines to all government agencies and academic institutions on prevention of sexual harassment at the workplace, in accordance with a directive issued by the country's supreme court. Belize and Côte d'Ivoire adopted legislation against sexual harassment in school and at work.

Various measures to monitor progress in realizing equality for women were reported. For example, some countries are studying law enforcement methods with a view to strengthening proper implementation of the law. The Czech Republic reported on the introduction of a system to monitor court cases concerning discrimination on the basis of sex, and cases of the violation of other rights of women. The Mexican National Commission on Human Rights undertook a study comparing federal and State standards containing provisions related to women and children with the Convention on the Elimination of All Forms of Discrimination against Women and the Convention on the Rights of the Child. Based on the findings, recommendations were made for legislative reform/ revisions in the areas of health, population, social assistance system, civil, judicial and procedural codes. China has developed targets and measures for the protection of women's rights in various areas, including eradication of women's poverty, education, and health care, and is combining the protection of women's rights with the promotion of women's participation in development. In the Russian Federation, the State Duma adopted guidelines on legislative action to ensure equal rights and equal opportunities for women and men.

(e) Institutional mechanisms to support
implementation of the human rights of women

Many Governments in all regions continued their efforts to establish and/or strengthen institutional mechanisms in support of realization of women's human rights. For example, several Central and Latin American countries, including Colombia, Ecuador, El Salvador and Peru, created separate offices for the defence of the human rights of women, or added specific mandates on the human rights of women to existing national human rights institutions such as the Office of the Ombudsperson and the Defensoria del Pueblo. Those institutions are also mandated to ensure the incorporation of a gender perspective in the work of these mechanisms, and to play an active role through interventions at the constitutional court aimed at law revision.

New machineries include the establishment of an Islamic Human Rights Commission with a department for women's rights in the Islamic Republic of Iran, the establishment of a National Commission on Woman Torture Elimination in Indonesia, and the creation of an office of the defence of the rights of women within the national police in Ecuador. Several countries reported the creation of Women's Ministries and Ministries for Equal Opportunities, of commissions on the rights of women, and of improved cooperation between such mechanisms and general human rights mechanisms and commissions. Turkey's Parliament formed, for the first time, a special parliamentary investigative commission for gender discrimination and issued several recommendations, *inter alia*, on the Government's reservations to the Convention on the Elimination of All Forms of Discrimination against Women, the integration of a gender perspective, and the adoption of temporary special measures in education, labour and politics so as to ensure equality.

Some Governments highlighted the fact that their national human rights plans both contained distinct chapters on women, and incorporated gender concerns as cross-cutting concerns in all parts of the plans. Cooperation in their development between the Government and civil society was noted, as was partnership between the national machinery on women and the national commission on human rights so as to ensure integrated implementation of the plan. Several countries noted that responsibility for preparation of all human rights reports had been assigned to inter-agency coordinating committees on human rights.

(f) Progress in achieving legal literacy
Several Governments have launched human rights and legal education programmes, with a focus on the human rights of women (including Albania, Burkina Faso, Chile, Ecuador and Senegal). These include training of judges and law enforcement officials on the human rights of women, as well as measures to strengthen capacity of women to defend their own rights. Human rights education programmes have been elaborated, and seminars and workshops on the human rights of women have been held involving grass-roots women. The Mexican National Commission for Women issued a handbook entitled "How to legislate from a gender perspective" and used it in information workshops for legislators.

Awareness-raising and sensitization efforts on the human rights of women were carried out in many countries. National machineries are instrumental in the systematic dissemination of information to women about their rights, and about avenues for claiming them. Such outreach creates "listening channels" between the Government and women, and allows for incorporation of their concerns into policies. International conventions and domestic codes, such as the family code, have been translated into local languages, and widely disseminated. Some Governments have given particular attention to improving popular knowledge of family, marriage and civil codes. Radio and other programmes of outreach and information on women's human rights continue to be offered. The creation of legal aid centres continues to be a focus in the implementation of this critical area of concern, as are programmes of free legal assistance by justice ministries. Areas frequently covered are violence against women, and women's human rights in general.

Within non-governmental organizations, the creation of chapters/groups dedicated to women's rights has been encouraged and supported by a number of Governments. This included the establishment of national committees on the Convention on the Elimination of All Forms of Discrimination against Women to monitor implementation of the Convention, and of affirmative action, and to serve as watchdogs on women's rights in collaboration with other national human rights bodies. Coalitions for the protection of women's human

rights among non-governmental organizations and other private institutions have been launched.

(g) Attention to the needs of particular groups of
women

Several Governments reported progress in addressing the situation of
particularly vulnerable groups of women. For example, Finland pays
special attention to the status of immigrant and refugee women who
need education, information on their rights, and crisis support in their
own language. Bulgaria established a programme to promote the
rights of Roma women. Italian legislation and immigration policy
now include the right to family unity, and provisions against exploitation and abuse of women and children who are introduced illegally
into the country.

Several countries, including Canada, Colombia and Italy, reported
progress in improving the condition of women in detention and in
prison, including the operationalization of small facilities designed
and built for women offenders, and special provisions for aboriginal
women, as well as substance abuse and parenting support. Other efforts have included the introduction of a bill on alternative measures
to detention aiming at the protection of the relationship of detained
mothers and their children, and the examination of a plan to address
the situation of women in detention/prison. The plan suggests the
creation of an office for women and family within the national prison
and penitentiary institute to promote the elimination of discrimination
against detained women.

4. Obstacles in the implementation of strategic objectives

The replies to the questionnaire show that achievement of the strategic
objectives of this critical area of concern is affected by several obstacles. A frequent concern is insufficiency of legislative, regulatory and
policy measures in accordance with the Platform for Action, and the
Convention on the Elimination of All Forms of Discrimination against
Women. Replies noted that women's rights are still not systematically
addressed within all relevant forums. While the importance of legal
reform is acknowledged, it is also noted that such reforms lose effectiveness if judges interpret laws restrictively, and in the absence of

clearly set precedents within the body of jurisprudence. Non-ratification of the Convention, as well as delays in reporting to the Committee on the Elimination of Discrimination against Women, is mentioned by several States as an obstacle to the realization of the rights of women, as is the limited efficacy of international human rights instruments, especially as reflected in the gap between the substantive provisions and the measures for their enforcement.

According to the replies, gaps in the legal framework for the protection and promotion of women's human rights persist. Specific shortcomings include lack of protection of women's and girls' sexual and reproductive health, and the non-recognition of reproductive rights as human rights. Criminalization of abortion, and lack of political will, together with social consensus, to change the abortion law, remain a concern. Pregnant girls continue to be expelled from primary and secondary schools within church-run State education systems. The fact that appropriate legislation to address new trends, for example, the Internet-based search for mail-order brides, has yet to be formulated creates a protection gap. Harmful traditional practices, such as dowry-related cruelty, persist. Weak laws to address sexual harassment in public, as well as in places of work and entertainment, present obstacles to progress in implementation of action in this area. Slow response, especially from the private sector, with respect to adhering to directives on sexual harassment in the workplace is a concern. Women's rights in criminal procedure, especially concerning sex-related crimes, are not adequately safeguarded, and there is a continuing lack of protection against recidivist offenders, and against abuse and sexual assault. Penal codes, especially with regard to domestic and marital violence against women, continue to carry discriminatory provisions. Civil and family codes in a number of countries require further revision, and in some instances, existing provisions—for example, with regard to polygamy—are violated, or not enforced.

Replies identified as obstacles to progress the continuing existence of contradictory and inconsistent provisions among various codes, such as labour law and social security law, and family law and civil law, as well as the continuing existence of laws in contravention of human rights norms. Replies also noted that labour regulations were not adequately implemented, and that discriminatory practices in recruitment and the daily operations of public offices continued. According to some replies, violations of the human rights of women continued, and violence against women and the criminal activity of abducting women and girls also occurred.

Replies indicate that, even when the legal framework is considered adequate, laws continue to be applied in a discriminatory and insufficient manner. Replies noted that policies, laws, and practices in the justice system, and the persons responsible for implementing the law, did not yet systematically take into account a gender perspective consecuently, the different needs and experiences of women were not always accommodated, and the law frequently discriminated against them. Law enforcement is at times considered to be weak and improper.

Lack of systematic pursuit by women of their legitimate rights, reflected in women's fear of seeking justice because of negative social pressure and women's difficulties in accessing justice through courts, remains a concern in many countries. It is also recognized that women may encounter additional barriers to justice because of their racial or ethnic background, sexual orientation, age or disability. At the same time, women's knowledge of their rights is meaningless if conditions and mechanisms to exercise them are not available or are insufficient. The lack of knowledge, the insensitivity or even the unwillingness of public officials (including judicial and law enforcement officers, mayors and administrators) to support and facilitate women's use of legal means of redress may be noted. Sometimes, there is a tendency among officials involved in the administration of justice to hold women responsible for the crimes of which they are the victims. Inadequate legal aid services, lack of assistance to women in court procedures, and insufficient institutional support for legal aid and family counselling persist, as do women's lower literacy levels, especially in rural areas. Lack of strong mechanisms for promoting women's rights continues to be an obstacle.

Many Governments noted that the existence of cultural and social stereotypes that stressed the traditional role of women in society continued to impede the promotion of women's rights. Social and cultural norms continue to disadvantage women. Persistent social pressures on women to adhere to traditional role patterns, and the persistence of discriminatory practices and customs were noted.

Governments pointed out that socio-political difficulties and the deterioration of the economic climate did not favour implementation of national action plans. A shortage of financial resources, with foreign debt accounting for large parts of annual government budgets, place constraints on the implementation of policy and action plans. Poverty remains a main obstacle to the realization of women's fundamental rights. Limited land resources, rapid development with consequences such as rural women's loss of their land, the failure of economic development to create sufficient employment and the resulting greater competition for scarce jobs place greater pressure on women in the area of employment. Women's rights to education and health care in poverty-stricken areas are constrained by economic conditions. Cuba considered the use of unilateral coercive measures (blockade) to be an obstacle to work in the area of the human rights of women, as women were doubly affected by the consequences of the crisis on domestic life.

Replies to the questionnaire indicated that there continued to be a lack of information about women's human rights in general, and its relationship to other areas. Women's rights are not covered sufficiently in the media. Lack of adequate training, and lack of training and information materials on women's human rights are also obstacles to implementation of action in this area. Lack of capacity for gender analysis, and for the use of sex-disaggregated data are also seen as obstacles in implementing the human rights of women.

Some replies identified women's lack of rights as a cause for women's continuing disadvantage in terms of economic power. For example, women's access to financial and credit opportunities, and to property rights, remains inadequate. *De jure* equality, and equal opportunities guaranteed under the law, have not fully protected women against the negative consequences of economic restructuring, trade liberalization and/or privatization. Employment sectors dominated by women continue to have disproportionately low pay.

5. Conclusions and further actions

There has been progress in implementing the various actions recommended in the critical areas of concern on human rights of women, and many countries from all regions have taken measures in accordance with the Platform for Action. Legal reform has been accomplished in areas including civil and penal law, and discriminatory provisions have been eliminated in personal status law, laws governing marriage and family relations, women's property and ownership rights, and nationality laws. Steps have also been taken to accelerate implementation of non-discriminatory legislation in practice through better enforcement and monitoring mechanisms, as well as through incentives and other tools for the creation of an enabling environment. Efforts have also been undertaken to increase knowledge of the law, and to make legal, judicial and law enforcement mechanisms more gender-sensitive and increase their accessibility to women. Actions taken at the national level have been complemented by actions at the international level, especially through further development of norms, standards and mechanisms to realize women's full enjoyment of human rights.

Notwithstanding this progress, gaps in implementation remain. Discriminatory legislation still exists, especially with regard to women's personal status. Further efforts are needed to complete revisions of family, civil and penal codes so as to eliminate all aspects that appear to be discriminatory to women, as well as to make such codes gender-sensitive. Legislative and regulatory gaps in respect of issues such as women's property rights, and protection against violence in marriage, the family, the workplace and society need to be addressed. Women still face many obstacles in respect of taking full advantage of the law, especially in court systems, because of a lack of knowledge and resources, but also because of the insensitivity and gender bias of law enforcement and judicial officials. Traditional and stereotypic attitudes about women's roles and rights in the family and society constitute a challenge to women's enjoyment of their human rights.

Further actions to accelerate implementation of this critical area of concern should thus continue to focus on the realization of a non-discriminatory and gender-sensitive legislative environment. Further measures to ensure the application of such laws should include broader and more systematic availability and use of legal remedies and other means of redress for violations of rights. Legislative monitoring, mediation, and incentive systems to increase compliance, as well as better enforcement of non-discrimination law and regulations, should also be considered.

J. Women and the media

1. Introduction

Since the Nairobi Conference in 1985 and, more recently, since the Beijing Conference in 1995, a plethora of new information and communication technologies have flourished. "Media have been established in different parts of the world at different times, in different order and are used differently within various social and cultural milieux".[120]

Under critical area of concern J, "Women and the media", the Platform for Action notes that "the potential exists for the media to make a far greater contribution to the advancement of women" (PfA, para. 234). The Platform for Action recognizes the potential of the media to impact on public policy, private attitudes and behaviour and, in particular, calls for the elimination of negative and degrading images of women in media communications in order to provide "a balanced picture of women's diverse lives and contributions to society in a changing world" (PfA, para. 236). The Platform for Action also notes that pornographic, degrading and other violent media products negatively affect women's participation in society. The Platform for Action further notes that programming reinforcing women's traditional roles can be equally limiting.

The Platform for Action calls for women's empowerment through the enhancement of their "skills, knowledge and access to information technology" in order to "strengthen their ability to combat negative portrayals of women internationally and to challenge instances of abuse of the power of an increasingly important industry" (PfA, para. 237). It calls for the creation and development of self-regulatory mechanisms for the media and the development of approaches to eliminate gender-biased programming.

Additionally, the Platform for Action recommends that, in order to address the issue of mobilization of the media, Governments and other actors should be involved in the promotion of an active and visible policy of mainstreaming a gender perspective in policies and programmes.

Two strategic objectives are outlined under the critical area of concern on women and the media. The first calls for the increased participation and access of women to expression and decision-making in and through the media and new technologies of communication. It outlines 17 actions to be taken by Governments, national and international media systems, national machinery for the advancement of women, and non-governmental organizations and media professional associations. The second objective outlines 15 actions to be taken to promote a balanced and non-stereotyped portrayal of women in the media by Governments and international organizations, the mass media and advertising organizations, and by non-governmental organizations and the private sector in collaboration with national machinery for the advancement of women.

Just over 50 per cent of national action plans on the implementation of the Platform for Action received by the Secretariat consider media to be one of the priority critical areas of concern. While most of these countries follow the two strategic objectives listed in the Platform for Action, they tend to pay more attention to promoting a balanced and non-stereotypic portrayal of women in the media. Ninety-eight States responded to the questionnaire regarding implementation of action in respect of the media. The responses closely mirror activities planned in the national action plans, with some States doing much more than had been anticipated earlier in the plans.

2. Achievements in the implementation of strategic objectives

Advances in the participation of women in the media industry have occurred since the adoption of the Beijing Platform for Action. The number of women's media organizations and programmes has increased and there has been some placement of women in various high decision-making positions. Women are increasingly taking up careers as journalists, reporters and broadcasters. Most notable is the establishment of several women's media networks in every continent of the world.

Recruitment policies of a major media company in the United Kingdom increased the percentages of women in senior- and middle-level positions between 1995 and 1998. By the end of 1998, the proportion of women senior executives had increased to 29 per cent from 19 per cent in 1995. One of the goals of the British Broadcasting Corporation was for 30 per cent of senior executive and 40 per cent of senior and middle management posts to be held by women by 2000. In Burkina Faso, the proportion of women media professionals was 10 per cent, but by 1998 the proportion had increased to 11.66 per cent. Hungary saw an increase of women's participation as journalists from 10 per cent in 1987 to 33 per cent in 1997. Women accounted for 15.5 per cent of the public television sector in Algeria; and in Seychelles, women actually constitute the majority of the national broadcasting company's production and journalistic staff and occupy most senior posts.

From 22 to 26 August 1998, the Know How Conference on the World of Women's Information was held in Amsterdam, the Netherlands. One of many conferences, workshops and seminars on women and the media held since the Beijing Conference, it was designed to improve the visibility and accessibility of women's information, on the global and local level. Reaffirming the Platform for Action, the principal goal of the Conference was to develop a strategy whereby women involved in information work could promote the empowerment of women at the local and global levels. It was also convened for the purpose of establishing global and local networks among workers in women's information centres, archives and services throughout the world.

Among the efforts reported in responses to the questionnaire, overwhelmingly the most frequent and perhaps the most significant has been the establishment of women's media organizations and programmes that facilitate the aims of increased participation as well as promotion of positive portrayals of women in the media. Many countries have seen the creation of women's newspapers and journals, women's radio and television programmes, and other forms of media. The British Virgin Islands, for example, has seen the emergence of a women's column in one of three weekly newspapers, a television channel for women, and radio programmes providing valuable information on women's health, legal and other issues. In China, there were more than 80 women's journals in 1997, and seven of 32 television stations were running women's programmes in 1998. The programme "Half the Sky" run by China Central TV has become influential and runs regularly, broadcasting special topics of relevance to women. In Vanuatu, two local newspapers have space allocated to women's issues, two radio programmes are devoted to women's issues and violence against women, and a women's newspaper is published monthly. The Russian Federation has also indicated a considerable increase in the number of women's newspapers and magazines. In Guatemala, one daily newspaper produces the only feminist publication to appear in a national newspaper.

In many countries, both broadcast and print media that address women's issues are also staffed by women, many in senior positions. Yemen, for example, has two newspapers devoted exclusively to women's issues, both headed by female editors-in-chief. In addition, four quarterly women's magazines are headed by women. In Belarus, there are more than 1,000 periodicals registered, of which some specialize in women's issues. Practically all the publications cover some female issues and the number of women editors has increased. The editors-in-chief of 12 State-owned periodical publications are women, and in one region alone, there are ten female editors among 25 district newspapers.

In several countries, the number of women in a variety of powerful positions has increased through government appointments. In Italy, for example, there was an appointment of three women to the Board of Directors of the public radio and TV services. A woman was appointed as the presidential adviser in charge of press affairs in the Islamic Republic of Iran. In Burkina Faso, one woman director was appointed in private radio, and one in national television. In Hungary, two women were appointed chief editors of two nationwide daily newspapers; in Trinidad and Tobago, a woman was appointed chief executive officer of one of the three daily newspapers; and in Ghana, the current president of the Journalist Association is a woman. Other efforts have been made to this end, for example, the government requirement in Finland that the national broadcasting company ensure equality between genders at every level of personnel, a survey in Greece on the status of women creators in the audio-visual field, and advocacy in Algeria and Nigeria to increase the number of women holding important posts in print and electronic media.

Several women and media networks have been established at local, national and international levels as a means to disseminate information, and the exchange of views, and to support women's groups active in media work. Finland's Gender Portrayal Network, for example, pooled the resources of six broadcasting companies and produced materials for training in, and implementation of, fair gender portrayal to be used in TV production. Networks such as Women Feature Service in India have developed interactions among women media professionals and facilitated increasing participation of women in the communication sector.

The Women's Journalists' Network in Guatemala, for example, has promulgated a gender-oriented, feminist approach to communication, deeming it vital to transforming the state of women in the media. Additionally, in the Latin America and the Caribbean region in July 1999, the Mexican, Central American and Caribbean Journalists' Network was established.

Other examples of efforts in this area include the establishment of the Women and Media Association in Namibia, and the creation of the Women and Media Network in Botswana, the Women's Media Centre in Cambodia and the Uganda Women's Media Association, to name a few such organizations. Additionally, a directory of women media experts was compiled in the Philippines. In Angola, the Government has created a non-governmental organization called "Association angolaise des femmes journalistes", while the African Women's Media Centre, established in Senegal in 1997, offers opportunities for training and networking with existing women's media organizations. The Asmita Women's Publishing House in Nepal teaches women journalists basic skills. One example regionally is the Centre for Women in Media of Central Asia which also offers continuing workshops for women journalists, and produces a monthly newsletter covering national, regional and international mass media issues. These are just a few examples of the many strong and active media and women's organizations and networks formed since the Beijing Conference.

Aside from these major initiatives, other efforts to increase women's participation in media focused largely on training and education. A project in Dominica, for example, trains young women from poor areas in information technology. After having established a media studies programme, the University of Kuwait now offers media studies exchange programmes and study grants for both women and men students. In addition to being creative, these actions were also significant because they addressed areas that had largely been overlooked, namely, increasing all women's access to participation in media and education/training to promote young women in the field. Ghana actively encourages the promotion of journalism as a career for young girls. Yemen has created the Mass Media College with female students' enrolments having shown marked increases since the establishment of the facility.

The development of information and communication technologies (ICTs) has provided communication opportunities to people, organizations and Governments, and has influenced the participation of women in the media. Traditionally, although ICTs have been a male-dominated field, women have been empowered by the enhancement of their skills, knowledge and access to information technology. However, access to information technology has been limited to those societies and economic groups that can afford the technology, to women who are literate, and to those women located in urban centres. The problem of access is being decreased by the development of tele-centres or multi-purpose community centres that aim to increase access to telephones, fax machines, computers and the Internet of communities without these facilities.

The information revolution continues to be an ongoing and dynamic process. Most notable is the development of information and communication technologies through the remarkable growth of computer technology, the Internet and the global information superhighway. In 1995, women's on-line engagements were estimated at 8.1 million women globally. In 1998, this figure was estimated at 30.1 million, and was expected to grow to about 43.3 million in 2000.[121] The Platform for Action predicted that these advances in technology would facilitate a global communications network that would enable media to make far greater contributions to the advancement of women. The development of electronic mail (e-mail) has enabled women to distribute information in a faster and less expensive way. It also enhances networking, organizing and mobilization work among women, women's organizations and media organizations.

Rural women have special communication needs, as they have more problems than women in urban areas with respect to accessing communication channels and media as well as the knowledge and skills to use them. At the Food and Agriculture Organization of the United Nations (FAO) High-Level Consultation on Rural Women and Information, held at FAO headquarters in Rome from 4 to 6 October 1999, it was recognized that communication programmes should make use of all modern and traditional media infrastructure and channels available in a country, and appropriate technologies and media should be applied according to the prevailing cultural, social and economic conditions. The Consultation agreed that a concerted effort should be made to harness the potential of the new communication technologies for sharing information and knowledge with women in rural areas. Essential tasks included improving the quantity and accessibility of infrastructure, increasing the relevance of information to the needs of rural women, and training women in computer skills.

Government reports show that since the Fourth World Conference on Women countries have witnessed a major increase in the portrayal of women in the media, but not necessarily one that has been diverse and free of stereotypes. Countries in most regions have indicated that there has been an increase in general media coverage of women's issues and concerns. For the last three to four years in Ethiopia, for example, campaigns conducted by women's organizations and departments have generated a high degree of media attention and public awareness around various women's issues. Likewise, Cuba has reported seeing more appearances by women in various media programmes. This can be partially attributed to the surge of women's media organizations and programmes.

Some States have carried out gender-sensitization workshops for media personnel within government and private sectors. Botswana, for example, intends including gender training in the regular training curriculum for media courses. A government project in Finland encourages girls to choose information technology as a career and offers in-service training. Measures carried out in Belarus have made it possible to overcome the stereotypes that arose in relation to the social and psychological problems of women and their adaptation to new conditions.

In most countries, efforts to promote a balanced and non-stereotyped portrayal of women in the media have been undertaken through the activities of women's media organizations and programmes. The most common media outlets in such portrayals have been radio, television and print media, especially newspapers and journals, but several alternative forms have also emerged such as museum exhibitions, jingles, electronic media, folklore, films and songs. In every region using all means of communication, numerous activities have been undertaken to disseminate information to and about women and their concerns. For example, the Indian Ministry of Information Broadcasting, through a vast network of media tools, has been actively engaging in creating mass awareness with respect to presenting positive portraits of women in society. In Brunei Darussalam, the government newspaper included a special column highlighting women's achievements and activities in the country. Additionally, a women's programme was being aired weekly on local television portraying women's activities and achievements in that country.

Themes such as crimes against women, preference for the girl-child, the dowry system and the improvement of the status of women are highlighted through various means including television, radio, electronic print and film programmes in local languages. Nigeria, for example, has placed an increasing focus on successful women in traditionally male-dominated professions and has sponsored production and airing of five jingles in English and Hausa to promote positive images of women in Nigeria. Efforts in Hungary have included regular portraits of successful women in several daily newspapers, a women's journal *Noszemely* (Women-persons) on social discrimination against women, a museum exhibition entitled "Women's Lives" and a recent media campaign showing that women can be successful in different areas of life.

Women and media networks have been established as a means to disseminate information, and the exchange of views, and to support women's groups active in media work. The Gender Portrayal Network in Finland, for example, pooled the resources of six broadcasting companies and produced materials for training and implementation of fair gender portrayal to be used in TV production. Networks such as Women Feature Service, headquartered in New Delhi, develop interactions among women media professionals and facilitate increasing participation of women in the communication sector in India. The development of the International Women's Media Foundation (IWMF), although established in 1990, has done much to raise awareness, build networks and create media opportunities for women since 1995.

The creation of these networks has been particularly enhanced by developments in ICTs, especially the Internet. Examples of electronic networks are AVIVA, a "Webzine" run by an international group of women based in London, which provides free listings enabling women globally to contact each other. It also acts as web site "host" to women's groups and services globally. The Gender in Africa Information Network (GAIN) provides an electronic networking space in which to share news, information and activities across Africa on issues of gender justice. The Asian Women's Resource Exchange is an Internet-based women's information service and network in Asia working towards developing cooperative approaches and partnerships in respect of increasing access and exploring applications of new ICTs for women's empowerment.

During the preparation for, and at the Fourth World Conference on Women, a total of 158,722 requests were made to the Division for the Advancement of Women's Conference web site from 68 countries within a month, indicating the importance for women of this electronic tool for ensuring mobilization and information exchange. As a direct result of the Beijing Conference, and following a June 1996 Workshop organized by the Division for the Advancement of Women, UNIFEM and the United Nations International Research and Training Institute for the Advancement of Women (INSTRAW) on "Global information through computer networking technologies in the follow-up to the Fourth World Conference on Women", WomenWatch was launched in March 1997.[122] WomenWatch, the United Nations Internet gateway on the advancement and empowerment of women, encompasses all the critical areas of concern established by the Beijing Platform for Action, and in 1999 held on-line working groups on all the critical areas focusing on good practices and lessons learned, the results of which will be integrated into the Beijing five-year review. Although it is one of numerous electronic sites created by the United Nations organizations, WomenWatch receives among the highest number of hits, averaging over 10,000 per month (statistics from the Division for the Advancement of Women).

A significant effort has been undertaken in the area of gender-sensitive training for media professionals in various sectors including government, the private sector and other relevant organizations; and several countries in Europe, Africa, Asia and the Caribbean have held workshops, training sessions, conferences and other forums in gender-sensitization. In Austria, for example, gender-sensitization workshops have been held for media personnel within the Government as well as in the private sector, and efforts have been made to increase awareness about women's rights among journalists in Latvia. Similarly, national and zonal workshops were organized in Nigeria on "Positive Media Coverage for Women Activities" and similar gender-sensitization training was held in Swaziland. Jamaica's Women's Media Watch (WMW) has focused on working with media workers to change how women are depicted in the media, to influence broadcast policy and legislation, and to promote women's participation in cinema and international press committees. WMW has also collaborated in organizing over 150 workshops and helped in creating other WMWs in Trinidad and Tobago and Barbados.

Some work has been done to develop strategies to promote a balanced portrayal of women in the media, especially through research and educational materials, with Governments and organizations, especially in Western Europe, contributing to ensuring that fair gender portrayals are used in media production, monitoring and analysis. A media study being conducted in Iceland, for example, is examining prevailing gender images in news media. In the Netherlands, a "Guide to Effective Image Making" containing advice from professional "image makers" on how to identify and break stereotypic gender images is being completed this year, and a five-year pilot project to find practical ways to generate a broader and more varied image of women and men is being run by the national broadcasting corporation. In Seychelles, a manual for trainers was compiled for gender-sensitization practitioners such as curriculum developers, career guidance teachers, heads of schools, teacher trainers and teachers.

Coverage by the media of subjects of concern to women and girls, as well as programmes or features focusing on women and girls, has increased markedly. Wide press coverage of the critical areas of concern is evident. For example, Denmark initiated a project to produce radio programmes on the 12 critical areas of concern to be broadcast to Asia, Africa and Latin America. However, subjects traditionally seen as female still tend to dominate among those subjects that are being covered in the media, particularly maternal health and family planning, child-rearing, fashion, housekeeping and cooking, arts and crafts, and so on. This has been slowly changing, with subjects focusing on women in the labour market, educational opportunities and literacy, women's rights, violence against women, AIDS, alcohol and drug abuse, and women in armed conflict. Belarus, for example, notes that the priority goals and long-term objectives of State policy in relation to women, and methods of implementation continue to be covered extensively in the media.

In some countries, efforts have been made to combat negative images of women by establishing professional guidelines and codes of conduct encouraging fair gender portrayal and/or the use of non-sexist language in media programmes. Greece, for example, has developed a sensitivity code urging better treatment of women in programming and discouraging sexism in language and behaviour. Japan has provided guidelines for materials that are accessible from the Internet. The Netherlands published a guide on image-making containing advice for image makers such as government information workers, professionals in the advertising and media industry and authors of official and academic publications. The guide indicates how to identify and break with stereotypic gender images, and, using texts and illustrations, applies existing insights on the development of male and female images to the work of these image makers. The United Kingdom's Press Complaints Commission's Code of Practice for print media contains the requirement that the press must avoid prejudicial or pejorative reference to a person's sex, among other things, and the new Broadcasting Council issued a new code of practice for broadcasters that includes sections on stereotyping, sexual humour and innuendo.

Other ways of combating negative images of women have included a toll-free number for reporting offensive advertisements (in Spain), the institution of an award for non-sexist advertising in conjunction with advertising agencies (in Greece and Hungary), annual awards by international media organizations,[123] and the establishment or stricter enforcement of legal measures restricting violent, degrading or pornographic materials (in Japan and Singapore).

Increasingly, Governments have denounced advertisements degrading the dignity of women, by portraying them as sex objects or inferior persons, or representing them in stereotypic or discriminatory roles. Legislation and other forms of government pressure have led to the development by advertising associations of ethical guidelines, to guide their member organizations on a more balanced and less gender stereotyped image of women and girls. In most countries however, this type of legislation is still in the formative stages. In Hungary, for example, although a self-regulatory organization for advertisers exists, its guidelines are still in the making, and its efficiency is termed insignificant.

3. Obstacles in the implementation of strategic objectives

Despite advances resulting from the information revolution, the images of women continue to be negative projections and gender-stereotyped images still proliferate. Additionally, even though more women are employed in the media and communications industry, they are still not employed in sufficient numbers in key decision-making positions, and do not serve on governing boards and bodies that influence media policy. The media field is still male-dominated, and attitudes of journalists overall remain negative or biased with regard to women's issues.

Among the most pervasive obstacles to full implementation of the strategic objectives are the gender-stereotypic behaviour and attitudes in local and international media. Lack of data, especially disaggregated by sex, is another obstacle to gender-sensitization and it also impedes the full realization of the needs for improvement. Additionally, in most countries, women's equality in the media is consistently restrained by discriminatory cultural attitudes, beliefs and practices deeply rooted in patriarchal societies.

The lack of financial and human resources has been cited by most Member States as a factor affecting all the critical areas of concern, including media. Lack of funds to pay for airtime for women's programmes, or for newspapers devoted solely to women's issues, is one of the many recurring obstacles in this critical area of concern. Financial factors have also been given as one of the reasons for States' not having wide distribution of newspapers and other periodicals dealing with women's issues.

Despite some advances in recruitment policies and the numbers of women working in the media industry, the increased participation of women in the media is still limited in many cases, and the mere increase in the number of women as media workers does not necessarily indicate their full enjoyment of equality. In most cases, women's full participation in the media has been limited, primarily in the area of women's access to decision-making power. With a few exceptions, women have not had equal opportunity to hold influential posts in the media. In Viet Nam, for example, women in media account for 25 per cent of the media workforce but only a few of these women hold leadership positions. Likewise, in Suriname, more men than women are in management positions, with only two radio stations reported to have women in senior positions.

Increased participation of women in media does not imply their access to managerial positions. Likewise, it does not mean that greater coverage of women's issues and concerns is guaranteed. In Armenia, although the number of female journalists is high, most female journalists do not specialize in gender issues. Consequently, gender issues continue to be insufficiently covered in print or broadcast media in that country. Hungarian women in the field of journalism have increased in number but only as reporters and not as TV presenters. Notably, in Seychelles, there has been an increase in the employment of women in the ranks of technical operators and engineering staff.

Women's increased participation as media workers, particularly in decision-making positions, is not easily achieved. The majority of women in media are still denied access to the decision-making levels in the communications industry and denied positions in governing bodies that influence media policy. Specialized training courses for women designed to encourage them to enter the media industry are insufficient. Even when given the opportunity to enter the industry or to pursue training courses, their continued responsibility for household and child-rearing tasks limits their ability to succeed. In addition, sexual harassment is still a commonly used impediment to the full participation of women in the media. The glass ceiling phenomenon makes it difficult not only for women to penetrate the upper management positions traditionally dominated by men but also for mainstreaming and empowerment policies to be fully implemented. Other obstacles to progress in this area include slow responses to new policies promoting women's participation and overall resistance to change.

Perhaps even more difficult than increasing women's full participation in the media is effecting a change from the prevailing portrayal of women to one that is balanced and free of stereotypes. Although much has been done to promote a more balanced image, discriminatory and stereotypic images of women continue to be generated in mainstream media. Obstacles to combating negative portrayals include weak measures and loose enforcement of relevant laws, slow procedures for bringing about change, and a lack of self-regulatory mechanisms. In addition, such factors as the low level of skills in gender-sensitive reporting and the slow institutionalization and low participation of gender-sensitivity training often make it challenging to promote positive images of women.

Analysis of television and radio programmes indicate that news programmes still tend to be male-centred. Topics presented by men and women are separated in news programmes. For example, Hungary reported that men spoke about State, political and international affairs, while women presenters focused on affairs considered to be local, insignificant, and sometimes of a sensational or scandalous nature.

Several countries have indicated that negative images of women, stereotyped portrayals and pornography continue to exist and, in some cases, have increased. In Ecuador, for example, coverage of women's contribution to development has increased since 1995, but there has also been a considerable increase in stereotyped images of women on television. In the British Virgin Islands, despite numerous awareness-raising campaigns and programmes on a wide range of women's issues, women are still mostly portrayed in stereotypic roles. Georgia reports that women's images in the media are limited and usually negative, while Colombia reports that pornography has increased in recent years. In Asia, a workshop held in the Philippines revealed that sexual harassment is increasing, while discriminatory practices in promotion, hiring and compensation and stereotyping in job assignments remain prevalent.[124]

Another obstacle exists within the field of ICTs which tends to be male-centred and Western culture-oriented. The language barrier bars some groups of women from using the Internet. Additionally, a significant portion of women are technologically illiterate. Rural women are illiterate and poor and have no access to computers. The Internet infrastructure availability in some countries depends on many factors including politics, goodwill and financial considerations. Some Governments have different priorities, and do not have the budgets to spend on developing telecommunications and infrastructure, or in legislating universal access. Acquisition of computers by women is a costly venture, and those with computers sometimes do not have the latest technology, and are not equipped to handle the demands of the Internet.

4. Conclusions and further actions

Media, globally, is virtually unregulated in terms of promoting balanced and non-stereotyped portrayals of women. Governments do not seem to exert meaningful control or influence in respect of the promotion of equality, or the eradication of stereotypes, violence against women, pornography and other degrading images. Still more must be done in the area of information and media to promote an active and visible policy of mainstreaming a gender perspective in policies and programmes. There is the need for the development of information policies and strategies with clear gender-sensitive approaches.

Since technology can facilitate the creation of information systems that enable women to build and maintain networks, and in order that collection of information for, about and by women may proceed in communities that do not have access to modern technology, some States have begun to recognize that there is a need to make women's access to information and to the means of dissemination a priority of public policy. Also, it must be recognized that the Internet is an important tool, and it is vital that women contribute to producing the contents of the Internet, instead of just consuming information provided by others.

Further, media and women's organizations recognize that the practice of monitoring the world's media, which is principally a research activity, could be used to raise consciousness about the issue of gender in the media. Monitoring groups from more than 70 countries planned to carry out a study starting in 2000, namely, the second Global Media Monitoring Project (GMMP). The Project, which presents a global picture of women in the news, is being coordinated by the Women's Programme in association with Media Watch Canada and Erin Research. Taking place five years after the first GMMP, it aims to present the global picture of women's representation in the news media and to assess changes in the media situation in half a decade. Research can be used by activists to back up audience perceptions of media bias, stereotyping, misrepresentation and overcommercialization. The objective is to try to influence policy regulating the increasingly powerful media industries, so that changes can be more systemic and lasting. Lobbying and advocacy at various levels by civil society, women's organizations and media groups to put women and the media on the agenda remain important.

Journalists and media specialists, media associations, and educational institutions offering programmes in journalism need to be targeted in terms of promoting balanced and non-stereotyped portrayal of women. Similarly, the further development and, in some instances, the creation of codes of conduct, professional guidelines and other self-regulation guidelines are another important factor. It has been recognized that all regulatory mechanisms on media at the national and international levels should be guided by contemporary values and principles such as gender justice, preservation of human rights and diversity of cultural expression.[125]

Media is a powerful tool; and for it to be used effectively by women and for women, much remains to be done, despite some advances that have taken place since the Beijing Conference. The explosion in the field of communications and technology must be harnessed and its resources made accessible to women so as to effectively ensure impact on public policy, private attitudes and behaviour.

K. Women and the environment

1. Introduction

The Platform for Action addresses the issue of women and the environment and reflects the latest understanding of the linkage between gender equality and sustainable development that has developed cumulatively over a series of major United Nations conferences and summits. In dealing with the theme of environment under the objective of "Development" (chap. II), the Nairobi Forward-looking Strategies for the Advancement of Women (1985) essentially adopted a women-specific approach that called for the recognition of and support for women's contribution to managing natural resources and safeguarding the environment. This "women-specific" approach to the issue of women and the environment was further reflected in Agenda 21,[126] adopted at the United Nations Conference on Environment and Development in 1992. However, the 1994 International Conference on Population and Development, while recognizing the impossibility of sustainable development without the full participation and empowerment of women, shifted the debate on population from demographic concerns and targets towards the view that the well-being of women and men was at the centre of sustainable development. The Programme of Action of the International Conference on Population and Development,[127] with its strong emphasis on the reproductive rights of women, was bolstered considerably by the outcome of the 1993 Vienna Conference on Human Rights with its significant affirmation of the human rights of women.

The Platform for Action further augmented the shift from the women-specific approach to a focus on gender relations by identifying gender mainstreaming, a human rights approach and the development of partnership between women and men as the strategic bases for the pursuit of gender equality and the advancement of women. Critical area of concern K, "Women and the environment", of the Platform for Action asserts that "human beings are at the centre of concern for sustainable development" and that "women have an essential role to play in the development of sustainable and ecologically sound consumption and production patterns and approaches to natural resources management" (PfA, para. 246).

The Platform for Action draws attention to the fact that, because of existing patterns of gender inequality, environmental degradation affects women and girls disproportionately in terms of their health, well-being and quality of life. Also, resource depletion and increasing dangers of polluting substances are destroying fragile ecosystems and displacing communities, especially women, to the detriment of their productive capacities. Therefore, the Platform for Action calls for attention to, and recognition of, the role and situation of rural women and those women involved in agricultural production through interventions, such as access to credit and land, that will strengthen their capabilities to participate fully in the process of sustainable development. The Platform for Action also notes the dearth of women at all levels of decision-making in the areas of natural resources and environmental management in spite of their role as key users and consumers of these natural resources.

Building on preceding conferences, the Platform for Action identifies specific actions to be implemented by Governments, international and regional organizations, and civil society, including non-governmental organizations and the private sector, in order to pursue the three strategic objectives for achieving gender equality and sustainable development.

A number of national action plans developed to implement the Platform for Action consider women and the environment a priority. Of the national action plans that were reviewed by the Division for the Advancement of Women, 50 per cent dealt with this critical area of concern, and they followed the conclusions and recommendations of the Platform for Action. Many other plans consider this critical area of concern in the broader context of development, underlining the importance of mainstreaming a gender perspective into policies and programmes, and recognizing the importance of increasing women's participation in environmental decision-making. In their responses to the questionnaire, several countries referred to these national action plans.

2. Achievements in the implementation of strategic objectives

(a) Mainstreaming a gender perspective in
sustainable development

Strategic objective 2 of Platform for Action critical area of concern K on women and the environment calls for the integration of gender concerns and perspectives in policies and programmes in pursuit of the goal of sustainable development.

Responses to the questionnaire indicate that a number of States have taken steps to incorporate a gender perspective in their national environmental activities and plans. Colombia's Ministry of the Environment, for example, has given support to the entities of the National Environment System with respect to incorporating gender perspectives in the planning, management and evaluation of projects. Also, in 1999, Colombia's national machinery, the National Directorate for the Equality of Women, agreed to work with the Ministry of Environment on the objective of incorporating a gender perspective in the planning and carrying out of political programmes. Côte d'Ivoire has developed a National Action Programme on Environment (PNAE) which takes into consideration gender concerns. Japan's Plan for Gender Equality 2000 states that "in view of the fact that the resolution of environmental problems is greatly enhanced by the participation of women, it is necessary to support and promote environmental protection initiatives by establishing partnerships that encompass a broad spectrum of society".

Canada has sought to incorporate the Platform for Action's principles on the environment at the international level. Canada promoted the integration of a gender perspective in the texts of international sustainable development agreements, including the review and assessment of the Rio Summit and recommendations of the Commission on Sustainable Development. Canada also proposed and supported texts that promoted gender equality or the integration of a gender perspective in a number of areas of sustainable development, including all levels of decision-making, poverty alleviation, health, population, human settlements, capacity-building, science, education and awareness, information and tools for measuring progress. Furthermore, Canada promoted the mainstreaming of a gender perspective in sectoral issues, such as sustainable management of freshwater, oceans and forests, protecting biodiversity and combating desertification, including the efforts of the FAO Forestry Department to mainstream gender concerns in its activities.

(b) Participation of women in decision-making for sustainable development

Strategic objective 1 of the critical area of concern K calls for the active involvement of women, including indigenous women, in environmental decision-making at all levels, *inter alia*, as managers, designers and planners, and as implementers of environmental projects.

In pursuit of this objective, many States have undertaken various steps to ensure the participation of women, including indigenous women, in international meetings and workshops. In Canada, for example, indigenous women have been fully active in the Government's efforts to meet commitments under the Convention on Biological Diversity.[128] Canada has provided financial and policy support for their participation both at the Canadian Open-ended Working Group on the Biodiversity Convention and at international meetings, such as the fourth meeting of the Conference of the Parties to the Convention and the Madrid Workshop on the United Nations Biodiversity Convention/Traditional Knowledge. The Government of Canada facilitated the participation of the delegation from the Pauktuutit Inuit Women's Association in the 1997 Northern Women, Northern Lives Conference in Norway, the objective of which was to enhance the contribution of women in achieving sustainable development.

There has been a positive, albeit tentative, trend towards greater involvement of women in government decision-making positions that deal with the environment. For example, China reports that, in 1997, 38 per cent of its total staff working in environmental protection departments were women. In Tunisia, women constitute 36 per cent of the total staff of the Ministry of Environment and Regional Development, 19 per cent of that 36 per cent occupying senior management positions. Jamaica reports positive changes in recruitment which have raised the participation of women to 69 per cent of the administrative staff of the environmental sector and 37 per cent of the technical staff of the Forestry Department. Italy also reports a positive and significant professional presence of women in agriculture. Other countries report the appointments of women at the highest decision-making level in this area as ministers (Portugal), as members of cabinet (Suriname) and as heads of environmental agencies (Islamic Republic of Iran).

Other Member States report efforts to extend women's equal participation in the international arena. For example, Germany submitted the resolution on "Personnel Questions: Women in the Secretariat" to the fortieth General Conference of the International Atomic Energy Agency in 1996.

(c) Strengthening women's capabilities

The Platform for Action encourages countries to further women's participation in environmental decision-making at all levels. Strategies include increasing women's access to information and education, especially in the areas of science and technology and economics, thus enhancing their knowledge, skills and opportunities for participation in environmental decisions. In pursuit of this objective, Governments report on a range of activities from awareness-raising to training programmes and seminars for women in the area of natural resource management and environmental protection.

Several countries reported on women's participation in environmental awareness campaigns. The Government of China, for example, launched an awareness campaign for the whole nation in which women's organizations actively participated. In 1997, the State Bureau of Environment Protection and the All-China Women's Federation jointly carried out a publicity activity with the theme "Women, Home and Environment" in more than 20 provinces. Close to 190,000 copies of the pamphlet entitled "100 questions about the knowledge on women and the environment" were distributed as part of the "March 8 Green Works" campaign, which has involved the participation of 100 million women annually in a campaign for reforestation, creation of shelter forests and soil and water conservation.

Other countries set up workshops designed to increase women's participation in environmental decision-making. The Islamic Republic of Iran, for example, organized workshops on women's participation in environmental protection in order to increase the proportion of women in preserving natural resources. The Government of Jamaica, with the support of the CIDA, launched a Trees for Tomorrow project which seeks to involve women in agroforestry extension programmes. Germany initiated a project called "Girls for an Ecological Europe", which motivates and supports girls who want to become involved in the field of ecology, while Costa Rica created an "International Eco-Peace Village" to train women and youth about ecological isues and sustainable development.

Numerous reports from Member States show that training was the strategy of choice employed to increase women's capabilities. The Islamic Republic of Iran, for example, has created a special department in the Environmental Protection Office for training and programming with the aim of promoting rural women's contribution to environmental protection activities. Likewise, Jordan has embarked on the training of rural women in the proper use of agricultural pesticides and fertilizers as well as in following sound irrigation techniques by using modern irrigation methods. Countries as diverse as the Congo, Malaysia, Mali and the Republic of Moldova have implemented training programmes to raise the environmental consciousness of women, to transfer know-how on agricultural technologies and methods, to organize women into cooperatives, to provide technical support by local agents, and to infuse into the policy framework an awareness of women's key role in environmental protection. An example of an activity with the last-mentioned objective is a seminar organized by the Islamic Republic of Iran on women's key contribution in coping and dealing with the aftermath of humanitarian crises such as earthquakes.

(d) Involving civil society
Member States have actively sought to involve non-governmental organizations and women's organizations in their work in the area of women and the environment. The United Kingdom, for example, promoted the involvement of non-governmental organizations in the Local Agenda 21 Steering Group of which the National Federation of Women's Institutes and Women's Environment Network are members.

Governments also indicated their commitment to supporting women's environmental non-governmental organizations in their own initiatives on environmental management. For example, Colombia has promoted the participation of women's organizations in decision-making and their representation in Regional Independent Corporations, as well as the elaboration and design by women's organizations of a plan of environmental management in Colombian family life.

Some non-governmental organizations led by women have taken the lead in efforts towards environmental protection and sustainable development. For example, in Côte d'Ivoire, women's non-governmental organizations are active in undertaking environmental conservation activities through conferences, cultural and recreation activities, and training on how to make and use improved stoves. In India, women's groups are playing an important role in activities aimed at environmental conservation through a diverse range of programmes.

(e) Carrying out gender analysis and research

A number of Member States have embarked on gender-sensitive research in the area of the environment. Some examples include: Zambia's participation in the worldwide gender assessment of water and sanitation by the WHO; a study conducted in Tunisia on the role of women in the management of natural resources and efforts to combat desertification; and a contextual analysis on gender and the environment completed by Environmental Action (ENACT), a non-governmental organization in Jamaica whose outcome will be used as a basis for a strategy for the recruitment of women into professional and technical levels. In Germany, the State of Baden-Wηrttemberg has promoted exemplary programmes and reports on "women-oriented regional planning" and "mobility in the Stuttgart region", through which ongoing women's research on the subjects is supported. Furthermore, in 1997, the Government of Germany funded the publication of a directory entitled "Who's who in the women's environmental sector".

In the Congo, the Government encouraged the direct and active participation of women researchers in the activities of the National Centre on Documentation and Scientific and Technical Information (CNDIST) and of the Research Centre for Initiating Technology Projects (CRIPT), while in Namibia, the Ministry of Environment and Tourism has launched a programme for women to specifically research the environmental effects of development on their communities.

(f) Empowering women economically

The link between poverty and environmental degradation is well established and was recognized both at the Rio Conference and at the Beijing Conference. Hence, the Platform for Action calls for all States and all people to "cooperate in the essential task of eradicating poverty as an indispensable requirement for sustainable development" (PfA, para. 247). Women, particularly rural women, have a higher incidence of poverty, and their economic empowerment is a necessary aspect of any environmental conservation strategy.

A number of Member States have included economic activities by women within their environmental conservation strategies. Botswana, for example, trains rural women in harvesting veld products in a sustainable manner. El Salvador is providing technical assistance for the production of 334,000 young trees in community nurseries tended by women. Tunisia cited its efforts to improve women's access to credit in order to strengthen their capacity to participate in sustainable development.

Several countries are involving women in projects to combat desertification. For example, Tunisia has launched a pilot project on fighting desertification through improving living conditions of rural women and promoting handicraft activities. Moreover, Tunisia set up a National Fund to combat desertification and support local capacity-building and sensitization efforts. Uzbekistan's Aral Sea Project is another effort at combating desertification that involves the full participation of women, and similar efforts are underway in Mali and Swaziland.

Some of the developed countries have announced initiatives to involve women in sustainable development in other parts of the world. The United Kingdom, for example, has launched a three billion dollar programme called the New Deal for Regeneration designed to tackle the problems of the most deprived areas. The New Deal focuses on enhancing economic and employment opportunities, improving quality of life and offering better management. Through the Aga Khan Foundation, Canada supported a women's organization in India that has reclaimed unproductive wasteland lost to salt damage. The women also set up their own savings clubs to provide small loans to members and follow up on new drinking-water projects.

Other developed countries have supported UN or other agencies in such initiatives. Through its support for UNIFEM, for example, Canada has made possible a project in Mali to train, equip and provide credit to women for the purpose of their establishing a waste-disposal business in Bamako, which currently provides garbage removal services to 18,000 residents.

(g) Other developments
The Platform for Action calls for the effective protection and use of the knowledge of women, especially indigenous women, including practices related to traditional medicines. In this regard, Tunisia reported that it has undertaken measures to promote women's traditional knowledge in the management of natural resources. Singapore, on the other hand, asserts that no inequality is practised between the sexes in respect of the intellectual property rights of the practices and knowledge in the field of traditional medicine and therefore no legislation on the practice of traditional medicine has been introduced.

The provision of safe water supply and sanitation has a positive impact on women. It enhances the health of women and girls and also removes the need for water collection, which is a major cause of their time burden. A number of countries such as China, Viet Nam and Zambia implemented initiatives in this area, which increased access to safe water and sanitation of the rural and urban poor, especially women.

The Platform for Action asserts that "environmental risks in the home and workplace may have a disproportionate impact on women's health because of women's different susceptibilities to the toxic effects of various chemicals" (PfA, para. 247). Some Member States have taken action in this area. For example, India has implemented the *Baghaa* (survival) project to monitor health conditions for carpet weavers, 70 per cent of whom are women, so as to improve their awareness of hazards of their workplace, while Denmark has arranged training workshops on the safety of women working with chemicals so as to reduce risks to women from identified environmental hazards.

3. Obstacles in the implementation of strategic objectives

Member States consistently identified the low level of management and technical skills among women and within small rural women's groups as constraints on the implementation and realization of the goals of the Platform for Action. This constraint, caused by socio-economic and cultural factors as well as low educational levels of women, results in women's lack of access to resources, information and scientific and technological skills, which leads to lower participation of women in environmental protection and management.

Some Member States pointed out that there is also a lack of awareness on the part of the population about environmental issues, in general, and about the benefit of gender equality considerations in environmental protection and management, in particular.

The low participation of women in the formulation, planning and execution of environmental policy was mentioned by almost all countries as a major constraint on the achievement of the goals of the Platform for Action. Member States discussed the insufficient numbers of women in responsible positions, the male monopoly on the management of the country's environmental resources with few women as token members on management committees, the insufficient participation of women in decision-making, the lack of adequate influence in decision-making in the sphere of natural resources on the part of women and so forth. Member States did not provide explanations, however, for the persistence of women's under-representation in environmental decision-making. A lack of technical skills cannot be the only determinant. For example, the Republic of Moldova reports that, although women possess knowledge and experience in the sphere of administration and conservation of natural resources, their role continues to be limited. The Republic of Moldova also reports that, although women have professional training that allows them to participate in natural resource decision-making, they are poorly represented in official bodies, as well as in planning and technical positions in the environmental sphere or in ecological reconstruction.

Perhaps the explanation lies in the absence of deliberate strategies to ensure women's participation in decision-making. The United Kingdom reports that there are no mechanisms or funding for monitoring women's involvement at the local level. Germany, on the other hand, ascribes the persistent under-representation in decision-making to the fact that women continue to be under-represented in research and teaching in the natural sciences, with the result that the percentage of women in the federal Government's advisory bodies in the environmental sector is still low.

Another factor is policies and programmes that are not gender-sensitive. These policies disregard issues such as the different and heavier time burden of women, due to their unpaid work and their greater share of responsibility for reproductive activities, which limits their ability to participate fully and equally in institutions.

Unpredictable climatic conditions and negative impacts of natural disasters, ranging from cyclones in Asia to hurricanes in the Caribbean and droughts in Southern Africa as well as earthquakes in Japan and Turkey, are making it difficult for Governments and other actors to formulate long-term plans. At the same time, these conditions impose constraints on the effective implementation of any such plans as are developed.

The perennial issue of insufficient financial resources, human resources and technology is mentioned, especially by developing countries, as constraints on the implementation of national plans for gender equity, including the issue of the environment.

Governments report that there is a persistent lack of skills and access to resources and information on the part of women, which curtails their capacity to participate fully in environmental decision-making. Governments are also reporting that the dearth of women in decision making still persists and this is also a constraint on the implementation of the Platform for Action. These factors are mutually reinforcing and contribute to gender inequality and, in turn, hinder the realization of the objectives of the Beijing Declaration and Platform for Action.

4. Conclusions and further actions

In the light of the existing constraints, Governments need to take urgent action to accelerate the advancement of women to ensure that women are empowered with the necessary know-how and technical skills and have access to critical resources and decision-making processes. In this regard, Governments should take cognizance of the relevant provisions of the Convention on the Elimination of All Forms of Discrimination against Women as they embark upon urgent actions in the area of women and the environment as follows:

- Ensure the full and equal participation of women in environmental decision-making as called for in the Platform for Action. Particular reference should be made to articles 4, 7 and 8 of the Convention on the Elimination of All Forms of Discrimination against Women. These articles call, respectively, for the adoption of temporary special measures to combat discrimination to establish equality in political and public life at the national level and to establish such equality at the international level;

- Design programmes that would contribute to developing the capabilities of women to enable them to participate fully in environmental policy-making and implementation. Special reference should be made to articles 3 and 4 of Convention on the Elimination of All Forms of Discrimination against Women, which call respectively for appropriate measures and for temporary special measures to combat discrimination, as well as to articles 10 and 12 of the Convention, which call, respectively, for equality in education and equality in access to health facilities;

- Improve the situation of rural women: article 14 of the Convention on the Elimination of All Forms of Discrimination against Women calls for appropriate measures to ensure the application of the provisions of the Convention to women in rural areas, in view of the particular problems they face despite their considerable role in ensuring the socio-economic security of their households.

There is also need to pay attention to the following emerging issues in order to further the implementation of the goals of the Platform for Action:

- The humanitarian crises that result from natural disasters and environmental degradation require gender-sensitive emergency responses as well as the full and equal participation of women in order to ensure that the subsequent reconstruction efforts are successful and sustainable;

- The past two decades have witnessed a steady increase in female participation in the labour market and a consequent rise in their income, in spite of the persistent gender gap in wage income. At the same time, women still have the main responsibility for meeting household needs and thus determine household consumption patterns substantially. As a result, women have emerged as a major force in determining consumption trends. Sustainable consumption patterns are critical to the effective and successful outcomes of environmental policies. Given the role that women play in determining household consumption, in addition to their own consumption, their full and equal participation in environmental policy-making and implementation is crucial for the achievement of sustainable development.

L. The girl-child

1. Introduction

The Beijing Platform for Action seeks to promote and protect the full
enjoyment of the human rights and fundamental freedoms of all women
throughout their life cycle. Critical area of concern L, "The girl-child",
recognizes that, in many countries, the girl-child faces discrimination
from the earliest stages of life, through childhood and into adulthood,
despite the progress in advancing the status of women worldwide. Reasons for this derive in large part from the resistance stemming from
traditional attitudes and practices. The Platform for Action expresses
concern at the effects of such attitudes on girls, which often take the
form of harmful practices, son preference, early marriage and gender
violence, including sexual exploitation. The Platform for Action argues
that, owing to this discriminatory environment, girls often receive limited opportunities for education and consequently lack knowledge and
skills needed to advance their status in society. The Platform for Action
further emphasizes the importance of implementing gender-sensitive
curricula and educational materials in schools.

The Platform for Action underscores the responsibility of Governments
to protect and promote the rights of the girl-child and recommends
eliminating all barriers in order to enable girls without exception to
develop their full potential and skills through equal access to education
and training, nutrition, physical and mental health care and related information. The Platform for Action also notes that girls are encouraged
less than boys to participate in and learn about the social, economic and
political functioning of society; and it urges Governments to take action
to provide access for girls to training and information so as to enable
them to articulate their views and to promote the equality and participation of girls in society. The Platform for Action points out that girls
are often treated as inferior to boys and are socialized to put themselves
last, thus undermining their self-esteem. The Platform for Action further recognizes that during adolescence girls could be receiving a variety of conflicting and confusing messages on their gender roles from
their parents, teachers, peers and the media.

The Platform for Action reaffirmed the commitment of Governments to eliminate discrimination against women and the girl-child and to remove all obstacles to equality between women and men. Governments also recognized the need to ensure the inclusion of a gender perspective in their policies and programmes.

At the Fifth African Regional Conference on Women, held at Dakar from 16 to 23 November 1994, where the issue of the girl-child was recommended for inclusion in the Beijing Platform for Action, participants pointed out that all available indicators showed that the African girl-child was discriminated against from birth, and that this resulted in less parental appreciation and care, poor nutrition and unequal access to education. The economic conditions as well as the high poverty ratio in developing nations, coupled with lower sociocultural value placed on the girl-child, constrain her development and the attainment of her full potential.

At the Beijing Conference, 13 countries made a firm commitment to promote and protect the rights of the girl-child and increase the awareness of her needs and potential. Out of these, nine stated their intention to focus on education by, for example, providing financial assistance to girls, developing an enabling environment for girls to continue schooling, and securing resources for programmes targeted at girls. Although the initial efforts were to be made in the area of primary education, five countries made a reference to girls' and young women's access to further education.

An Expert Group Meeting on Adolescent Girls and their Rights, jointly organized by the Division for the Advancement of Women, UNICEF, UNFPA and ECA in 1997, concluded that adolescent girls were often discouraged from developing their full potentials and self-esteem and that there was an urgent need to create an enabling environment for the empowerment of adolescent girls whose particular needs had not been adequately addressed.

At its forty-second session, the Commission on the Status of Women adopted agreed conclusions on the girl-child,[129] proposing actions to be taken in order to accelerate the implementation of the strategic objectives of the Platform for Action on the girl-child. The agreed conclusions called for elaboration of an optional protocol to the Convention on the Rights of the Child and measures to prevent and eradicate the sale of children, child prostitution and pornography; and also suggested actions to enable girls, including pregnant girls and teenage mothers, to continue their education, and proposed that teaching materials be reviewed and revised to highlight women's effective role in society. The agreed conclusions called for the elimination of traditional and customary practices and stated that Governments, civil society and international organizations should establish recovery programmes for children who had been abused or sexually exploited. In addition Governments were encouraged to enact and enforce laws that prohibited sexual exploitation including prostitution, incest, abuse and trafficking of children with special attention to girls, and to prosecute and punish offenders.

Both the Convention on the Elimination of All Forms of Discrimination against Women and the Convention on the Rights of the Child emphasize the needs of the girl-child. The Convention on the Rights of the Child mandates that the State protect children from any form of discrimination based on sex, and the Convention on the Elimination of Discrimination against Women ensures the girl-child the right to freely choose if, when and with whom she will enter into marriage. Both Conventions also afford girl-children the right to participate in community and recreational activities that, while not essential to survival, are an integral part of the child's growth and development.

Out of 116 national action plans that were reviewed by the Secretariat, more than 40 plans focused on the girl-child as a priority issue in implementing the Beijing Platform for Action. Several plans aimed at the realization of equal opportunities for girls as well as promotion and protection of the rights of the girl-child in school, the family and society, through revising an existing legal provision and putting appropriate measures in action. Lack of disaggregated data by age and sex was a concern reflected in several plans. The need to analyse existing policies and programmes for children from a gender perspective was recognized.

2. Achievements in the implementation of strategic objectives

Much progress has been noted in various parts of the world in the area of primary education, as well as, to a lesser extent, in the areas of secondary and tertiary education. Many Governments reported on measures taken to retain girls in schools, including creating a more gender-sensitive school environment, establishing support mechanisms for pregnant girls and teenage mothers, and more non-formal education opportunities, and encouraging girls to take up science and technology classes. Furthermore, different forms of violence against girl-children have been recognized, and a number of legal measures have been taken to protect girl-children from violence. The importance of teaching girls and boys their equal value and their human rights has also been widely appreciated, and various advocacy measures have been taken to increase the awareness of the public in this regard.

The four most frequently addressed issues in the Governments' replies in the context of the girl-child were: education; health, including reproductive and sexual health; violence against women, including harmful traditional practices; and human rights of girls. Another priority was the eradication of violence against girls, often with a focus on sexual exploitation, prostitution, child pornography, trafficking and harmful traditional practices such as female genital mutilation.

Measures taken or planned by Governments, as indicated in their replies to the questionnaire, are categorized under four types:

- Legal measures to ensure equality between girls and boys (women and men);

- Policy measures to create and promote an enabling environment;

- Temporary and short-term measures to accelerate the process of creating an enabling environment;

- Capacity-building measures specifically designed for girls and women, and for societies in general.

(a) Legal measures
Government replies cited a number of legal measures that have been introduced or enacted in order to ensure *de facto* equality between girls and boys as well as to promote human rights of the girl-child. Many Governments, including Bhutan, Ghana, Jordan, Oman, Singapore and Trinidad and Tobago, emphasized the need to set a higher minimum legal age of marriage. Law reforms took place in several other countries with regard to harmful traditional practices. For example, the practice of female genital mutilation has been banned in Ghana, and the United Republic of Tanzania also introduced new legislation that criminalized female genital mutilation and established penalties, including fines and imprisonment. Currently ten countries where female

genital mutilation is widely practised (Burkina Faso, the Central African Republic, Côte d'Ivoire, Djibouti, Egypt, Ghana, Guinea, Senegal, Togo, and the United Republic of Tanzania) have enacted laws to criminalize the practice. Several other States with immigrant or refugee populations that practise female genital mutilation, including Canada, have enacted legislation to prohibit it.[130] In Singapore, the registration of every child born has been enforced.

Some countries have introduced legislation to encourage girls to continue and complete their schooling and to ensure that this is possible. In Nigeria, for example, legislation now prohibits withdrawal of girls from school. Grenada introduced legislative reform in education, health and construction of public facilities regarding the girl-child with disabilities.

Many countries reported on new legislative initiatives and laws such as a proposed law on children's rights, promulgation of a bill on children including the girl-child, laws to protect and promote rights of children and their health, laws on child protection and care, especially the girl-child, and a revision of laws to intensify protection of the girl-child. Countries that reported such measures include Albania, China, Cuba, Ghana, Italy, the Republic of Moldova and Viet Nam. Relevant international and national legal instruments such as the Convention on the Rights of the Child have been implemented to protect children including girls.

Violence against the girl-child including sexual abuse and exploitation, and trafficking of the girl-child are a concern of many countries. Initiatives to enact laws against the production of child pornography, and for the criminalization of perpetrators were reported by several countries, including Italy, Japan, Mexico, Myanmar, the Philippines and Sweden. Penalties for the offenders in cases of domestic and family violence have been enforced in countries such as the Dominican Republic, Greece and the Philippines, among others. In 1998, Sweden set up a Parliamentary Law Committee on Sexual Offences that, *inter alia*, examined to what extent the offence of rape should focus on lack of consent rather than on force. Mauritius amended its Criminal Code to increase penalties for the commercial sexual exploitation of children, while the National Assembly of Viet Nam has decided to increase the penalty for prostitution procurers and sex abusers of the girl-child, including adolescents. In some countries, including Seychelles, Singapore and the Philippines, provisions have been made for children and/or women who are giving evidence against a crime of violence so that their security is ensured. In Seychelles and the Philippines, family tribunals have been set up to deal with legal aspects of family problems, with a view to providing legal support to women and children.

Concerning the issues of child labour, several countries have taken legal measures to prohibit child labour and protect young people at work. Such measures include implementation of international labour agreements, various ILO Conventions and the Convention on the Rights of the Child, as well as enactment of domestic laws on employment.

(b) Policy measures
Many Governments focused on policies measures that are intended to benefit girls and boys equally. These measures include education policies, vocational and skills training policies, youth/children policies, health policies including reproductive and sexual health, policies aimed at eliminating violence against children and policies on poverty. Some Governments reported on policy measures that addressed the specific needs and the situation of the girl-child, particularly with regard to education, health and violence against the girl-child.

Many Governments have made commitments to carry out surveys and research efforts in order to reflect their findings in future policy measures. In Oman, for example, a database has been established on the situation of the girl-child. Topics of surveys and research that have been launched include: the extent of violence against women and children in Botswana and the Republic of Moldova; the situation of girls' education in Uganda; reasons for girls dropping out of school in the Islamic Republic of Iran and Burkina Faso; the extent of sexual exploitation of children in Mexico and Trinidad and Tobago; the situation of child labour in Trinidad and Tobago; and the rights of the girl-child in rural areas in Myanmar. Lack of sex- and age-disaggregated data has become a policy concern in many countries including Albania, Saint Vincent and the Grenadines, Seychelles and Spain.

A number of countries have implemented policy measures aimed at creating an environment conducive to encouraging girls, including teenage mothers and pregnant teens, to continue their education, in particular formal education. For example, Ethiopia, Malaysia, Nigeria, Peru and Spain have implemented policies aimed at increasing enrolment of girls, and several other States have adopted laws or policies to support pregnant girls and/or teenage mothers in continuing/re-entering education. Measures have been taken in many countries to make the school environment more gender-sensitive through, *inter alia*, reviewing and developing gender-sensitive curriculum and teaching materials, reviewing career guidance to encourage girls to take up traditionally male-dominated careers and courses, and supporting pre-service and in-service education programmes. For example, policies aimed at increasing opportunities for non-formal and vocational education have been established in India, Myanmar, Trinidad and Tobago and Uganda.

Several countries have taken policy measures to address issues of reproductive and sexual health of adolescent girls with a view to reducing teenage pregnancy. These measures include development of health programmes and training materials for adolescent girls, provision of reproductive and sexual health education, provision of contraceptives and provision of health care for young mothers and children of young mothers.

Many countries have adopted measures to eliminate violence against women. For example, a special police task force was set up in Botswana, while centres to investigate child abuse cases were established in the Philippines. A number of States have included in their policy documents plans to eliminate sexual exploitation of children, and sexual and domestic violence against the girl-child, and the provision of support to victims of violence against women and girls. Others, such as Greece, India, Myanmar, Nepal and Viet Nam, have specifically addressed the need to eliminate trafficking of women, while the exploitation of child labour was addressed by countries including Finland, Malaysia, Peru, the Philippines and Viet Nam.

Many countries have committed themselves to the implementation of international policies and norms concerning girl-children such as the Convention on the Rights of the Child. Establishing an institutional mechanism to promote rights of children including the girl-child reflects the commitment of Governments at policy level, as reported by Grenada, Italy, Nigeria and Singapore.

Other policy measures reported include the provision of funding for sports and youth policy in Finland, the provision of assistance to street children in Indonesia and Viet Nam, the establishment of a telephone hotline to report violation of the rights of the child in Benin, the organization of a National Summit on the Girl-Child in the Philippines and the promotion of cultural activities for all children in Viet Nam.

(c) Temporary measures

Action-oriented temporary measures have been implemented in order to expedite the realization of girls' equal rights and equal opportunities as well as the creation of an enabling environment to empower the girl-child. Measures such as non-formal classes including literacy classes and vocational training for girls were reported by Bhutan, Myanmar and Nigeria. Other measures include the setting up of a Vesico-Vaginal Fistula theatre and rehabilitation centres to provide care for under-age married women affected by female genital mutilation in Nigeria, and more vocational and professional training for girls, with a view to providing them with more employment opportunities in Bhutan, the Czech Republic, Myanmar, Portugal and Saint Lucia.

A number of countries including Austria, Dominica, the Islamic Republic of Iran, Japan, Mexico, Portugal and Zambia introduced affirmative action to encourage female students to take up science and technology and/or non-traditional subjects, while Austria provided computer and Internet courses for girls. Zambia provided scholarship schemes for girls, and Burkina Faso adopted affirmative action to ensure that the proportion of girls represented in basic and literacy educational institutions is 50 per cent. Programmes to improve school education with a focus on female literacy was introduced in India, and girls in Indonesia were encouraged to participate in the designing and planning of the policies and programmes that affected them. Setting up of technical and vocational schools dedicated to girls in the Islamic Republic of Iran and Myanmar has been reported.

(d) Capacity-building measures

Responses to the questionnaire indicated that countries have undertaken two types of capacity-building measures. One type is designed to build the capacity of girls themselves so that they can articulate and assert their own rights. The other is designed to build the capacity of those who interact with girls, such as boys, family members, community members, teachers, health-care providers and law enforcement officers. Advocacy work and public information campaigns aimed at the general public can benefit both girls and all the other actors involved.

In the area of education, several countries have initiated capacity-building measures targeted at girls, such as, for example: gender–sensitization in Botswana and China, a science clinic for girls to encourage them in non-traditional subjects in Ethiopia, establishment of a National Centre for the Project to Educate Women and Young Girls in Mathematics and Science in Africa (FEMSA) in Burkina Faso, comprehensive education strategies including reproductive health and vocational training aimed at girls under age 20 in Mexico, education and career guidance and counselling services in Bhutan, Nigeria and Uganda, the provision of educational opportunities for underprivileged girls through non-governmental organizations in Trinidad and Tobago, establishment of a school environment that caters to the needs of the girl-child in China, Finland, Saint Vincent and the Grenadines, Uganda and Zambia and an advocacy campaign in Burkina Faso.

Concerning the health issues, countries reported taking several measures, including, for example, setting up rehabilitation facilities for teenage girls with reproductive disorders in the Russian Federation, advocacy work for girls on health including nutrition in Georgia, India and Mexico, and a campaign to promote a healthier lifestyle aimed at young women in Spain.

With regard to socialization skills, several countries have implemented measures to empower girls to actively participate in all aspects of public and private life. Such measures include leadership and advocacy skills training in Indonesia, the use of female role models in Uganda, peer education and life skills training in Namibia, confidence-building programmes in Vanuatu and the establishment of sports and recreational clubs for girls in the Islamic Republic of Iran. Other reported examples of capacity-building measures targeted at girls include programmes for indigenous girls incorporating their mothers' indigenous knowledge in Mexico.

Several other measures to build the capacity of both girls and boys were reported by different countries. For example, Botswana, Greece, Mexico, Oman and Turkey reported on capacity-building measures with regard to socialization skills and respect for women and their equal human rights. The organization of campaign and information networks has aimed at empowering youth and children in Greece. Facilities for young people in which they can discuss their sexuality have been set up in Botswana and Portugal. Education programmes for young people on HIV/AIDS have been implemented in some countries including the Czech Republic, Grenada, Indonesia and Swaziland. Educational programmes on sex/reproductive health were developed, *inter alia*, in the Czech Republic, Dominica, Indonesia, Latvia and the Russian Federation. Workshops on teenage pregnancies and sexually transmitted diseases were organized in Saint Lucia. Information campaigns to prevent teenage pregnancy were reported in the Netherland Antilles and Saint Vincent and the Grenadines. A 24-hour hotline to provide social services to children who are victims of child abuse has been set up in the Philippines.

Other capacity-building measures with a targeted audience other than girl-children include training of teachers in countries such as Burkina Faso, Ethiopia, Greece, Indonesia, Oman, Trinidad and Tobago and Zambia, training of reproductive health workers in Finland, training of promoters of the defence of the rights of children in Mexico and training of media personnel in Oman. Gender-sensitization activities have been implemented for those involved in education including policymakers in Oman and Swaziland, as well as for those involved in private and public services dealing with violence against women and girls in Portugal and Sweden. The Islamic Republic of Iran supported activities of non-governmental organizations and community-based organizations to change negative attitudes and practices towards girl-children. Information materials on the issues of the girl-child have been produced to sensitize policymakers in the Philippines. Public leaders in Indonesia have been encouraged to advocate for youth, and in Palestine awareness-raising programmes for men about women's and children's rights have been implemented. In Cuba, a nationwide programme to enable parents to develop a non-sexist perspective has been organized.

Various public advocacy campaigns targeting a wider audience have been organized. For example, China, India and Indonesia have organized campaigns to promote development of the girl-child, while countries such as India, Indonesia, the Islamic Republic of Iran, Italy, Nepal and Nigeria organized campaigns to promote girls' rights. Campaigns to promote children's rights were organized in China, and campaigns were organized in India, Mexico and Peru to promote the importance of girls' education. Viet Nam organized campaigns to address the protection of children, especially girl-children, and Dominica, Jamaica and Mexico organized campaigns for the elimination of violence against women and children, while Japan advocated against child abuse. Uganda organized campaigns to advocate for a change in customs and practices that violate the dignity and rights of girls and women.

A workshop was held in Botswana to raise public awareness on issues relating to the socialization of girls and boys, round-table discussions on the girl-child took place in Guyana and advocacy meetings relating to negative cultural attitudes and practices against the girl-child were organized in Myanmar. Various forms of information materials to advocate on behalf of and promote the issues of the girl-child have been produced. These included videotapes on negative consequences of early marriage as well as information materials on health of the girl-child produced in Nigeria, and information materials on violence against girls produced in Austria and Greece. Greece also produced information materials on trafficking of women and girls. The Convention on the Rights of the Child and the proceedings of the Committee on the Rights of the Child have been disseminated in Mexico, and the Annual National Awareness Week of Child Sexual Abuse and Exploitation has been established in the Philippines.

3. Obstacles in the implementation of strategic objectives

Responses to the questionnaires reveal that many countries face similar obstacles to providing for the full enjoyment of equality and human rights by the girl-child. Most common among these is the lack of adequate financial and human resources, as well as the inadequate sensitivity and awareness towards the girl-child that still deny her access to education, health and other benefits equal to that enjoyed by her male counterpart. Many Governments face the additional problem of inadequate technical, financial and material resources to carry out innovative programmes and projects. The vast majority of countries are confronted with the lack of statistical data, especially data disaggregated by sex, on education, health and other indicators of factors affecting girl-children.

At the institutional level, a number of obstacles hinder the full implementation of the Platform for Action. In many countries, especially those that are still trying to develop their economic and social infrastructures, low priority is given to gender issues, and thus fewer resources are invested in gender-specific programmes. In addition, weak and infrequent liaison with support agencies, both in Governments and in non-governmental organizations, results in inadequate coordination to support the implementation of programmes and projects. Slow institutionalization of gender-mainstreaming, backlog in the adjustment of laws to meet international standards, and lack of formal monitoring mechanisms are also obstacles to the full realization of improving the status of women and the girl-child.

Many communities, especially those that are rural or poverty-stricken or where harmful traditional attitudes prevail, face similar hurdles in ensuring girl-children full access to education throughout her life cycle. Girls are not encouraged to the same extent as boys to further their studies and develop their careers. Aside from the lack of basic educational facilities and teachers, many communities assign very low priorities to a girl-child's education and instead place emphasis on her marrying and/or becoming pregnant early or on the demand for her labour either inside or outside the home. Any of these three conditions, early marriage, early pregnancy or child labour, prevents her from attending school.

Although progress has been seen in providing opportunities for re-entry of young mothers and pregnant teens into the educational system, many countries still do not have such provisions owing to insufficient resources, and lack of full administrative will and general support to implement these programmes. Many pregnant teens are still either expelled or pressured into dropping out of school because of a social stigma. In some countries, especially in Africa, sexual abuse or harassment and school-based discrimination create a hostile environment where girls are discouraged from receiving an education. Other factors contributing to discrimination in schools are inadequately trained teachers; gender-biased curricula, teaching methodologies or textbooks, and materials; too few or overcrowded schools; and long distances between home and school, especially in rural areas.

Despite the prioritization of health-related issues for women and children in many countries, many children still lack adequate care and services, especially in poverty-stricken areas where malnutrition and disease are rampant. Owing to harmful traditional practices and negative attitudes, girl-children especially run the risk of being denied the ability to fulfil their health needs. The Special Rapporteur on violence against women, its causes and consequences submitted to the Commission on Human Rights at its fifty-fifth session her report on policies and practices that impact women's reproductive rights and contribute to, cause or constitute violence against women.[131] She analysed cultural practices such as female genital mutilation, child marriages and early childbearing, and sex-selective abortion/female infanticide and demonstrated that they were a consequence of son preference and the lack of measures to redress the situation. Furthermore, those who are forced and socialized into early marriage face the additional dangers of early pregnancy or too closely spaced pregnancies.

Although many countries agree that there is a need for more dissemination of sexual and reproductive health information to children, especially young adolescents, cultural barriers and attitudes, lack of trained personnel or facilitators with sufficient experience, and lack of education programmes teaching responsibility in sex all create obstacles.

Concerning the issue of violence against children, particularly in the forms of sexual exploitation, child prostitution, child pornography and incest, several factors, both institutional and societal, impede the eradication of these abuses against girl-children. The inadequate structure of mechanisms to successfully prosecute perpetrators of criminal acts against girl-children is one common obstacle, as is the lack of financial and human resources to sufficiently meet the needs of abused children. Many countries note that awareness and understanding of child abuse are still very limited.

Despite widespread progress in improving the health, nutrition and education of children, the situation of girls continues to be disadvantaged compared with that of boys in many parts of the world. Parents in many countries often prefer to have a son rather than a daughter owing to the higher cultural, social and economic values associated with male children.

4. Conclusions and future actions

Neglect or abuse of girls in childhood generally leads to, or is linked to, their lower status as women. If girls are given equal opportunities to develop themselves to their fullest potential, they are more likely to grow up to be empowered women. Transforming the social, economic and political environment so that girls can fully enjoy their rights and develop their potential is fundamentally related to the broader struggle for gender equality. Attention to women's equality has proved, in some instances, capable of filtering down to adolescent girls. However, the effects of discrimination against girls, including abuse, sow the seeds for discrimination throughout the life cycle.

Although *de jure* progress has been noted, in particular in the area of primary education in various parts of the world, *de facto* progress has not been satisfactory. Much more needs to be done in terms of creating an enabling environment, in schools, in the family and in communities, where the value of educating girls is recognized and appreciated. The first step towards the creation of an enabling environment for empowering the girl-child is to recognize their specific needs and situation, as well as their right to participate in decision-making about their own lives. To this end, resources need to be mobilized and secured so that in-depth assessments of the situation of the girl-child may be carried out. Collection of sex- and age- disaggregated data is also necessary in order to formulate effective policy measures as well as concrete actions. Visibility of human rights and the specific needs of the girl-child must be increased, through the dissemination of the findings of such assessments.

Ensuring equal opportunity for girls alone is not enough. The importance of instilling positive attitudes in both girls and boys about their equal value as well as mutual respect must not be underestimated. Girls and boys need to be socialized as equals, while their equal participation in social, cultural, political and economic activities must be ensured. At the same time, proactive efforts need to be undertaken to sensitize parents, other family members, community members and decision makers to the rights and needs of the girl-child. For example, prevailing attitudes towards women and girls that excuse parents and decision makers for not sending girls to school to receive formal education need to be revised.

The rights and needs of adolescent girls require further action and attention. It is important that the development of the life skills and self-esteem of adolescent girls be emphasized in policies and programmes across the board. Governments should, in coordination with partners in civil society, develop and implement gender-sensitive strategies to address the rights and needs of adolescent girls, including special action for their protection from sexual exploitation and abuse, harmful traditional practices, including early marriage, teenage pregnancy and vulnerability to sexually transmitted diseases, and for the development of their life skills and self-esteem. Targeted programmes allow the specific requirements of adolescent girls to be examined in a more detailed manner, and this can help in effectively implementing the policy measures to improve the status of adolescent girls. Such efforts can be best organized in coordination with non-governmental organizations and community groups whose work involves close interaction with adolescent girls, and who are familiar with and sensitive to local culture and social arrangements.

In particular, the increase in the number of girls infected with HIV has raised an alarm and calls for urgent action by Governments and international organizations in coordination with non-governmental organizations. Adolescent girls are particularly at high risk of becoming infected with HIV. Their lower social status often pressures them into situations where they have no choice but to have sexual intercourse with men despite the potential exposure to HIV. When the adults in the family become ill, young daughters are often left with the responsibilities of nursing them; and when the sick are gone, it is the young daughters who may be forced to leave school to help at home and to work in the fields. Until recently, not enough attention was given to such implications for the girl-child in the context of her status in the family and community and her particular gender role. Along with preventive measures, Governments need to take steps to ensure that the rights of the girl-child are not neglected.

Notes

[16] *Official Records of the Economic and Social Council, 1996, Supplement No. 6* (E/1996/26), chap. I, sect. C.2.

[17] World Bank, *World Development Report 1999/2000: Entering the 21st Century* (New York, OUP Press, 2000), see Introduction, subsect. entitled "The record and outlook for comprehensive development", pp. 24-25.

[18] Report of the Secretary-General on the implementation of the first United Nations Decade for the Eradication of Poverty (1997-2006) (A/53/329).

[19] UNDP, *Human Development Report 1997* (New York, OUP, 1997), chap. 2, subsect. entitled "Years of life", p. 28.

[20] World Bank, *World Development Report, 2000/2001: Attacking Poverty* (New York, OUP, 2001).

[21] J. Dreze and A. Sen, *The Political Economy of Hunger: Selected Essays* (New York, OUP, 1995); and A. Sen, "Editorial: human capital and human capability", *World Development*, vol. 25, No. 12 (1997), pp. 1950-1961.

[22] UNDP, *Poverty Report 1998: Overcoming Human Poverty,* (United Nations publication, Sales No. E.99.III.B.2), p.34.

[23] *The State of World Population, 1990* (New York, UNFPA, 1990), p.15.

[24] *Investing in Women: The Focus of the 90s* (New York, UNFPA, 1989), p. 22.

[25] Report of the Secretary-General entitled "Improvement of the situation of women in rural areas" (A/54/123-E/1999/66, sect. IV.A).

[26] N. Cagatay, "Gender and poverty", Working paper, No. 5 (New York, UNDP, May 1998).

[27] *Final Report of the World Conference on Education for All: Meeting Basic Learning Needs, Jomtien, Thailand, 5-9 March 1990*, Inter-Agency Commission (UNDP, UNESCO, UNICEF, World Bank) for the World Conference on Education for All, (New York, 1990), appendix 1.

[28] UNESCO, *Education for All: Achieving the Goal. Final Report of the Mid-Decade Meeting of the International Consultative Forum on Education for All, Amman, Jordan, 16-19 June 1996* (Paris, UNESCO, 1996).

[29] Joint communiqué of the Second E-9 Ministerial Review Meeting of the Nine High-population Countries; and *Mobilizing for Progress: Second E-9 Ministerial Review Meeting of the Nine High-Population Countries, Islamabad, Pakistan, 14 to 16 September 1997* (Paris, UNESCO, 1997).

[30] *Official Records of the Economic and Social Council, 1997, Supplement No. 7* (E/1997/27), chap. I, sect. C.1.

[31] Concluding comments on Armenia of the Committee on the Elimination of Discrimination against Women (*Official Records of the General Assembly, Fifty-second Session, Supplement No. 38* (A/52/38/Rev.1), part two, para. 49); on Bangladesh (ibid., para. 455); on Bulgaria (ibid., *Fifty-third Session, Supplement No. 38* (A/53/38/Rev.1), part one, para. 249); on China (ibid., *Fifty-fourth Session, Supplement No. 38* (A/54/38/Rev.1), part one, para. 295); on Colombia (ibid., para. 356); on Greece (ibid., para. 202); on Iceland (ibid., *Fifty-first Session, Supplement No. 38* (A/51/38), para. 95); on Indonesia (ibid., *Fifty-third Session, Supplement No. 38* (A/53/38/Rev.1), part one, para. 289); on Italy (ibid., *Fifty-second Session, Supplement No. 38* (A/52/38/Rev.1), part two, para. 346); on Slovenia (ibid., part one, para. 113); on South Africa (ibid., *Fifty-third Session, Supplement No. 38* (A/53/38/Rev.1), part two, para. 122); and on Thailand (ibid., *Fifty-fourth Session, Supplement No. 38* (A/54/38/Rev.1), part one, para. 233).

[32] Thematic debate: women and higher education: issues and perspectives, World Conference on Higher Education, UNESCO, Paris, 5 to 9 October 1999.

[33] Paris, UNESCO, 1998.

[34] Hamburg Declaration on Adult Learning and Agenda for the Future, Fifth International Conference on Adult Education (UNESCO), Hamburg, 14 to 18 July 1997.

[35] *Report of the International Conference on Population and Development, Cairo, 5-13 September 1994* (United Nations publication, Sales No. E.95.XIII.18), chap. I, resolution 1, annex.

[36] ECOSOC resolution 1999/17

[37] ESA/P/WP/148.

[38] General Assembly resolution S-21/2, annex.

[39] *Official Records of the General Assembly, Fifty-fourth Session, Supplement No. 38* (A/54/38/Rev.1), part one, chap. I, sect. A.

[40] E/CN.6/1998/6 and E/CN.6/1999/2/Add.1.

[41] Report of the Administrative Committee on Coordination (ACC) Subcommittee on Nutrition on its twenty-sixth session, Geneva, 12 to 15 April 1999 (ACC/1999/9), para. 10.

[42] OECD Working Party on Gender Equality, *Reaching the Goals in the S-21: Gender, Equality and Health*, vol. II (DCD/DAC/WID(99)2).

[43] World Health Organization, *Beijing Platform for Action: a review of WHO's activities* (Geneva, WHO, 1999), pp. 17-18.

[44] Ibid., p. 36.

[45] Ibid., p. 39.

[46] General Assembly resolution 48/104.

[47] ECOSOC resolution 1998/12 of 28 July 1998, sect. I.

[48] *Official Records of the General Assembly, Forty-fourth Session, Supplement No. 38* (A/44/38), chap. V, para. 392.

[49] Ibid., *Forty-seventh Session, Supplement No. 38* (A/47/38), chap. I.

[50] Ibid., *Forty-fifth Session, Supplement No. 38* (A/45/38), chap. IV, para. 438.

[51] Commission on Human Rights resolution 1994/45 of 4 March 1994 (*Official Records of the Economic and Social Council, 1994, Supplement No. 4* (E/1994/24 and corrigendum), chap. II, sect. A). The mandate of the Special Rapporteur was extended for a further three-year period in 1997, by Commission resolution 1997/44 of 11 April 1997 (ibid., *1997, Supplement No. 23* (E/1997/23), chap. II, sect. A).

[52] ECOSOC Agreed Conclusions 1997/2, op. cit.

[53] PCNICC/1999/INF/3. This document incorporates the corrections circulated by the Depositary on 25 September 1998 and 18 May 1999.

[54] A/54/69-E/1999/8 and Add.1.

[55] E/CN.4/Sub.2/1994/10/Add.1 and Corr.1.

[56] E/CN.4/Sub.2/1999/14, annex.

[57] Communication to the Council and the European Parliament for Further Actions in the Fight against Trafficking in Women (COM (1998) 726 final).

[58] *Human Rights: A compilation of International Instruments*, op. cit.

[59] OEA/Ser.L/V/II.100, Doc.13, 1998.

60 With regard to Latin America and the Caribbean, see Guidelines for a Policy to Protect Women from Violence (Inter-American Commission of Women, General Secretariat, Organization of American States, Washington, D.C., 1998).

61 *Report of the World Conference to Review and Appraise the Achievements of the United Nations Decade for Women: Equality, Development and Peace, Nairobi, 15-26 July 1985* (United Nations publication, Sales No. E.85.IV.10), chap. I, sect. A, chap. III.

62 A/CONF.157/24, op. cit.

63 General Assembly resolution 48/104, op. cit.

64 Report of the Secretary-General to the General Assembly and Security Council on the causes of conflict and the promotion of durable peace and sustainable development in Africa, of 13 April 1998 (A/52/871-S/1999/318), para. 4; and report of the Secretary-General to the Council on the protection of civilians in armed conflict, of 8 September 1999 (S/1999/957), paras. 8-11.

65 Report of the Secretary-General to the Security Council on the protection of civilians in armed conflict (S/1999/957), para. 18.

66 United Nations, *Treaty Series*, vol. 75, Nos. 970-973.

67 Ibid., vol. 1125, Nos. 17512 and 17513.

68 Security Council resolution 955 (1994) of 8 November 1994, annex.

69 *Official Records of the Security Council, Forty-eighth Year, Supplement for April, May and June 1993*, documents S/25704 and Add.1.

70 (IT/32/Rev.6)

71 Before the International Tribunal for the former Yugoslavia, see in re *Karadzic and Mladic*, indictment (*Prosecutor* v. *Radovan Karadzic and Ratko Mladic*) 1995 ICTY, No. IT-95-5-1 (25 July); before the International Tribunal for Rwanda, see in re *Jean Paul Akayesu*, amended indictment (*Prosecutor* v. *Jean Paul Akayesu*) ICTR-96-4-T, 30 July 1997; *Furundzija* case, IT-95-17/1, amended indictment 2 July 1998.

72 PCNICC/1999/INF/3, op. cit.

73 Ibid., article 6.

74 Ibid., article 7.

75 Ibid., article 7, para. 3.

76 Ibid., article 8, para. 2 (b) (xxii).

77 Ibid., article 36, para. 8 (a) (iii).

78 Ibid., article 36, para. 8 (b).

79 Ibid., article 43, para. 6.

80 Ibid., article 68, para. 1.

81 Ibid., article 68, para. 4.

82 A/CONF.183/10, annex I.

83 PCNICC/1999/L.4.

84 *Sexual Violence against Refugees: Guidelines on Prevention and Response* (Geneva, UNHCR, 1995).

85 UNHCR, "Symposium on Gender-based Persecution, Geneva", *International Journal of Refugee Law* (New York, OUP, autumn 1997).

86 *The United Nations Disarmament Yearbook,* vol. 5: 1980 (United Nations publication, Sales No. E.81.IX.4), appendix VII.

87 Ibid.,vol. 5:1980.

88 A/50/1027

89 United Nations, *Treaty Series,* vol. 729, No. 10485.

90 A/53/78, annex.

91 Norwegian Institute for Foreign Affairs, 1999.

92 Economic and Social Council resolution 1998/12, sect. II.

93 *Arms Availability and the Situation of Civilians in Armed Conflict: A Study by the International Committee of the Red Cross* (Geneva, ICRC, June 1999).

94 General Assembly resolution 48/96, annex.

95 General Assembly resolution 44/25, annex.

96 International Labour Organization, *ILOLEX on CD-ROM: A database of International Labour Standards, 2000 edition* (Geneva, ILO, 2000), or access the ILOLEX database at http://www.ilo.org.

97 United Nations Conference on Trade and Development, *Trade, Sustainable Development and Gender*, papers prepared in support of the themes discussed at the pre-UNCTAD X, Expert Workshop on Trade, Sustainable Development and Gender (UNCTAD/EDM/Misc.78) (Geneva, UNCTAD, 1999).

98 International Labour Office, *Key Indicators of the Labour Market, 1999* (Geneva, ILO, 1999).

99 *Official Records of the Economic and Social Council, 1997, Supplement No. 7* (E/1997/27), chap. I, sect. C.1.

100 *Official Records of the General Assembly, Fifty-second Session, Supplement No. 38* (A/52/38/Rev.1), part two, chap. I, sect. A.

101 UNICEF, *The Progress of Nations, 1997* (Sales No. 97.XX.USA.1), Women's League table: women at top levels of government.

102 Division for the Advancement of Women research data.

103 A/50/691 and A/54/405.

104 Council of Europe, *Final Report of the Group of Specialists on Equality and Democracy* (EG-S-ED) (Strasbourg, 6 March 1997).

105 *Democracy Still in the Making: A World Comparative Study* (Geneva, IPU, 1997), p. 43.

106 ST/SGB/1999/4 of 20 May 1999.

107 General Assembly resolution 217 A (III).

108 ECOSOC Agreed Conclusions 1997/2, op. cit.

109 Economic and Social Council resolution 1999/17, sect. II.

[110] E/CN.6/1998/6 and E/CN.6/1999/2/Add.1.

[111] Information obtained from the *Directory of National Machinery for the Advancement of Women* (New York, United Nations Division for the Advancement of Women, 11 October 1999).

[112] Economic and Social Council resolution 1999/17, sect. II., op. cit.

[113] Economic and Social Council resolution 1998/12, sect. III.

[114] *Official Records of the General Assembly, Fifty-third Session, Supplement No. 38* (A/53/38/Rev.1), part one, chap. I, sect. A.

[115] General Assembly resolution 54/4.

[116] Austria, Belgium, Bolivia, Chile, Colombia, Costa Rica, the Czech Republic, Denmark, Ecuador, Finland, France, Germany, Greece, Iceland, Italy, Liechtenstein, Luxembourg, Mexico, the Netherlands, Norway, Senegal, Slovenia and Sweden.

[117] Report of the Secretary-General on integrating the gender perspective into the work of United Nations human rights treaty bodies (HRI/MC/1998/6), 3 September 1998.

[118] Donna Sullivan, "Trends in the integration of woman's human rights and gender analysis in the activities of the special mechanism", *Report of the Workshop on Gender Integration into the Human Rights System* (Geneva, 26 to 28 May 1999), pp. 46-63.

[119] Report of the Secretary-General on follow-up to and implementation of the Beijing Declaration and Platform for Action (E/1999/54), sect. III.D.

[120] *From Nairobi to Beijing: Second Review and Appraisal of the Implementation of the Nairobi Forward-looking Strategies for the Advancement of Women* (United Nations publication, Sales No. E.95.IV.5), sect. II, chap. J, para. 2.

[121] According to Kathy Bushkin of America On Line, and member of International Women's Media Foundation, and speaker at the "Caught in the Web: Women Journalists and the New Media" conference (Washington, D.C., February 1998).

[122] The three main partners in WomenWatch are the Division for the Advancement of Women of the United Nations Secretariat, the United Nations Development Fund for Women (UNIFEM) and the United Nations International Research and Training Institute for the Advancement of Women (INSTRAW).

[123] The International Women's Media Foundation awards the Courage in Journalism Awards, the Lifetime Achievement Award and the Judy Woodruff Award for women in journalism annually.

[124] Report of the National Consultative Workshop on the Women and Media Section of the Beijing Platform for Action (Quezon City, Philippines, 11 August 1999).

[125] Summary of the Women and Media Workshop and Recommendations/ Future Actions, Asia Pacific Women 2000 Regional Symposium (Bangkok, Thailand, 31 August-4 September 1998).

[126] *Report of the United Nations Conference on Environment and Development, Rio de Janeiro, 3 to 14 June 1992,* vol. I, *Resolutions Adopted by the Conference* (United Nations publication, Sales No. E.93.I.8 and corrigendum), resolution 1, annex II.

[127] *Report of the International Conference on Population and Development, Cairo, 5-13 September 1994,* op. cit.

[128] United Nations Environment Programme, *Convention on Biological Diversity* (Nairobi, UNEP Environmental Law and Institution Programme Activity Centre), June 1992.

[129] ECOSOC resolution 1998/12, sect. IV.

[130] Report of the Secretary-General on traditional or customary practices affecting the health of women (A/54/341).

[131] E/CN.4/1999/68/Add.4.

II. Institutional arrangements

A. Introduction

The Platform for Action places primary emphasis on the establishment of clear actions to lead to fundamental change in women's empowerment and gender equality. At the same time, it emphasizes the importance of institutional arrangements and highlights the role of a wide range of institutions in the public, private and non-governmental sectors necessary to provide an adequate structure and framework for implementing these actions. In addition to containing a chapter (v) on institutional arrangements, the Platform for Action addresses institutional mechanisms for the advancement of women as a critical area of concern, with a focus on the role of national machineries and other governmental bodies in support of implementation of the Platform for Action at the national level. That critical area of concern is covered in an earlier section of this report. An assessment of the implementation of the system-wide medium-term plan for the advancement of women, 1996-2001, covering programme activities of the United Nations system in support of implementation of the Platform for Action, is contained in a separate report of the Secretary-General.[132]

The Platform for Action covers institutional arrangements for implementation at the national, subregional/regional and international level, as well as within the United Nations system. It calls for networking and linkages among institutions at all levels, stressing the need for transparency and a consistent flow of information among all concerned. In addition, it underlines the role of non-governmental organizations in ensuring progress in Platform for Action implementation and highlights the importance of effective national machineries, strategies and national action plans, and of targets for their implementation, for translating the Platform for Action into practice.

The Platform for Action directs the regional commissions of the United Nations to contribute to the implementation process through the provision of technical assistance and operational activities. The roles of intergovernmental bodies, including the General Assembly, the Economic and Social Council and the Commission on the Status of Women, in Conference follow-up are addressed, as is the contribution of the Committee on the Elimination of Discrimination against Women and other treaty bodies. The Platform for Action further suggests institutional arrangements for the United Nations Secretariat, highlighting, in particular, the functions of the Executive Office of the Secretary-General, the Division for the Advancement of Women and other units of the United Nations Secretariat, as well as INSTRAW and UNIFEM. It concludes with a discussion of the role of the specialized agencies and of other institutions and organizations in facilitating implementation.

B. Recent developments

Linkages and information exchange among actors at different levels have grown exponentially since the Fourth World Conference on Women. A variety of tools are available and are increasingly used to facilitate the creation and strengthening of such linkages to support implementation of the Platform for Action.

Knowledge about, and access to, institutional mechanisms is a prerequisite of increased networking among various actors. The Division for the Advancement of Women of the Department of Economic and Social Affairs maintains, and updates twice yearly, a Directory of National Machinery for the Advancement of Women. This Directory is made available to Governments, to the organizations of the United Nations system and to civil society. As of October 1999, the Directory had 151 entries from 140 countries. ECLAC and ESCAP maintain directories of national organizations dealing with programmes and policies on women in the Latin America and the Caribbean region, and the Asia and the Pacific region, respectively. The role of the Presiding Officers of the Regional Conference on Women in the Latin American and

Caribbean region in liaising with national machineries has been strengthened. Expert group meetings on the role and opportunities of national machineries to support implementation of the Beijing Platform for Action and the realization of gender equality were convened by the Division for the Advancement of Women and ECLAC in 1998, and by ESCAP for the Asia and the Pacific region in 1996.

Web sites have become an important outlet for distributing information, and for interaction among individuals and organizations from all regions, on particular issues. The use of the Internet, and of thematic web sites, as advocacy and outreach tools is growing. Building on its successful use of information technology in the preparatory process for and during the Fourth World Conference on Women, the Division for the Advancement of Women, in cooperation with UNIFEM and INSTRAW, developed WomenWatch, a United Nations Internet site on the advancement and empowerment of women. The site facilitates global information exchange through the use of computer networking technology. The site, which also contains archival information on the Beijing Conference and other global United Nations conferences, provides a single on-line source for key information and data on global women's issues. It is also linked to other relevant Internet sites, *inter alia*, of United Nations entities, Governments (national machinery for the advancement of women) and non-governmental organizations. Since WomenWatch was endorsed as an inter-agency project by the Administrative Committee on Coordination (ACC) Inter-Agency Committee on Women and Gender Equality(IACWGE) in 1998, new entities from the United Nations system and from Government have joined the site, which is increasingly becoming a gateway for all gender-related information and activities of the United Nations system. WomenWatch has also forged a partnership with a non-governmental organization web site, Women Action 2000, with the aim of providing training in the setting up of regional web sites on Beijing+5, and of working with non-governmental organizations to redisseminate Web-based information through traditional means of communication, such as the radio.

The importance of WomenWatch has been further recognized through its receipt of major financial contributions for outreach and a series of on-line conferences, conducted during 1999 and 2000, on the Platform for Action's 12 critical areas of concern in preparation for the special session of the General Assembly entitled "Women 2000: gender equality, development and peace for the twenty-first century". The results of these on-line dialogues were made available, in March 2000, to the Commission on the Status of Women acting as the preparatory committee for the special session of the Assembly.[133]

Non-governmental organizations and women's groups are increasingly forming international coalitions, using information and communications technologies to advocate for implementation of the Beijing Platform for Action in general, or in particular areas of concern. Global campaigns against violence against women have used Internet technology to reach a larger audience in a greater number of countries, as have women working in community radio. Women's human rights organizations from different parts of the world use Internet technology to link organizations, to conduct on-line discussions on women's human rights issues, to provide a virtual resource centre to support advocacy, education and research, and to share information on national, regional and international events. Global communications networks have also been set up with the specific purpose of enabling women in every region of the world to participate more fully in the Beijing+5 process, and to monitor progress. Other networks focus on the synergies between gender and development, bringing a subregional approach to these issues, while at the same time linking them to the global level.

C. National level

Governments committed themselves in the Platform for Action to developing implementation strategies or plans of action, and reaffirmed this commitment subsequently in resolutions adopted by the General Assembly. A total of 116 Member States and two Observer States provided their national action plans or strategies to the Secretariat. In addition, five interregional, subregional and regional plans were received. Many of the plans were prepared in cooperation with non-governmental organizations and relevant actors in civil society, and frequently mobilized efforts and commitments at many levels. National machineries played a key role in their preparation, supported in many developing countries by the international community, in particular the United Nations system. However, only a few national action plans established comprehensive, time-bound targets and benchmarks or indicators for monitoring. Most national action plans made no reference to sources of financing for the actions identified.

D. Regional level

The five regional commissions of the United Nations continue to play a special role owing to their strategic location at the intersection of support for implementation of both the Beijing Platform for Action and the regional plans and platforms for action that emanated from the five regional preparatory conferences leading up to Beijing. The regional commissions bring a multidisciplinary orientation and integrated approach to their core competencies and functions. They focus on regional policy development and also have an operational dimension, reflected in their provision of technical assistance to member States in their region. The regional commissions are therefore in the unique position of mediating the regional and the global dimensions of the empowerment of women and gender equality, for the benefit of women at the national level.

All five commissions are carrying out activities in support of the special session of the General Assembly in the year 2000.[134] ESCAP convened a high-level meeting to review the implementation of the Jakarta Declaration and Plan of Action for the Advancement of Women in Asia and the Pacific and the regional implementation of the Beijing Declaration and Platform for Action from 26 to 29 October 1999 in Bangkok, Thailand. ECA convened the Sixth African Regional Conference on Women to assess progress in the implementation of the Beijing Platform for Action and African Platform for Action, from 22 to 27 November 1999 in Addis Ababa, Ethiopia. The ECA conference on the occasion of its fortieth anniversary in April 1998, entitled "Women and economic development: investing in our future", drew attention to women's access to resources, information technology and human rights. It featured a Forum of Heads of State, in which Government leaders from six African countries reaffirmed their commitment to the implementation of the Beijing Platform for Action. ESCWA held the Second Meeting to Follow up Beijing from 15 to 18 December 1998, and convened an Arab Conference on Integrated Follow-up to Global Conferences from 29 November to 1 December 1999 in Beirut, Lebanon. ECE held a Regional Preparatory Meeting on the 2000 Review of

the Implementation of the Beijing Platform for Action to review economic issues, problems and policies relating to women in the ECE
countries from 19 to 21 January 2000 in Geneva, Switzerland. ECLAC
held the eighth regional conference on the integration of women into
the economic and social development of Latin America and the Caribbean from 8 to 10 February 2000 in Lima, Peru.

Representatives from the regional commissions have regularly participated in the sessions of the Commission on the Status of Women since
1996, and have informed the Commission about programmatic and
institutional aspects of their work as it pertains to regional and global
conference follow-up. Such information has also been regularly included in the Secretary-General's report to the Economic and Social
Council on the follow-up to Beijing. The programmatic work of the
regional commissions is addressed in the report of the Secretary-
General on the assessment of the implementation of the system-wide
medium-term plan for the advancement of women, 1996-2001.[135] Over
the period under review, regional commissions have partnered with the
Division for the Advancement of Women in selected expert group
meetings organized in the implementation of the Platform for Action.
ECE cooperated with the Division in convening a meeting on the
preparation of national action plans, held in Bucharest, Romania, in
1996; ECA, in the convening of an expert group meeting on adolescent
girls, held in Addis Ababa, Ethiopia, in 1997; and ECLAC, in the convening of an expert group meeting on national machineries, held in
Santiago, Chile, in 1998. ESCWA hosted a Division meeting on Beijing
follow-up in Beirut, Lebanon, in 1999; and ESCAP hosted a workshop
of the ACC/IACWGE in Bangkok, Thailand, also in 1999.

Recent reform efforts in the regional commissions have also been
shaped in those bodies with regard to follow-up to recent global conferences, including the Fourth World Conference on Women. The session
of the Economic and Social Council in May 1998 on integrated and
coordinated implementation and follow-up of the major United Nations
conferences and summits provided an opportunity to assess follow-up
at regional level. Based on the discussions during the session, the
Council concluded, *inter alia*, that the regional commissions should
pursue conference follow-up on a systematic basis and enhance their
interaction with other parts of the system, in particular the functional
commissions.[136] The most important follow-up decision taken by ECE
after Beijing, and which is featured in its reform, was to mainstream the

gender perspective in the work programme of its principal subsidiary bodies. Gender mainstreaming has been made a cross-cutting concern in all ECE activities, supported by gender focal points in all ECE divisions. ECE is the convener of meetings of United Nations and non-United Nations organizations active in women's and gender issues in the region to enhance support to the implementation of the regional and global platforms in the region.

The capacity of ECA's African Centre for Women, which is the institutional gender focal point for the Commission, has been strengthened. The Centre's leadership has been upgraded to the level of Director (D-1), as is the case in other substantive divisions, and its professional staff has been increased. In order to promote gender mainstreaming within the Commission, gender issues have been officially defined as cross-cutting. Every substantive division is now required to integrate gender concerns in its work programme. To ensure this, gender focal points have been appointed in each division, and in each of the five ECA Subregional Development Centres; and training for senior staff has taken place.

The Executive Secretary of ESCWA set up an *ad hoc* working group to formulate a plan of action for mainstreaming a gender perspective into ESCWA policies, plans and programmes. In pursuance of this plan, an overall coordinator, and gender focal points in each division, have been designated. Gender mainstreaming is being introduced on a gradual and phased basis into the planning and programming process in ESCWA, and work-months have been earmarked for gender activities to facilitate monitoring and evaluation of the process. The first training in gender mainstreaming has been held for senior staff.

ECLAC undertook a project with the German Development Cooperation Agency (GTZ) on institutionalizing the gender perspective in its substantive work in order to strengthen and consolidate this approach and to reflect a gender perspective explicitly and systematically in the work of ECLAC. It has also reinforced the activities of the Board of Presiding Officers of the Regional Conference and has strengthened their liaison function with national machineries for the advancement of women in the region.

At ESCAP, the reform process led to the institutionalization of a thematic approach. ESCAP has established an inter-divisional mechanism to promote mainstreaming of a gender perspective and attention to women's issues, and the integration of the priorities of the Beijing and Jakarta Platforms for Action into ESCAP's work programme. ESCAP is the convener of the Regional Inter-agency Committee for Asia and the Pacific (RICAP) Subcommittee on the Advancement of Women which provides the institutional framework for joint and collaborative activities based on these two platforms.

E. International level

1. Intergovernmental bodies of the United Nations

(a) General Assembly

The General Assembly set out the framework for follow-up to the Fourth World Conference on Women and full implementation of the Platform for Action.[137] Accordingly, the Assembly, the Economic and Social Council and the Commission on the Status of Women constitute a three-tiered intergovernmental mechanism that plays the primary role in overall policy-making and follow-up, as well as in coordinating the implementation of the Platform for Action. The Assembly has considered Beijing conference follow-up on an annual basis,[138] supported by reports provided by the Secretary-General. The Assembly has directed the attention of all of its committees and bodies to the need to mainstream a gender perspective systematically into all areas of their work. Apart from the Assembly's regular consideration of items on the advancement of women and on follow-up to Beijing, allocated to its Third Committee, the Assembly has continued, on a biennial basis, to review the question of women in development in the Second Committee. Discussion of this item by that Committee continues to be an essential entry point for greater attention to the impact of gender on other items in the Second Committee's agenda, such as macroeconomic questions, sustainable development, and population and development issues. Efforts have also been undertaken to increase awareness of, and attention to, gender issues in the work of other committees of the General Assembly. The Committee for Programme and Coordination (CPC), for example, has used the review of the system-wide medium-term plan for the advancement of women, as well as of the biennial programme budget of the United Nations as an opportunity to draw attention to the need to mainstream a gender perspective programmatically in all areas of work of the Secretariat. The Special Committee on Peacekeeping Operations took up the subject of gender balance and of gender mainstreaming in peacekeeping operations in March 1999. At the session of the Working Party on the Medium-Term Plan and the Programme Budget of the United Nations Conference on Trade and Development (UNCTAD) (Geneva, 25 to 29 January 1999), representatives of member States requested that, in the work planned for the biennium 2000-2001, the gender dimension of development be included in UNCTAD's five subprogrammes as a cross-sectoral issue.

(b) Economic and Social Council

As directed in the Platform for Action, the Economic and Social Council reviewed and expanded the mandate of the Commission on the Status of Women to reflect the task of implementation of the Platform for Action. In 1996, it decided on a multi-year work programme for the Commission, thus providing the basis for a systematic review of progress in implementation.[139] The schedule for consideration of the Platform for Action's 12 critical areas of concern took into account follow-up processes for other conferences, such as the World Conference on Human Rights (1993) and the International Conference on Population and Development (1994), setting the stage for mutual inputs by the functional commissions in respect of work in their respective reviews. The Council has taken a proactive coordinating and management role in the follow-up to Beijing. It reviewed over the period all agreed conclusions and resolutions of the Commission on follow-up to the Platform for Action. As recommended by the Platform for Action, the Council considered the advancement and empowerment of women and implementation of the Platform for Action at each of its three main segments.

At the coordination segment of the substantive session of 1997 of the Economic and Social Council, 1997, the Council considered the question of mainstreaming a gender perspective into all policies and programmes in the United Nations system. The resulteing agreed conclusions 1997/2[140] provided the definition and principles of gender mainstreaming. Recommendations are addressed to the General Assembly, to the Council itself and to its subsidiary bodies, including the Commission on the Status of Women, and to the funds and programmes and regional commissions. The agreed conclusions cover institutional requirements for gender mainstreaming into all policies and programmes, and put forward recommendations concerning the role of gender units and focal points in gender mainstreaming; capacity-building for gender mainstreaming; and gender mainstreaming in the integrated follow-up to United Nations conferences. The Council also called for full implementation of its recommendations at the latest by the year 2000.

In the operational activities segment of the substantive session of 1998 of the Economic and Social Council, the Council considered the role of operational activities in promoting, in particular, capacity-building and resource mobilization for enhancing the participation of women in development. The Council emphasized the need for gender analysis to be an integral part of all operational activities and called for information on follow-up to the Beijing Conference to be incorporated in the triennial comprehensive policy review. The General Assembly acted on this recommendation later in 1998 in its triennial policy review when it identified gender as a cross-cutting theme, stressing the need for gender mainstreaming in operational activities of the United Nations system in all fields, in particular in support of poverty eradication. The next triennial policy review, to be conducted in 2001, has been set as the target for a comprehensive analysis of operational activities, including effective gender mainstreaming therein.

The Economic and Social Council considered the theme "The role of employment and work in poverty eradication: the empowerment and advancement of women" at its high-level segment of 1999. The gender dimensions of poverty and the need to combat gender inequalities in poverty eradication efforts, components of successful poverty eradication strategies, the promotion of productive employment and the achievement of gender equality, including the role of the international community, are outlined in the ministerial communiqué[141] adopted by the Council on 7 July 1999.

In addition to these specific follow-up activities, the Economic and Social Council has increasingly endeavoured to apply a gender-sensitive approach in its sectoral work, both institutionally and programmatically. This was the case when it considered follow-up to the Vienna Declaration and Programme of Action at its 1998 coordination segment. At the time, the Council paid explicit attention to the equal status and human rights of women, and called for increased attention to the human rights of women and to gender aspects in the protection and promotion of human rights in general human rights mechanisms. At its

1999 humanitarian affairs segment, the Council recognized that all humanitarian emergencies had gender-specific impacts.

Equally, in its ongoing work on the restructuring and revitalization of the United Nations in the economic, social and related fields, the Economic and Social Council has addressed the need for gender mainstreaming in terms of the working methods of the functional commissions, the documentation to be prepared by the Secretariat in these fields and the Council's relations with its functional commissions. Gender mainstreaming was also a focus at meetings of the Bureau of the Council with the bureaux of its functional commissions in 1998. The Council has also emphasized the need for gender mainstreaming in the coordinated and integrated follow-up to United Nations conferences and summits: it did so, for example, during its session on this topic in May 1998. At that session, the President of the Council identified the mainstreaming of a gender perspective as a cross-cutting theme in the follow-up process as one of the challenges that remained to be confronted so as to ensure effective follow-up to conferences and the implementation of their outcomes at the country level.[142]

(c) Commission on the Status of Women
The Economic and Social Council, in its resolution 1996/6, confirmed the existing mandate of the Commission on the Status of Women, and expanded it to include responsibilities for monitoring, reviewing and appraising progress achieved and problems encountered in the implementation of the Platform for Action at all levels. The Commission is also responsible for ensuring support for mainstreaming a gender perspective in United Nations activities and for developing further its catalytic role in this regard in other areas. It identifies issues where United Nations system-wide coordination needs to be improved, identifies emerging issues, trends and new approaches to issues affecting the situation of women or equality between women and men that require urgent consideration, and maintains and enhances public awareness and support for implementation of the Platform for Action. Its annual agenda reflects these broadened terms of reference. The Commission's multi-year work programme culminates in a quinquennial review and appraisal of the Platform for Action in the year 2000. The Council affirmed that the Commission will continue to meet annually beyond the year 2000, for a period of ten working days. The Commission maintains its practice of electing its Bureau for a two-year period.

The Commission on the Status of Women reviewed its own methods of work for dealing with the implementation of the Platform for Action so as to increase its effectiveness and efficiency. Since 1996, it has invited experts to participate in the substantive debates on the implementation of action in the 12 critical areas of concern, and the results of these dialogues were normally reflected in action-oriented agreed conclusions. From the Commission's fortieth to its forty-third session, a total of 14 panel discussions were convened. An additional two panel discussions were held in 1999 at the second session of the Commission acting as the preparatory committee for the special session of the General Assembly on "Women 2000: gender equality, development and peace for the twenty-first century". The number of States participating in each session of the preparatory process has increased, with the Commission's Bureau having assumed a greater role. The Bureau regularly convenes consultations of all States on issues affecting the conduct of the Commission's sessions and its substantive work.

The Commission on the Status of Women has further developed its catalytic role, especially in support of gender mainstreaming, by ensuring that its work is available to other functional commissions when dealing with an issue also addressed in the Beijing Platform for Action. It forwarded, for example, its agreed conclusions 1997/1 on women and the environment,[143] adopted in 1997, to the Commission on Sustainable Development acting as preparatory body for the special session of the General Assembly for the purpose of an overall review and appraisal of the implementation of Agenda 21 (Rio +5). It provided its agreed conclusions on human rights of women, women and armed conflict, and violence against women[144] to the Commission on Human Rights in 1998 as input into its follow-up to the Vienna Declaration and Programme of Action. Its agreed conclusions on women and health[145] served as input into the preparations for the twenty-first special session of the General Assembly on an overall review and appraisal of the implementation of the Programme of Action of the International Conference on Population and Development (Cairo +5). The Commission on the Status of Women focused on older women in 1999 and provided input into the International Year of Older Persons. The Chairperson of the Commission on the Status of Women has also participated in the work of other commissions, most notably, the Commission on Human Rights.

Under the guidance of the Economic and Social Council and its President, the Bureau of the Commission on the Status of Women has met with the bureaux of other functional commissions, *inter alia*, by video-conference (as was the case with regard to the Bureau of the Commission on Human Rights in 1999) to discuss issues of common concern, increase coordination, exchange experiences with regard to working methods, and ensure that the agendas and work programmes complemented each other. The Commission on the Status of Women has followed up on Council agreed conclusions and decisions, as requested. Starting with its forty-fourth session in 2000, the Commission on the Status of Women will include a separate item in its agenda to follow up on Council resolutions, agreed conclusions and decisions.

Between 1996 and 1999, the Commission, through the Open-ended Working Group on the Elaboration of a Draft Optional Protocol to the Convention on the Elimination of All Forms of Discrimination against Women, elaborated the Optional Protocol to the Convention on the Elimination of All Forms of Discrimination against Women, which was adopted by the General Assembly in its resolution 54/4 of 6 October 1999.

In accordance with General Assembly resolution 52/100, the Commission on the Status of Women serves as the preparatory committee for the special session of the General Assembly on "Women 2000: gender equality, development and peace for the twenty-first century", to be held from 5 to 9 June 2000. The Commission acting as preparatory committee has elected its own Bureau consisting of ten members.

(d) Other functional commissions
Functional commissions (such as the Commission on Human Rights, the Commission on Population and Development and the Commission for Social Development) responsible for follow-up to recent global conferences, including the World Conference on Human Rights, the International Conference on Population and Development and the World Summit for Social Development, have taken steps to strengthen attention to gender-specific recommendations contained in those conference results. This was facilitated by the adoption of Economic and Social Council agreed conclusions 1997/2 on gender mainstreaming, which called on all the Council's functional commissions to mainstream a gender perspective in their work. Subsequently, the Commission on Crime Prevention and Criminal Justice adopted a decision in

1998 to mainstream a gender perspective in its work,[146] and the Working Group on International Statistical Programmes and Coordination of the Statistical Commission, at its nineteenth session, adopted a statement in response to the Council's agreed conclusions 1997/2 in 1998.[147] At the same time, functional commissions continue to focus on issues of particular relevance to women within their sectoral mandates, using a women-specific approach.

2. Inter-Agency Committee on Women and Gender Equality of the Administrative Committee on Coordination

Based on the Platform for Action's support for system-wide coordination and participation of United Nations entities in Conference follow-up, the ACC decided, in April 1996, to regularize the *ad hoc* inter-agency arrangement that had existed since the first United Nations conference on women in 1975. It established the ACC Inter-Agency Committee on Women and Gender Equality (IACWGE) as a standing sub-committee, on a par with the Inter-Agency Committee on Sustainable Development and the Consultative Committee on Programme and Operational Questions (CCPOQ). The Inter-Agency Committee on Women and Gender Equality seeks to ensure the largest possible participation of focal points on gender issues from the United Nations system in its annual sessions, and in its inter-sessional activities, including those from departments and offices of the United Nations Secretariat, the regional commissions, funds and programmes, specialized agencies and international financial institutions. The Committee is chaired by the Special Adviser to the Secretary-General on Gender Issues and Advancement of Women, on behalf of the United Nations.

According to its terms of reference, IACWGE has two major responsibilities: to support implementation of the Platform for Action and of gender-related recommendations emanating from other recent United Nations conferences and summits, especially by ensuring effective cooperation and coordination among entities of the United Nations system; and to support the mainstreaming of a gender perspective in the work of the United Nations system. To this end, the Committee facilitates action and monitors progress in achieving gender-related goals of United Nations conferences in the areas of policy, operational activities, coordination, research, training and public information. It identifies emerging issues that require the attention of the system, and prepares practical tools, such as guidelines, background notes and checklists, to strengthen women-specific activities and increase gender mainstreaming. It compiles good practices and performance indicators to ensure accountability for progress. Through joint workshops, and collaboration in the preparation of reports, and in electronic information dissemination, the Committee ensures implementation of a cohesive system-wide approach to its mandate. It seeks to achieve links with other bodies of ACC so as to ensure attention to women and gender issues and mainstreaming, and it exchanges information with subsidiary bodies of ACC in this regard. Information on the work of the Committee is regularly provided to the Commission on the Status of Women and the Economic and Social Council so as to strengthen links between the inter-agency and intergovernmental mechanisms.

The approach of IACWGE to its mandate has, from its inception, been guided by the need to achieve, in the short term, visible outputs and to contribute to work elsewhere in the ACC system on Conference follow-up. At the same time, it remains acutely aware that its role as a standing committee of ACC goes beyond the accomplishment of well-defined, specific tasks to ensuring that, in the long term, the United Nations system remains at the cutting edge of efforts to realize equality between women and men.

Coordinated support for implementation of the Platform for Action is centred around the system-wide medium-term plan for the advancement of women, 1996-2001. This plan was prepared after the adoption of the Beijing Platform for Action and submitted to the Economic and Social Council by the Secretary-General in his capacity as Chairman of ACC. A mid-term review of the implementation of the plan, taking into account the comments provided thereon by the Commission on the Status of Women and CPC in 1996, was conducted in 1998. The Council requested that an assessment of the activities undertaken by the United Nations system and of obstacles encountered and lessons learned from the present plan and the system-wide process of its implementation be prepared for 2000. A new plan for 2002-2005 is to be submitted to the Council, through the Commission, in 2001, and is to reflect a growing emphasis on action and delivery.

From the point of view of integrated conference follow-up, gender mainstreaming is cross-cutting and deals with the interface of gender with sectoral issues. While many women-specific activities are being supported by the United Nations system at the national, regional and international levels and progress, therefore, is being made in implementation of the Platform for Action, the gender dimension as a cross-cutting issue must be addressed as an essential and integral part of all conference follow-up. In its effort to support such gender mainstreaming, the Inter-Agency Committee on Women and Gender Equality places special emphasis on refining methodology, and transforming analytical frameworks, institutional culture, and policy and programme processes. It undertook follow-up action to ensure implementation of Economic and Social Council agreed conclusions 1997/2 on gender mainstreaming. The Committee contributed to the preparation of the CCPOQ guidance note for resident coordinators on field-level follow-up to global conferences to ensure systematic and across-the-board attention to gender. It held a workshop on the issue of gender mainstreaming, together with members of the OECD/DAC Working Party on Gender Equality in 1997. Two subsequent workshops of these groups, on a rights-based approach to gender equality in 1998, and on women's empowerment in the framework of human security in 1999, also contributed to clarifying the practical implications of gender mainstreaming in these areas.

The importance of gender concerns to all sectoral areas was highlighted in the development of the Generic Guidelines for a Strategic Framework Approach for Response to and Recovery from Crisis, which were developed under the aegis of CCPOQ, and which address gender considerations. The experience gained and the recommendations made by the inter-agency gender mission to Afghanistan, led by the Special Adviser on Gender Issues and Advancement of Women from 12 to 24 November 1997, which looked at the critical situation of women and girls, *inter alia*, in the health, education, employment and human rights sectors, were instrumental in this regard. The report and recommendations of the gender mission to Afghanistan guided subsequent inter-agency and planning documents concerning humanitarian assistance in that country, and have also been considered by intergovernmental bodies. They have facilitated the development of a more coherent, effective and consistent political strategy that takes into account human rights and gender equality, in respect of the humanitarian assistance provided by the United Nations system, by bilateral donors and by other development actors on the ground.

ACC adopted a statement on gender equality and mainstreaming in the work of the United Nations system as a follow-up action to Economic and Social Council agreed conclusions 1997/2. In preparation for the special session of the General Assembly on Beijing +5, ACC held a substantive discussion on the gender aspects of globalization at its second regular session of 1999. An ACC statement to serve as input into the special session was prepared.

3. Committee on the Elimination of Discrimination against Women and other treaty bodies

The Platform for Action recommends that the Committee on the Elimination of Discrimination against Women, within its mandate, take account of the Platform for Action in the consideration of reports of States parties. States parties are invited to include in their reports information on measures taken to implement the Platform for Action in order to facilitate the Committee's effective monitoring of women's ability to enjoy the rights guaranteed by the Convention. Increased coordination is called for with other human rights treaty bodies, who are invited to ensure the integration of the equal status and human rights of women in their work.

The Committee revised its reporting guidelines at its fifteenth session in 1996. It now includes in its dialogue with reporting States questions on the follow-up to the Platform for Action undertaken by the State party. In its concluding comments, the Committee requests reporting States to continue to disseminate widely the Convention, the Committee's general recommendations and the Beijing Declaration and Platform for Action. In 1999, the Committee also submitted to the Commission acting as the preparatory committee for the special session a report on progress achieved in implementation of the Platform for Action, based on the Committee's review of reports of States parties to the Convention since 1996.[148] This report highlights progress made, identifies challenges to implementation of the Convention and the Platform for Action, and summarizes the specific recommendations addressed by the Committee to reporting States directed towards accelerated implementation of the Platform for Action. Recommendations included introducing temporary special measures, conducting law reforms, and undertaking measures to address stereotypic attitudes. Recommendations also emphasized the role of human rights education, the importance of the availability of data disaggregated by sex and the need for high-level national machinery. With regard to particular issues, the Committee called for measures directed towards the implementation of gender equality in employment, gender-sensitive poverty eradication strategies, and measures to address various forms of violence against women. The Committee also made recommendations concerning trafficking in women and the exploitation of prostitution, and issues related to women's health.

The Committee, through its Chairperson, regularly participates in the annual meeting of persons chairing human rights treaty bodies. The agenda of that meeting now regularly includes an item on mainstreaming a gender perspective in the work of the treaty bodies. At the request of the Chairpersons, a report assessing the integration of a gender perspective in the work of five general human rights treaty bodies was prepared by the Division for the Advancement of Women for their tenth meeting in September 1998. The report also reviewed interaction between the five treaty bodies and the Committee on the Elimination of Discrimination against Women.

A workshop on gender integration in the human rights system, convened jointly by the Division for the Advancement of Women, the Office of the United Nations High Commissioner for Human Rights (UNHCHR) and UNIFEM in May 1999, brought together Chairpersons of human rights treaty bodies, and Special Rapporteurs and Representatives to assess progress made and obstacles encountered, and to identify opportunities for strengthening attention to gender issues in their work. The workshop developed a series of recommendations on when, how and where experts had opportunities to integrate gender concerns in their work.

4. United Nations Secretariat, specialized agencies and other entities

After the 1975 Mexico World Conference of the International Women's Year, many institutions were established at the national and international levels specifically devoted to the advancement of women. Two such institutions were established at the international level, namely, UNIFEM and INSTRAW. These, together with the Division for the

Advancement of Women as the secretariat of the Commission on the Status of Women, became the main institutions in the United Nations specifically devoted to women's advancement globally. Following the Beijing Conference, the Secretary-General was invited to establish a high-level post in his Office for a special adviser on gender issues.

(a) Special Adviser on Gender Issues and
*   Advancement of Women*

Following the recommendation contained in paragraph 326 of the Beijing Platform for Action, an Assistant Secretary-General in the Office of the Secretary-General was designated in 1996 to assume also the responsibilities of Special Adviser on gender issues in order to further strengthen the programme on the advancement of women. Since 1997, the Secretary-General has appointed a Special Adviser on Gender Issues and Advancement of Women in the Department of Economic and Social Affairs to perform the tasks of follow-up to the Beijing Platform for Action and to provide overall oversight and direction of the Division for the Advancement of Women. The Special Adviser also reports directly to the Secretary-General on policy issues with regard to gender; on matters of improving the number of women in the United Nations Secretariat and in the secretariats within its system of organizations; and on gender mainstreaming. The Special Adviser is a member of the Executive Committees on Economic and Social Affairs, on Political Affairs, and on Humanitarian Affairs.

The core functions of the Special Adviser include: to facilitate, monitor and advise the Secretary-General on the overall policy goals, as well as policy direction, of the Organization with regard to gender analysis and mainstreaming a gender perspective into all activities of the United Nations; to advocate for gender issues and gender mainstreaming throughout the United Nations system; and to assist in the design of policies and strategies to achieve targets set for the improvement of the status of women in the Secretariat, and for gender balance. Another new focus of work is to stimulate and monitor the extent to which gender dimensions are mainstreamed into the work of intergovernmental bodies, departments and offices of the United Nations Secretariat and system-wide, as well as at national and regional levels. The Special Adviser offers advice and support to, and seeks the views of, senior managers of the United Nations Secretariat, and of the heads of funds, programmes and specialized agencies of the entities of the United Nations system on gender-related issues, in order to promote gender equality. She participates in the work of intergovernmental bodies, especially functional commissions, and meets with representatives of Member States, non-governmental organizations and women's groups to advocate for implementation of the Beijing Platform for Action. Another new focus of work is to stimulate and monitor the extent to which gender dimensions are mainstreamed into the work of intergovernmental bodies, departments and offices of the United Nations Secretariat and system-wide, as well as at national and regional levels. The Special Adviser is supported by the Division for the Advancement of Women, to which she provides guidance and policy advice through its Director.

As Chairperson of the ACC/IACWGE, the Special Adviser works with all entities in the United Nations system to ensure system-wide support for the implementation of the Platform for Action.

(b) Division for the Advancement of Women
The Division for the Advancement of Women's primary functions are the provision of substantive servicing to the Commission on the Status of Women and other intergovernmental bodies when they are concerned with the advancement of women, as well as to the Committee on the Elimination of Discrimination against Women. It plays a coordinating role in the preparation and assessment of the system-wide medium-term plan for the advancement of women, serves as the secretariat for inter-agency activities and maintains a flow of information with national machineries and non-governmental organizations with regard to the implementation of the Platform for Action, and the Convention on the Elimination of All Forms of Discrimination against Women.

As of 1996, the work of the Division was refocused and three structural units were established, on gender analysis, on women's rights, and on coordination and outreach. As a result of the Secretary-General's reform of the Secretariat in the economic and social field as approved by the General Assembly, the Division is part of the Department of Economic and Social Affairs. A fourth unit on gender advisory services has been added. The addition of gender advisory services strengthens the Division's analytical and normative work.

Since the Fourth World Conference on Women, the Division has undertaken policy research in support of intergovernmental consideration and action on the Platform for Action's critical areas of concern. It has convened expert group meetings to prepare policy recommendations for accelerated implementation of the Platform for Action, and organized workshops to support attention directed towards the human rights of women in general human rights activities.

Reports have been prepared for the General Assembly's annual, or biennial, consideration of the advancement of women and follow-up to Beijing, including the situation of women in rural areas, violence against women migrant workers, trafficking in women, and traditional practices harmful to women and girls. Biennial reports on the situation of women in development have been prepared, and one issue of the (quinquennial) *World Survey on the Role of Women in Development* was prepared in 1999.[149] Some of the work undertaken was published in *Women2000*, a regular publication of the Division for the Advancement of Women. Reports in support of work of the Committee on the Elimination of Discrimination against Women were also prepared, *inter alia*, on issues such as reservations, and the transformation of international law into domestic legal systems. The Division continues to collaborate with the United Nations Statistics Division of the Department of Economic and Social Affairs in the preparation of *The World's Women*, a publication of trends and statistics in respect of women, which is co-sponsored by a number of United Nations partners.

The Division has continued to maintain a flow of information with many institutions and organizations, including non-governmental organizations. In cooperation with United Nations entities, donor governments and non-governmental organizations, it has facilitated the participation of non-governmental organization representatives from developing countries in the annual sessions of the Commission on the Status of Women, including the organization of panel discussions to present national experiences. The Division regularly provides information on Beijing follow-up to non-governmental organizations, and receives information from them about their activities, examples of which have been submitted to the Commission in reports on conference follow-up. Representatives of non-governmental organizations have also participated in expert group meetings and workshops organized by the Division for the Advancement of Women.

(c) Other units of the United Nations Secretariat
The preparation of the revised system-wide medium-term plan for the advancement of women offered an opportunity to a number of departments and offices of the United Nations Secretariat, in addition to

those that had traditionally been involved in efforts to advance the status of women, to begin the process of assessing the implications of the Platform for Action, and in particular its mainstreaming directive, for their work. Since then, other departments have also taken steps to contribute to implementation, to develop capacity for gender mainstreaming, and to reflect women-specific activities in their work programmes. The Secretary-General, in his 1997 reform proposals submitted to the General Assembly, called for gender mainstreaming in all policies and programmes.

Based on CPC direction for the proposed programme budget for the biennium 2000-2001, the budget document presents gender mainstreaming as one of its underlying factors.[150] It discusses the implications of gender mainstreaming for the Organization's work at the programme level, and the opportunities that this strategy offers to programme managers to define more accurately the intended beneficiaries and thus to formulate clearer objectives that take gender into account. Although gender mainstreaming in budget preparation is still a relatively new concept, several departments gave specific attention to this strategy, including the regional commissions, the Department of Economic and Social Affairs, the Department for Disarmament Affairs, the Department of Political Affairs and the United Nations International Drug Control Programme (UNDCP). Their experience, and the monitoring of how these programmes adequately address the concerns and meet the needs of the beneficiaries of the Organization's work, will provide valuable insights for future budget preparations.

The Special Adviser on Gender Issues and Advancement of Women and her staff in collaboration with the Division for the Advancement of Women work in a catalytic and advisory manner to support the implementation of mainstreaming in the Secretariat. Several departments have sought opportunities to integrate aspects of the Platform for Action within their own work programmes, and cooperative links between the Office of the Special Adviser, the Division for the Advancement of Women and other offices and departments have increased, reflected in joint preparation of workshops and expert group meetings, contributions to reports, and exchange of information, data and materials. Gender focal points of departments and offices are members of the ACC Inter-Agency Committee on Women and Gender Equality, and are thus part of the United Nations system-wide network of gender experts.

The General Assembly and the Commission on the Status of Women continue to monitor annually the improvement of the status of women in the Secretariat, based on reports of the Secretary-General.[151] The Assembly has reaffirmed the goal of 50/50 gender distribution by the year 2000 in all categories of posts within the United Nations system, especially at the D-1 level and above, with full respect for the principle of equitable geographical distribution, in conformity with Article 101 of the Charter of the United Nations. A comparison of the number and percentage of women at the Professional and higher levels with appointments subject to geographical distribution over a 10-year period (1989 to 1999) shows an increase from 26.9 to 38.1 per cent. Gender balance is almost achieved at the P-2 level (47.5 per cent as compared with 44.9 per cent in 1989). Visible progress has been made at several levels, most notably, at the Assistant Secretary-General (from 0 to 17.6 per cent), the D-2 (from 8.2 to 23.2 per cent) and the D-1 (from 13.5 to 31.6 per cent) levels.

The Secretary-General continues to place the highest priority on achieving gender balance in his efforts to bring about a new management culture in the Organization. This includes full implementation of the strategic plan of action for the improvement of the status of women in the Secretariat (1995-2000), and of the special measures governing the recruitment, placement and promotion of women. The Secretary-General has issued revised terms of reference of the Steering Committee for the Improvement of the Status of Women in the Secretariat in June 1999.[152] The Committee is chaired by the Special Adviser on Gender Issues and Advancement of Women to provide policy guidance, monitor actions and review human resources measures, with a view to achieving gender balance and to creating a more gender-sensitive work environment.

Building upon steps taken by the Assistant Secretary-General for Human Resources Management to develop human resources action plans, the Special Adviser on Gender Issues and Advancement of Women works with departments and offices to ensure that gender balance goals are fully addressed in such plans. Gender issues are also increasingly incorporated into staff development programmes, such as for people management and supervisory skills; and several offices and departments are implementing training on gender mainstreaming and gender-sensitivity.

(d) International Research and Training Institute for the Advancement of Women (INSTRAW)

The Platform for Action invites INSTRAW to review its work pro-gramme and to develop a programme for implementing those aspects of the Platform for Action that fall within its mandate. The Institute func-tions under the authority of its Board of Trustees, which reports annu-ally to the Economic and Social Council. The Secretary-General sub-mits a report on the activities of the Institute to the General Assembly every other year, or as otherwise requested, in accordance with relevant General Assembly resolutions.

Guided by its Board of Trustees, the Institute identifies research and training activities within biennial work programmes. During the period since the Beijing Conference, its main research activities have focused on time-use surveys, use of communication technologies by women's organizations, women migrant workers, and engendering public poli-cies; and its training activities have concentrated on the environment and compilation of sex-disaggregated data. The Institute also partici-pated in inter-agency activities and produced women in development-related publications.

The Institute is an autonomous institution operating within the frame-work of the United Nations, funded from voluntary contributions. Over the past years, the Institute experienced financial constraints that af-fected its staffing situation and its capacity to deliver its work pro-gramme. Efforts have been undertaken at different levels, *inter alia*, by the Under-Secretary General for Economic and Social Affairs as the Secretary-General's Special Representative to INSTRAW the Special Adviser on Gender Issues and Advancement of Women, the Director of INSTRAW and its Board of Trustees, to create a stable financial and staffing situation that would allow the Institute to contribute fully to the implementation of the Platform for Action.

At its fifty-fourth session, the General Assembly, in its resolution 54/140, endorsed Economic and Social Council resolution 1999/54 on the revitalization of the Institute, and the decision of Member States to engage in the revitalization of the Institute. The endorsement was based on proposals for a new working method through the establishment of an electronic Gender Awareness Information and Networking System (GAINS), a reduced core staff, and project-specific staffing and fi-nance. A feasibility study of GAINS, including the work plan and budget for 2000-2001, will be submitted by the Director to the next session of the Board of Trustees of INSTRAW. The Assembly expressed its satisfaction with the new approach of GAINS and the reduced staffing structure.

(e) United Nations Development Fund for Women
   (UNIFEM)

The Platform for Action invites UNIFEM to review and strengthen its work programme in the light of the Platform for Action, focusing on women's political and economic empowerment. UNIFEM is an autonomous organization working in close association with UNDP. The Fund functions under a Consultative Committee that advises the Administrator of UNDP on all matters affecting its activities. The Secretary-General transmits annually to the General Assembly a report on the activities of UNIFEM and submits it to the Commission on the Status of Women for its information. He also submits annually to the Commission on the Status of Women a report prepared by UNIFEM in pursuance of Assembly resolution 50/166, on its activities undertaken to eliminate violence against women.

UNIFEM put in place a strategy and business plan that delineates areas of focus and operations for the period 1997-1999. The plan is designed and guided by an empowerment framework based on the promotion of women's rights, opportunities and capacities. It focuses on three thematic areas: strengthening women's economic capacity; engendering governance and leadership; and promoting women's human rights, and the elimination of all forms of violence against women. It also plays a catalytic role in promoting gender mainstreaming within the United Nations system of operational activities. UNIFEM has adopted a results-based management approach and the principles of a learning organization. Strategies and activities, geared towards the policy level as well as the microlevel, focus on capacity-building of women and women's organizations, gender-sensitive national planning, participation of women in peace-building and conflict resolution, information-sharing on successful strategies, and training.

Efforts to strengthen the United Nations system's capacity for women's empowerment and gender mainstreaming focused on the resident coordinator system at the country level, collaboration with the entities of the United Nations system, and involvement in the United Nations Development Assistance Framework (UNDAF) and United Nations Development Group (UNDG) processes to ensure gender integration.

UNIFEM consolidated the programme by placing at the country and sub-country level ten senior UNIFEM gender advisers, who work in tandem with the resident coordinators to increase gender mainstreaming, and to help implement the Beijing Platform for Action at the country level. UNIFEM, UNDP and the United Nations Volunteers Programme (UNV) have together fielded a number of volunteer gender specialists to strengthen support for the United Nations system as a whole at country level.

(f) Specialized agencies and other organizations
of the United Nations system
The Platform for Action invites all entities of the United Nations system to contribute to its implementation, *inter alia*, through technical assistance. Agency heads are urged to support the roles and responsibilities of focal points on women's issues. Organizations are called upon to accord greater priority to the recruitment and promotion of women so as to achieve gender balance.

Following the adoption of the Beijing Declaration and Platform for Action, the ACC/IACWGE served as institutional mechanism for revising the system-wide medium-term plan for the advancement of women (1996-2001), as directed by the Economic and Social Council.[153] Specialized agencies, funds and programmes, and other entities of the United Nations system indicated the types of activities that they intended to implement in support of the Platform for Action. Progress in implementation of the system-wide medium-term plan for the advancement of women, together with the comments thereon adopted by the Commission on the Status of Women and CPC in 1996, was assessed in 1998.[154] A final assessment is available to the preparatory committee in a separate report.[155]

Steps have been taken by many entities of the United Nations system to strengthen institutional capacity in support of implementation of the Platform for Action and gender mainstreaming. The role of gender focal points in these efforts was highlighted in the Secretary-General's report[156] submitted to the Economic and Social Council for its 1997 coordination segment, after having been extensively discussed in the Inter-Agency Committee on Women and Gender Equality. The report highlighted the role of gender units/focal points, and suggested a series of recommendations, which were taken up by the Council in its agreed conclusions 1997/2. The agreed conclusions, and a subsequent letter of the Secretary-General bringing them to the attention of all heads of agencies and senior officials in the United Nations system, proved a critical tool for gender focal points within their own organizational settings, *inter alia*, with respect to emphasizing the importance of adequate institutional and resource support. IACWGE is conducting a survey of the role and functions of gender focal points in the system, both at Headquarters and at field level. It is also surveying system-wide management commitment to gender mainstreaming. The results of both surveys will be available to the General Assembly at its special session.

Many recent directives and initiatives of United Nations entities have been targeted at increasing the capacity of staff to use gender analysis in designing, implementing and assessing plans and projects with regard to their gender implications. There is also general agreement that the catalytic role of gender and women-in-development focal points is essential to gender mainstreaming, but questions remain about how best to institutionalize this role so that attention to gender becomes irreversible.

Steps have been taken to ensure that the Beijing Platform for Action is given full attention in the coordinated and integrated follow-up to United Nations conferences at the country level, and to gender mainstreaming. The March 1998 ACC guidance note for the resident coordinator system on field-level follow-up to global conferences stresses the potential of coordinated conference follow-up for achieving the goal of gender equality. It gives examples of appropriate action at the country level to incorporate gender equality and women's empowerment strategies in the country strategy note (CSN) and UNDAF processes, and in the common country assessments (CCAs). As a cross-cutting issue, gender mainstreaming is increasingly being used by the United Nations system as an underlying approach in its operational activities. The establishment of theme groups, the development of gender-sensitive monitoring and evaluation tools, and the use of gender-related measures as advocacy tools and for policy dialogues are among the steps most commonly taken by the United Nations system at the country level.

The Inter-Agency Committee on Women and Gender Equality maintains links with the Consultative Committee on Administrative Questions (CCAQ) to ensure that issues of gender balance are a central component in the work of that Committee. The Special Adviser has also addressed the International Civil Service Commission (ICSC) in support of the goal of gender equality in the organizations of the common system, and the role of the ICSC in monitoring gender balance within these organizations.

Notes

132 E/CN.6/2000/3.
133 E/CN.6/2000/PC/CRP.1.
134 E/CN.6/1995/5/Add.1-5.
135 E/CN.6/2000/3.
136 ECOSOC resolution 1998/44, para. 6.
137 General Assembly resolution 50/203 of 22 December 1995.
138 General Assembly resolutions 51/69, 52/100, 53/120 and 54/141.
139 ECOSOC resolution 1996/6.
140 ECOSOC Agreed Conclusions 1997/2, op. cit.
141 A/54/3 and Add.1 and 2, chap. III, para. 23.
142 *Official Records of the General Assembly, Fifty-third Session, Supplement No. 3* (A/53/3 and Corr.1 and Add.1), chap. III, "Summary by the President of the Council", para. 6 (e).
143 *Official Records of the Economic and Social Council, 1997, Supplement No. 7*, op. cit.
144 ECOSOC resolution 1998/12.
145 ECOSOC resolution 1999/17, sect. I.
146 *Official Records of the Economic and Social Council, 1998, Supplement No. 10* (E/1998/30 and Corr.1), chap. I, sect. D. (see resolution 7/1).
147 E/CN.3/1999/20, para. 21.
148 E/CN.6/1999/PC/4, annex.
149 *World Survey on the Role of Women in Development: Globalization, Gender and Work* (United Nations publication, Sales No. E.99.IV.8).
150 *Official Records of the General Assembly, Fifty-fourth Session, Supplement No. 6*, vol. I, *Foreword and introduction* (A/54/6/Rev.1), paras. 44-49.
151 For example, A/54/405.
152 ST/SGB/1999/9.
153 ECOSOC resolution 1993/16.
154 E/CN.6/1998/3.
155 E/CN.6/2000/3.
156 E/1997/66.

III. Financial arrangements

A. Introduction

The Platform for Action states that "the primary responsibility for implementing the strategic objectives of the Platform for Action rests with Governments" (PfA, para. 346) and calls upon Governments to undertake the necessary institutional, budgetary and other such measures to implement these objectives. It further calls upon Governments to allocate sufficient resources to the implementation of the Platform for Action in general, and to the national machineries for women's advancement in particular. The Platform for Action also calls for resources to be allocated to other institutions, such as non-governmental organizations, that can contribute to the implementation of the strategic objectives.

As no specific methodology for assessing allocations and expenditures in the process of implementation is mentioned in the Platform for Action, Governments report a mix of approaches. These range from mainstreaming the entire national budgets, and totalling allocations that benefit women in one or more sectors, to channelling resources exclusively through the national machineries. In most instances, it is not possible to determine comprehensively, from the available data and the replies of Member States to part two of the questionnaire, any particular approach of Governments. A comprehensive analysis of financial arrangements at the national level is therefore not possible at this stage.

The Platform for Action calls for the commitment of sufficient financial resources at the international level for implementation of the objectives in developing countries, especially those in Africa, the least developed countries and the countries in transition. In this context, the

Platform for Action calls for the speedy realization of the agreed target of 0.7 per cent of the GNP of developed countries for official development assistance (ODA). The Platform for Action calls for a greater share of that assistance to be directed towards activities designed to implement the Platform for Action.

Provision of adequate financial resources at the international level for the implementation of the Platform for Action in the developing countries is called for under financial arrangements (PfA, paras.345-361). International financial institutions are invited to examine their grants and lending policies, and to allocate loans and grants to programmes for implementing the Beijing Platform for Action. Fourteen international donor countries and five multilateral agencies provided information to the Secretariat on the extent to which the Beijing Platform for Action had impacted upon their institutional policies, budget processes, women-specific expenditures, and so forth. This information serves as the basis of the analysis contained in the present chapter.

B. Bilateral arrangements

1. Institutional policies of bilateral development agencies

In terms of institutional policies, all international donor countries report that the Platform for Action had a profound effect on their development assistance programmes. For example, Denmark reports that the Fourth World Conference on Women and the Platform for Action resulted in a fundamental shift in its development cooperation approach from the more women-oriented strategy of the 1980s to a focus on gender equality. As a result, there is now an ongoing process of revising most general policies, country strategies and sector policies to conform to the new focus. On the other hand, Switzerland reports that the Platform for Action merely reinforced an existing trend in its development assistance (policy) that focused on gender-balanced development.

The Beijing Platform for Action serves as the basis for Sweden's Action Programme for Promoting Equality between Women and Men in Partner Countries. Since 1995, gender equality has been one of four priority areas and informs the overall as well as sectoral work of the SIDA. SIDA's development cooperation covers all 12 critical areas of concern; however, there is a special focus on the empowerment of women in the area of political decision-making.

Germany reports that the Platform served as a basis for its July 1997 Concept on Gender Equality, which states that women and men should have equal influence on shaping development cooperation measures and should derive equal benefits from them. There are cases, however, where there is a need for women-specific assistance and in recognition of this fact, the German Parliament in 1999 introduced new, women-specific special terms for German development cooperation that provide for "measures that serve to enhance the status of women in society" to be supported by grants instead of loans (even in countries that are not least developed countries).

The United Kingdom reports that its policy on gender equality in development cooperation is entirely consistent with, and supports the implementation of, the Beijing Platform for Action.

The Netherlands reports that its policy on women and development is shaped by several priority areas that are drawn from the Platform for Action. These areas include equal rights for women, women's contribution to the prevention and resolution of conflicts and to post-conflict reconstruction, and prevention of violence against women.

The Platform for Action significantly influenced Australia's decision to replace, in March 1997, the Women in Development Policy with the Gender and Development Policy emphasizing strategies to address gender inequalities as part of all Australian aid activities. Another priority is the provision of assistance so as to increase women's access to education, health care and economic resources as well as to encourage women's participation in decision-making and the promotion of their human rights.

Canada reports that the promotion of gender equality, as a human rights, social justice and development issue (long a part of Canada's foreign and aid policies), has been strengthened by the Platform for Action. In order to reflect the priorities and outcomes established at Beijing, CIDA made specific efforts to ensure that policy and strategic orientation conformed to the Platform for Action's goal of gender equality between women and men so as to ensure sustainable development.

Finland's development cooperation in all contexts promotes implementation of the Platform for Action of the Beijing Fourth World Conference on Women to improve the status of women and girls, and to encourage equal participation by women in society and production. At a practical level, the Ministry of Foreign Affairs as part of its Equality Action Plan advises that employees involved in project work should analyse the importance of the gender component in each project by means of a retrospective project interpreter so as to enable follow-up. In mid-term and final evaluations, the aim is to attach importance to the gender components as well as the factors of importance to the project. The project managers are instructed to maintain equality at each stage of implementation.

The United States Agency for International Development (USAID) has finalized a Gender Plan of Action which ensures gender mainstreaming throughout the Agency's policies and programmes. The plan ensures that gender issues as key development issues are addressed in the strategic framework that now guides all of USAID programming. Also, the Plan includes the building of internal capacity to address gender in all Agency programmes as well as incentives for consideration of gender issues.

Irish Aid, Ireland's official development agency, is committed to the Platform for Action and this is reflected in the following gender principles it has elaborated:

* Gender issues will be integrated in Irish Aid ODA during policy formulation, and dialogue, and at all stages of the project cycle;

* In Irish Aid-supported projects, a gender perspective is favoured rather than regarding women as an isolated group and developing women-specific projects. Some circumstances will require women-specific projects or project components;

* Women, as well as men, must be viewed as active participants in development. This will require the identification of obstacles to their participation and inclusion of measures to overcome these obstacles in projects and programmes;

* Women in their own right must be included in the development process. This participation is over and above their roles as mothers and caregivers in the family and community;

- Women and men will be treated equally in the allocation of paid work in Irish Aid projects. Care must be taken to avoid using women's unpaid time unless there are compensatory measures to relieve their existing workload;

- Building local capacities of Government, institutions and women's groups to undertake measures that promote gender equality will be supported;

- Gender and development will be a strong component of development education policy.

In Spain, the Agency for International Cooperation (AECI) mainstreams a gender perspective in all its policies and programmes, using the Beijing Declaration and Platform for Action as the basis. AECI is currently conducting a pilot project in Guatemala in which gender equality is fully integrated as part of the project's objectives. The lessons learned from this project are being incorporated into AECI's programming.

In France, the Agency for Development (AFD) has, since 1997, been in the process of redefining a new strategy in order to reinforce efforts towards the pursuit of gender equality in its development cooperation as part of its commitment to the Platform for Action. Some of its new approaches are being piloted in a few partner countries with a view to incorporating them into future programming.

2. Budget processes of bilateral development agencies

Several donors have revised their budget processes in line with recommendations of the Platform for Action. Denmark now requires the inclusion of gender analysis at all levels of preparation, implementation and evaluation of a programme submitted for funding to the Board of the Danish International Development Agency (DANIDA). The United Kingdom's Department for International Development (DFID) uses a Policy Information Marker System (PIMS) to track expenditure commitments in its bilateral programme against key policy objectives, including the removal of gender discrimination. Since 1994, the proportion of new bilateral spending commitments that explicitly seek to support DFID's gender equality objective has increased from 23.2 per cent in 1994-1995 to 46 per cent in 1998-1999.

The Netherlands requires that all development cooperation spending be screened in advance to ensure that it takes into account the theme of women and development. Also, since 1998 there has been a gender criterion for the award of macrolevel support (balance of payments support, debt relief and programme aid). Furthermore, as part of the monitoring and evaluation process, gender-country profiles are currently being developed for the 20 countries with which the Netherlands has a structural bilateral aid relationship.

Gender analysis is a key tool in designing programmes and budgets, and gender equality is now incorporated in the design and implementation of Canada's bilateral projects. To further assist gender-sensitive programming and to measure the development effectiveness of such programmes and projects, CIDA, in 1997, published a Guide to Gender-Sensitive Indicators with an accompanying project-level handbook. CIDA has an annual reporting process that includes reporting on results achieved against the policy priority of gender equality. Also, specific efforts are under way to examine reporting systems in order to ensure a more systematic inclusion of sex-disaggregated data at the results level of reporting.

As a consequence of applying the gender mainstreaming approach to development assistance, Finland, Denmark and Sweden are unable to indicate the specific amount spent on advancing gender equality through women-specific programming. However, Finland spent 16 per cent of development assistance on gender and development- and women in development-related programmes. Also, no separate statistics are kept on the percentage of assistance targeted at women-specific activities. Switzerland also reported the absence of data on expenditure on women-specific programmes.

Germany reported that a number of projects have been funded within the framework of its commitment made at Beijing to make available US $40 million by 2000 for legal and social policy advice for women in developing countries. The Netherlands set aside an annual sum of 45 million guilders (US $20.87 million) as total resources for the Women's Fund which are used to support innovative activities and capacity-building in local women's movements and other relevant organizations.

The Republic of Korea has spent approximately US $4.5 million since 1991 on women-specific project and programme support as part of its overall development assistance. Canada has spent approximately 4 to 5 per cent of its overseas development assistance disbursements annually on activities directly addressing gender equality. During 1998-1999, for example, CIDA spent approximately Can $76 million (4.7 per cent of overseas development assistance) on such activities.

C. Multilateral arrangements

1. Institutional policies of multilateral development agencies

The Platform for Action calls upon international and regional financial institutions to examine their grants and lending frameworks in order to incorporate a gender perspective into their policies and funding modalities and to allocate loans and grants to programmes for the implementation of the Platform for Action, especially in developing countries and countries in transition. The Platform for Action also calls upon international and regional financial institutions to take action in the areas below, as follows:

- Increase resources allocated to eliminating absolute poverty;

- Support other financial institutions that serve low-income, small-scale and micro-scale women entrepreneurs and producers;

- Increase the funding for the education and training needs of girls and women;

- Give higher priority to women's health;

- Revise policies, procedures and staffing in order to ensure that investments and programmes benefit women.

At the World Bank, the Platform for Action has stimulated a variety of new initiatives on gender, in accordance with the Bank's overall policy of mainstreaming gender into all its activities. The Country Assistance Strategy (CAS), which guides the Bank's country lending programmes, will address gender issues, along with other cross-cutting issues. A body of best practices on mainstreaming gender in CAS is emerging.

Gender is addressed as a cross-cutting issue within the Comprehensive Development Framework (CDF), which focuses Bank assistance on a range of prerequisites of sustainable growth and poverty alleviation beyond the traditional emphasis on macroeconomic policy. Attention is drawn to gender issues in relation to such topics as good governance, an effective legal and judicial system, social safety nets and social programmes, education and knowledge transfer, health and population issues, water and sewerage, energy, roads, transport and communications, environment and cultural issues, and rural, urban and private sector development strategies. Handbooks focusing on how to integrate gender issues in different sectors, such as agriculture, water and sanitation and transport, have been issued to assist staff in mainstreaming gender. In addition, a number of new initiatives on gender activities are being piloted in country lending programmes.

Within the framework of its mandate and expertise, the International Monetary Fund (IMF) pursues the implementation of the Platform for Action in the overall context of its policy advice to member countries. In this regard, the IMF places considerable emphasis on broadening women's participation in the economic process and ensuring their gain from the economic process by, *inter alia*, protecting budgetary outlays in education, health care and basic social services.

The gradual shift, since 1992, from a women-in-development approach to a gender-and-development approach consisting of mainstreaming gender into all operations of the Asian Development Bank has been strengthened by the outcome of the Beijing Conference. In June 1998 the Asian Development Bank adopted a policy on gender and development that completely replaced its women-in-development policy. This policy is operationalized by mainstreaming gender considerations in its macroeconomic and sectoral work, including policy dialogue, lending and technical assistance operations. Furthermore, increased attention is given to directly addressing gender disparities, by designing an increasing number of projects to address women's concerns in health, education, agriculture, natural resource management, and financial services including microfinance, while ensuring that women's considerations are addressed in other Bank projects, including those in the infrastructure sector.

In order to accelerate the process of addressing gender issues, the Asian Development Bank is establishing new institutional mechanisms together with some additional resources and changes in the skills mix. Such mechanisms include: (a) the preparation of a Bank-wide Gender and Development Action Plan; (b) increased in-house gender-and-development capacity with the recruitment of two additional gender-and-development specialists to work primarily on projects, bringing to four the number of gender-and-development specialists; (c) the enhancing of institutional gender capacity of developing member countries through funding and training; (d) the establishment of a regional technical assistance programme to support small gender-and-development initiatives, Governments and non-governmental organizations; (e) the development of a database on gender-and-development best practices to be used in training Bank staff and member country officials; (f) the establishment of an External Forum on Gender to facilitate outreach in this area of work; and (g) the coordination of all Bank aid on gender.

At the African Development Bank, the Beijing Conference has acted as catalyst for a number of activities, at both the policy and operational levels. The Bank's new Vision Statement, adopted early this year, identifies poverty reduction as the primary development challenge facing Africa, and focuses on the mainstreaming of gender as a priority across all activities financed by Bank resources. The Vision Statement, *inter alia*, requires the Bank to work closely with regional member countries to mainstream gender in all aspects of its operational work and to promote the empowerment of women through programmes that seek to:

- Provide increased support for functional literacy that addresses women's issues in business, agroprocessing and marketing, water management and sanitation, primary health care, nutrition and family planning;

- Eliminate gender disparities in primary and secondary education;

- Reduce infant and maternal mortality.

The African Development Fund VII Lending Policy and Guidelines require the Bank to mainstream the gender perspective in all policies and programmes in order to facilitate a dynamic and central role for women through strengthening the gender competence of Bank staff and officials of regional member countries. The guidelines also emphasize the application of gender analysis tools to development planning and the utilization of gender-sensitive indicators to assess the effectiveness of the Fund's approach.

The Bank has also adopted the Country Policy and Institutional Assessment (CPIA), making women's empowerment an element of assessment on the basis of which decisions to allocate resources to Regional Member Countries are taken. CPIA examines the quality of the member country's policy, legal and institutional framework for the advancement of women in areas such as education of girls, health services and the implementation of pro-equality legal reforms. It assesses government action in implementing international conventions and norms in respect of enhancing gender equality.

Over the years, the African Development Bank has adopted a two-pronged approach that focuses on women as development agents in their own right on one hand, and on the mainstreaming of gender issues on the other. From 1990 to 1998, the Bank financed a total of 134 social sector projects of which 12 were women-in-development stand-alone projects. These projects were designed to provide women with basic literacy and functional skills, and training in entrepreneurship and business management, and to build the capacities of women at the grass-roots level to implement, monitor and evaluate the impact of development interventions in their communities, as well as credit. In the same period, a total of 122 projects incorporated gender concerns in a wide range of development sectors such as agriculture, health and public utilities.

In 1998, the Bank established the African Development Fund Microfinance Initiative for Africa—also known as the AMINA Programme—designed to increase the capacity of existing microfinance institutions to deliver an appropriate range of financial services to microentrepreneurs, especially women microentrepreneurs. To date, AMINA has provided support to over 36 non-governmental organizations delivering savings and credit services. Most of these devote between 40 and 100 per cent of their loan portfolio to women in rural and urban areas.

The EU has drafted an Action Plan for Mainstreaming of Gender designed to ensure that its project planning system, based on logical framework analysis, will be made gender-sensitive. As a consequence, monitoring and evaluation of projects will also reflect the gender equality issues that are part of all projects. A joint Help Desk for gender and poverty issues to assist project staff in Brussels and in delegations has also been established. This will be followed by the establishment of a resource bank for useful models of terms of reference and project documents as well as best practices of gender- or women-focused actions from a great range of countries and sectors.

Furthermore, gender issues have been integrated in the ongoing negotiations with the African, Caribbean and Pacific countries about a New
Partnership Agreement to replace the Lomé Convention[157] dealing
with tariff and trade policies.

In 1996, the EU Directorate General for Development established gender focal points in all operational units. Gender focal points are responsible for:

- Coordination and organization of the activities related to the gender questions within the unit;

- Strengthening of the communication between the various gender
  focal points on the one hand, and between the gender focal points
  and the Gender and Development Desk at the Directorate General
  for Development on the other hand;

- Contact with external resource persons;

- Collection and consultation of specialized documentation on the
  questions of gender;

- Gender tasks specific to the Unit of Delegation of the Gender Focal Point.

A Quality Support Group within the Directorate General has been mandated to integrate the gender aspects in a more transparent manner. A
new format for project identification, reflecting clearly gender, poverty
and environment integration aspects, was scheduled for introduction
during autumn 1999.

2. Budget processes of multilateral development agencies

The Asian Development Bank has redesigned its lending and technical
assistance operations to facilitate women's participation and access to
benefits. Gender-and-development objectives and components are systematically monitored and reported. Project completion and post-
project evaluation reports are expected to assess any project's impact
on women.

The World Bank has facilitated the mainstreaming of gender throughout Bank operations by means of the Gender Sector Board, part of the
Poverty Reduction and Economic Management Network, which cuts

across regions and sectors. Supported by a small anchor group, the Board sets priorities and determines budgets for the network anchor, and monitors the implementation of gender policies and programmes. Several gender thematic groups have specific budgets to address special issues such as gender and law, and gender and transport.

The Operations Evaluation Department has pioneered evaluations of gender mainstreaming in the World Bank assistance programme. These include reviews of "Gender Issues in Bank Lending: An Overview" (1994) and "Mainstreaming Gender in World Bank Lending" (1997). An ongoing evaluation of "The Gender Impact of Bank Assistance" is expected to be published in 2001.

The budgeting process of the African Development Bank had to undergo considerable transformation in order to accommodate the new priorities on gender mainstreaming and women's empowerment. Instead of lending to assist "the people" as an undifferentiated or non-specific mass of "beneficiaries" thus concealing gender priorities and needs, current Bank practice increasingly dictates that, first, beneficiaries have to be disaggregated by sex and, second, that projects and policies have to be formulated and implemented through a participatory approach in order to ensure gender equity. Accordingly, budget procedures were restructured to take into account:

- The inclusion of gender expertise throughout the project cycle in order to ensure an adequate level of gender analysis;

- The involvement of the civil society in the planning, implementation and evaluation of projects;

- The formulation of women-in-development stand-alone projects focusing on sectors that are of significance to women as specified above;

- The specification of gender targets in "mainstream" projects such as poverty, agriculture and rural roads;

- The need to enhance gender competence through training;

- The recruitment of more gender specialists.

Apart from mainstreaming efforts, the EU Directorate General for Development supports women-in-development projects and projects aiming at specific equality problems. The first category is mainly financed from the budget for co-financing with European non-governmental organizations in developing countries, which is approximately 200 million euros per year. In 1998, 47 actions were gender-specific for a total amount of 45 million euros. The European Commission (EC) contribution to those projects was 19 million euros. The second category consists of a few small projects, either of an awareness-raising/experimental character or designed to demonstrate the feasibility of involving women in specific sectors or institutions of society. Four projects in this category have received approximately 2 million euros, while four more projects are in the process of being approved.

A third category under the heading of "Democracy and Human Rights", include a number of projects focused on women, among them, three projects for an amount of 383,414 euros (in Ghana, Sri Lanka and Yemen) in 1996; six projects for an amount of 605,851 euros (in Burkina Faso, Cambodia, Nepal, the Philippines and Togo) in 1997; and three projects for an amount of 846,098 euros (in Burkina Faso, Ethiopia and Togo).

The World Bank emphasizes the mainstreaming of gender issues into all activities, rather than separate projects for women. Since the Beijing Conference, the proportion of projects addressing gender issues has increased modestly, from 37 to 41 per cent of total lending.

Health, education and agriculture accounted for 64 per cent of all investment projects addressing gender in fiscal year 1999. Most of these address the education of girls and the health and nutrition of women. Over 100 projects address women's reproductive health and over 50 address girls' education. New lending for projects that target women's health and nutrition have reached almost US$600 million a year since 1995, while lending for girls' education averaged US$900 million in fiscal years 1996-1998.

The African Development Bank's predominant approach is gender mainstreaming with a smaller number of women-in-development targeted projects. The total African Development Bank Group approvals for the social sector projects that emphasize this approach, as well as women-in-development projects, amount to US $17,179.12 million which represents 11.12 per cent of the cumulative African Development Bank Group approvals for the period 1990-1998.

D. Conclusions and further actions

In their replies, all Member States and multilateral development agencies emphasized their intention to accelerate or continue the implementation of the Beijing Platform for Action by strengthening their institutional mechanisms and by using the available financial and human resources in a more focused manner. The Member States and the multilateral development agencies further reported a high level of mainstreaming a gender perspective in their institutional policies and budget processes to the extent that some could not report on actual women-specific expenditure. While this is a very good development, it is important for the following factors to be considered:

- Mainstreaming a gender perspective, especially in the budget processes, entails the establishment of a clear and effective monitoring, follow-up and evaluation framework. Without that, gender equality objectives might not be fully pursued and realized;

- The advancement of women is an essential element of efforts to attain gender equality because of existing inequalities and persistent discrimination against women. Targeted spending on women-specific projects and programmes is therefore a necessary tool in closing the gender gap.

No detailed picture emerged from the reports about the size of ODA and the extent to which it is engendered, as well as the full extent of expenditure on women-specific projects and programmes. The average net disbursement of ODA has consistently been far below the agreed target of 0.7 per cent of GNP. There is a danger that, with such limited resources being made available for ODA, women's concerns and the goal of gender equality might be marginalized. Therefore, the monitoring, evaluation and reporting on the extent to which ODA expenditures are targeted towards the advancement of women and the pursuit of gender equality should be systematically analysed.

Some of the multilateral development agencies outlined some specific areas in which they propose to pursue further actions and undertake new initiatives. For example, the EU proposes to strengthen gender mainstreaming efforts especially in terms of country strategies and co-ordination with other donors. Development cooperation financed from thematic budgets will focus on women's rights, as part of the support for human rights, women's roles in conflict resolution and peace-building, and the gender aspects of the fight against HIV/AIDS, in particular men's roles in this context.

The World Bank reports that a major research programme on gender and development, scheduled for publication in the spring of 2000, focuses on ways in which taking account of the links among gender, policy and development outcomes can improve policy formulation and development effectiveness. Designed to strengthen the analytical and empirical linkages between gender and development and clarify the value added of a gender perspective, this report is expected to provide policy guidance to the Bank's lending programme. Gender is also integral to the annual World Development Indicators report, which now includes gender differentials among all development indicators.

This report of the World Bank will also identify gender-related results that the Bank strives to achieve in client countries, specify goals for Bank operations, identify obstacles to achieving these goals and design a strategy (including resource needs and proposals for budget planning, implementation, and monitoring) to overcome these obstacles.

Further analytical work on gender will be carried out in *World Development Report 2000/2001*, which is focused on poverty. A *World Development Report* on gender and development is planned for 2004 in order to carry this work forward and place gender more firmly on the Bank's development agenda.

The African Development Bank is in the process of developing a new gender policy, focused on the achievement of gender equality results. It will sharpen the Bank's financial and institutional policies in order to enable the Bank to adopt a more proactive stance in areas such as the three-year work plan and the establishment of mechanisms for gender-sensitive resource allocation.

The African Development Bank will also develop gender-sensitive indicators in order to monitor and evaluate its own progress and to determine the degree to which its policies, programmes and projects have succeeded in achieving results related to gender equality and women's empowerment. One of these indicators will be the size of the investments committed for gender mainstreaming purposes as well as women in development-targeted projects. Training will continue to feature as an instrument for enhancing competence of Bank staff in gender analysis, and gender planning, as well as gender budgeting.

The Platform for Action states that the advancement of women has not received adequate financial and human resources and this has contributed to the slow progress in the implementation of the Nairobi Forward-looking Strategies for the Advancement of Women. Unless adequate resources are made available for the implementation of the Beijing Platform for Action and the commitments made at other United Nations conferences and summits, progress towards gender equality will be slow. Therefore, urgent action is needed, especially in the following areas:

- The continued and concerted effort to assist the process of development and transformation in developing and transition countries. In this regard, action should be taken by developed countries to reach the agreed target of their setting aside 0.7 per cent of their GNP for ODA;

- Ensuring that both women and men benefit equally from that assistance and other budgetary expenditures and that they fully and equally participate in decision-making pertaining to the design, implementation, monitoring and evaluation of development plans, projects and programmes;

- The accelerated implementation of the 20/20 initiative as well as of the Cologne Debt Initiative for the reduction of the debt of many developing countries. The proviso that the funds saved through debt reduction as part of this latter initiative should be used for the eradication of poverty ought to be carried through with due cognizance of the gender dimension of poverty;

- The consideration of financing for development and issues related to a new global financial architecture should incorporate a gender perspective and involve the full and equal participation of women in order to ensure that the pursuit of gender equality will be central to the evolving policy framework and that women, especially poor women, will not be marginalized.

Notes
[157] A/AC.176/7.

Part Three

Trends and challenges of global change

In the closing statement of Boutros Boutros-Ghali, Secretary-General of the United Nations, at the Fourth World Conference on Women, it was affirmed that the implementation of the goals and objectives contained in the Platform "... must be further strengthened, as needed, to take account of new developments as they emerge" (fourteenth paragraph).[158]

The report of the Secretary-General on the second review and appraisal of the Nairobi Forward-looking Strategies for the Advancement of Women, which set the framework for the Beijing Platform for Action,[159] focused attention on the long-term trends towards globalization, integration of markets and internationalization of production. The report asserted that "as a consequence of these trends, the world economy became more interdependent and thus more vulnerable to economic and political upheavals as national economic policies acquired widespread international ramifications. Together, these changes led to economic restructuring that has shaped the development process in recent years and has had a significant impact—both positive and negative—on women's participation and on their economic, political and social status".[160]

Part Three of the present review and appraisal of the implementation of the Beijing Platform for Action explores some of the developments anticipated in the Platform for Action that not only form the backdrop against which Beijing commitments have been implemented, but also increasingly pose further challenges to the process of full implementation.

A. Globalization

The implementation of the Beijing Platform for Action is being reviewed as the world becomes increasingly characterized by a globally integrated economy. As stated in the 1999 report of the Secretary-General on the work of the Organization,[161] globalization "is a summary term for the increasingly complex interactions between individuals, enterprises, institutions and markets across national borders. The manifold challenges it poses, challenges that cannot successfully be addressed by nation States acting on their own, provide the most immediate and obvious reason for strengthening multilateral cooperation. Globalization is manifest in the growth in trade, technology and financial flows; in the continuing growth and increasing influence of international civil society actors; in the global operations of transnational corporations; in the vast increase in transboundary communication and information exchanges, most notably via the Internet; in transboundary transmission of disease and ecological impact; and in the increased internationalization of certain types of criminal activity. Its benefits and risks are distributed unequally, and the growth and prosperity it provides for many is offset by the increasing vulnerability and marginalization of others—and by the growth of 'uncivil society'".

As indicated in the *1999 World Survey on the Role of Women in Development*,[162] government policy choices have shifted in favour of openness of trade and financial flows. Policies calling for lighter regulation of industry, privatization of State-owned enterprises and lower public spending have characterized the programmes of Governments around the world. Liberalization policies coupled with technological advances in communications accelerated the impact of economic integration, thus eroding conventional boundaries, particularly those of the State.

In many instances, Governments proceeded with deregulation without the introduction of mechanisms to ensure the observance of social and livelihood security and to provide for the needs of the people. This increased the risks of globalization for many social groups. As stated in the Platform for Action, these measures "... led to a reduction in social expenditures, thereby adversely affecting women, particularly in Africa and the least developed countries. This is exacerbated when responsibilities for basic social services have shifted from Governments to women" (PfA para. 18).

Studies such as the United Nations Conference on Trade and Development (UNCTAD) *Trade and Development Report, 1997*,[163] and the UNDP *Human Development Report, 1997*[164] and *Human Development Report, 1999*,[165] suggest that the economic growth fostered by recent liberalization policies can be accompanied by increased inequality and a decline in living standards. As the East Asian crisis has revealed, failures in financial markets can cause severe dislocations in the real economy around the globe.

The *1999 World Survey on the Role of Women in Development* also points out that the cultural, political and social correlates of increasing international integration have been profound as well. Populations around the world are being familiarized—through economic exchanges and exposure to advertising, the media and telecommunications—with a culture of instant gratification through material consumption. Additionally, globalization is tied to the momentous political changes of the present era such as the rise of identity politics, transnational civil society, new forms of governance and universalization of human rights.

The World Bank *World Development Report, 1999/2000: Entering the 21st Century*[166] draws attention to the strong reactions provoked by globalization, both positive and negative. According to this report, globalization is welcomed for the opportunities it brings, such as access to markets and technology transfer, but it is also feared and criticized because of the instability and risks that can accompany it. Foreign investment and international competition can help poor economies to modernize, increase their productivity and raise living standards. At the same time, it can threaten the livelihoods of workers, undermine banks and destabilize whole economies when flows of foreign capital overwhelm them.

Concerns have also been raised that globalization increases agricultural monoculture, thereby reducing the self-reliance of local populations. This has adverse effects on the poor, on the environment and on food production. These trends, coupled with global climate change, can endanger the sustainability of entire regions.

The significant gender differences and disparities with respect to decision-making powers, participation and returns for effort that prevail in different societies must be taken into account when responding to the diverse implications of globalization. Because of these gender inequalities and discrimination in all parts of the world, women can be affected negatively by globalization processes to a greater extent than men. On the other hand, there can be significant gains for women if the opportunities emerging with globalization are used for promoting gender equality. It is necessary to monitor systematically the impact of change so that the goals of gender equality and the expansion of human capabilities are not sacrificed in macroeconomic policies aimed at increasing economic growth.

B. Conditions in the world of work

Trends of globalization have had strong gender-specific impact on the world of work. With the change of economic policy environment towards greater economic liberalization and closer integration with the world economy, market-oriented activity has intensified, labour markets have become more flexible, and short and part-time employment has increased. Much of new employment creation in both developed and developing countries has involved *irregular* forms of work, characterized by the new casual forms of employment, such as outworking, informal subcontracting, part-time labour, homework, informal activities and other forms of labour that are unprotected by standard labour legislation.

The rise of irregular forms of work has been a part of business response to the changing market conditions under globalization, involving efforts to cut costs on the one hand and to make production responsive to increased volatility in demand on the other. As also indicated in the Secretary General" report *From Nairobi to Beijing*, part time and other forms of irregular employment are increasingly a female phenomenon (p. 28). Women, who have low opportunity cost in the market and who are socially considered to be flexible labour have been the prefered labour supply. Even though some women were able to break into better jobs that were previously male dominated, the majority of women are still in low-paying, *irregular* jobs, without social benefits, and with little training and promotion prospects. This includes also women migrant workers (see bellow).

The steady increase in the female share of employment during the last two decades has resulted from, among other factors, the overall shifts in the structure of output and employment from manufacturing to services in developed countries and from agriculture to manufacturing and services in developing countries. In the developed countries, the relocation of labour-intensive industries to developing countries resulted in loss of jobs for women who were concentrated in those industries. The shifts in the developing countries were accompanied by a movement of female labour from the unpaid household and subsistence (agriculture) sector to the paid economy. Industries where manufacturing production was heavily oriented towards exports, in particular exports of labour-intensive goods, have had the highest increase in the share of women. However, in countries where export production became more skill- and capital-intensive, the demand for labour has changed in favour of male workers. Despite this change, the labour participation of women has remained high.[167]

These changing employment patterns around the world and their gender dimension have been often called the "feminization of labour". The term has two specific connotations. First, it refers to the rapid and substantial increase in the share of women in paid employment. This resulted from faster growth in sectors where the labour force is predominantly female and from women's taking over jobs that were traditionally held by men. The term has also come to be used to describe the changing nature of employment, where *irregular* conditions that were once thought to be symbolic of women's "secondary" employment have become widespread for both sexes.

It is difficult to assess with certainty the current conditions in the world of work from a gender equality perspective and their implications for women and gender relations. On the one hand, there is a growing body of evidence that increased employment would give women greater autonomy and status, broaden their life options, and strengthen their self-esteem, thereby eventually enhancing their influence within and outside the household. On the other hand, the unequal burden of work at home and the marginal position of women in paid employment at work could simply reinforce each other, confining women to the role of secondary earner in the family. In addition, the shift of societal costs of reproduction and other welfare provisions from the public sector to a sphere where the costs are no longer visible—the household—also increases the workload of women, especially poor women. This becomes particularly acute during times of economic distress when the family becomes the welfare provider of last resort and women bear a disproportional burden of meeting these needs.

It is also important to note the impact of the changing nature of work on declining enforcement of labour standards. Standard labour legislation applies to fewer workers, either because Governments have not enforced regulations or because enterprises have been able to bypass or circumvent them. This has weakened the labour union movement which in the past provided many women with a mechanism for pursuing their claims for equality.

C. Migration

The Platform for Action states that "global trends have brought profound changes in family survival strategies and structures. Rural-to-urban migration has increased substantially in all regions. These massive movements of people have profound consequences for family structures and well-being and have unequal consequences for women and men, including in many cases the sexual exploitation of women" (PfA, para. 36).

Since the 1970s, long-term labour migration from the countries of the South to those of the North has been declining in large part owing to changing demand for labour and the adoption of restrictive immigration policies by labour receiving countries. New and complex patterns of labour migration have become particularly distinct in the past two decades. These new flows can be summarized under four interrelated categories: (a) reverse and return migration from North to South and from urban to rural; (b) shuttle between two or more worlds with strong links in all; (c) illegal forms of international migrant labour arrangements; and (d) temporary, short-term migration of "rented" labour.

While more conventional forms of migration continue, a large proportion of migration is related to changes in the structure of output in production and employment. Labour-intensive industries are being relocated in the search for cheaper labour and lower production costs or, when relocation is not an option, rented labour is moved to where the jobs are. Current trends increasingly favour short-term, temporary migrant labour.[168] There has been a significant increase in the number of women migrants and the ratio of women to men among migrants has risen. In 1990, the number of migrant women and men worldwide were, respectively, 57.1 million and 62.6 million.[169] However, it is likely that the real number of women migrants is much higher.

Changing patterns of demand for labour and the increasing need for women's income on the part of households of all types have resulted in an increasing number of women in new forms of employment. The global context of the service sector has also led to an increase in the involvement of migrant women in various occupations and professions of this sector. Women around the world have made impressive inroads into professional services such as law, banking, accounting and computing; into tourism-related occupations; and into the information services. The bulk of women's labour migration, however, remains in unskilled, low-paid jobs such as domestic work and caregiving. In countries where, owing to prevailing norms and conventions, women are less mobile (for example, in West Asia and parts of Africa), they have taken over the work on land or the non-farm family business, thus freeing male members of the household to migrate in search of work elsewhere.

While much research has been done on the impact of male migration on women who remain behind, less information is available on the impact of female migration on men and families, in particular on girl-children. At the receiving end, as indicated in the government responses to the questionnaire, increased migration of women has brought about greater attention to strengthening the integration and legal position of foreign women.

D. Issues of identity

The fact that political developments around the world have opened up new political spaces for women has facilitated diversification of women's political identities—their sense of belonging to a political entity and of being able to exercise their rights and obligations as active members within it. The emergence of non-State political actors has also facilitated the mobilization of women as key participants in all areas.

The bestowal of citizenship has defined the relationship between the State and the individual that operates to accord rights and obligations, including personal security and access to State provisions such as those for health, education, housing, law enforcement, childcare and other social services. Citizenship is the tangible status of dignity, legitimacy, participation, accountability and equality within society. The Committee on the Elimination of Discrimination against Women (general recommendation 21) has recognized that "… without status as nationals or citizens, women are deprived of the right to vote or to stand for public office and may be denied access to public benefits and a choice of residence".[170] Citizenship, and the rights and obligations that accompany it, depend for the most part upon nationality within a sovereign State.

While States retain control over the bestowal of citizenship, their role in meeting expectations of citizenship is lessening. Recent policy shifts of Governments and their response to the requirements of global markets have undermined the regulatory ability of the States to ensure social security and protection of its citizens. Privatization policies have reduced States' delivery of affordable and accessible health and educational services, and economic restructuring has necessitated cutbacks in welfare provision. This situation poses new challenges for women's personal identity, full citizenship and enjoyment of human rights.

Issues of identity also arise for women who are full citizens when they seek to enter into a relationship with a non-citizen, a situation that occurs more frequently because of the increased movements of peoples across national boundaries. Confiscation of passports of migrant and trafficked women means loss of proof of identity and creates obstacles to diplomatic protection. Refugees may have fled without documentation or had their documentation confiscated, or women's documentation may be controlled by men from whom they have become separated. Vulnerability to violence and exploitation is increased in such situations. In post-conflict reconstruction, women's identity is again contested in various ways.

E. Changing nature of conflict

Since the adoption of the Platform for Action trends discerned in regard to armed conflict have persisted and deepened. Although the threat of global armed conflict has continued to diminish (PfA, para. 11), the period since the adoption of the Platform for Action has been marked by increased localized conflicts. This has resulted in significant numbers of displaced populations, not only beyond borders, but within

States. This period has also been marked by apparent increased commitment to human rights and humanitarian responsibilities. At the same time, there has been little progress in identifying the root causes of conflicts so as to avoid their occurrence.

The shift of armed conflict from the global level to regional, national and even local levels is a major challenge to the implementation of the Platform for Action. Several characteristics of the current patterns of conflict can be identified. First, new actors have emerged in armed conflicts. Whereas in the past, those engaged in armed conflicts were predominantly regular soldiers or irregular militias, including liberation groups, contemporary conflicts increasingly see the participation of insurgents and irregular forces, including children, who are vulnerable to coercion as well as ideological persuasion, including that relating to ethnic, religious, cultural and class factors. These new actors are largely unconstrained by the rules of international law, especially in respect of non-combatants, in conflict situations.

Second, while casualties among armed forces during conflicts once significantly outnumbered casualties among non-combatant civilians, civilians are now the primary victims. Not only are non-combatant civilians involved in incidents of "collateral damage" in conflicts, but increasingly they arc also targets of aggression. Murder, torture and rape of civilians, as well as the execution of prisoners, are a matter of course in many conflicts. Patterns of behaviour in conflicts since the adoption of the Platform for Action have confirmed that, while women are affected by armed conflict in a variety of ways, they are at particular risk of gender-based persecution, including rape, sexual mutilation, sexual slavery and enforced pregnancy. These persecutions have been shown to constitute neither an accident of war, nor an incidental adjunct to armed conflict, but rather a deliberate strategy of war, which builds upon and exacerbates other aggressive acts towards non-combatants. Aggression towards non-combatants is also facilitated by the effectiveness of modern armaments which can create enormous damage with little risk for the aggressor.

Third, the rapid expansion of free trade and modern electronic communications technology has allowed easy access to military weaponry, particularly small arms and light weapons. In addition, the supply of illegally held arms has been facilitated by the persistence of corruption and growing international criminal networks, which also trade in illicit drugs and women and children.

Civilian displacement within and beyond borders as a result of intra-State and localized conflict is an increased phenomenon reported by Member States in their response to the questionnaire. Such movements have led to heightened political insecurity and threat of further conflict. Camps and other facilities established to provide humanitarian relief for non-combatants have themselves, in many instances, become sites of human insecurity, in particular for women. On the other hand, economic sanctions, which are often enforced indiscriminately in response to conflict situations, can cause the further deprivation for women and children.

The Platform for Action has recognized the value of women's involvement in peace processes, stating that "their full participation in decision-making, conflict prevention and resolution and all other peace initiatives is essential to the realization of lasting peace" (PfA, para. 23). There are already a substantial number of movements initiated by women that are seeking alternative solutions to conflict resolution and peace-building. Establishing and supporting such networks can enhance these approaches.

F. Natural disasters and epidemics

Another important source of population displacements is environmental degradation exacerbated by climate change and increased natural disasters and epidemics, which has uprooted individuals, families and entire communities from their homes and/or lands, creating additional constraints on women as refugees and other displaced women (para. 46). While the displacement problems associated with conflict situations as discussed above have received much attention in the past decade, the social and economic impact of natural disasters and epidemics remains relatively invisible as a policy issue, in particular the impacts on the achievement of gender equality. The social, political and economic repercussions of those situations reached such a magnitude in recent years that the sustainability of life in many parts of the world has become challenged. Local food security and nutrition are particularly threatened, and this has affected rural as well as urban areas.

Problems associated with environmental degradation are central to the concerns of the Platform for Action as they affect sustainability of livelihoods, subsistence and ecosystems (PfA, paras. 34 and 35 and critical area of concern K). Environmental degradation is linked with (a) habitat destruction; (b) introduction of alien species causing epidemics; (c) industrial pollution due to armed conflict; (d) poverty-driven, unsustainable land use or misuse; (e) excessive consumption by a minority of the world's population; and (f) global climate change increasing the possibilities of natural disasters and spread of disease. More needs to be known on the gender equality implications of these factors.

The Platform for Action placed emphasis on gender equality perspectives in the spread of diseases, especially HIV/AIDS (PfA, para. 37). Since the Beijing Conference, HIV/AIDS has emerged as the single most devastating epidemic experienced in modern history. At the end of 1999, there were 33.6 million people estimated to be infected with HIV. More than 95 per cent of HIV-infected people live in the developing world.[171] As indicated in the Platform for Action, young women and adolescents are particularly vulnerable. While HIV/AIDS was initially perceived mainly as a health problem, both the short- and long-term social and economic development impacts of HIV/AIDS are increasingly recognized, in particular the gender equality implications.

The increase in casualties and damage caused by natural disasters in recent years has brought about a renewed interest in the social and political characteristics of human organization that contribute to vulnerability in such disasters. It has also raised awareness of the inefficiency of the existing approaches and intervention methods in responding to such emergency situations where women, more often than men, must establish some semblance of order in the midst of disorder, so as to meet the immediate daily needs of their families.

Gender relations are central to understanding how communities are affected by, and respond to, natural disasters. Therefore, developing disaster mitigation and recovery strategies that incorporate a gender equality perspective can produce effective humanitarian and disaster management interventions.

G. Challenges of new communications technologies

The Beijing Platform for Action calls attention to the dramatic level of developments in the field of communications, noting that "with advances in computer technology and satellite and cable television, global access to information continues to increase and expand, creating new opportunities for the participation of women in communications" (PfA, para. 33).

Owing to the expanding reach of new ICTs in recent years, the use of technology for the empowerment of women has been impressive. For example, many women worldwide are making effective use of Internet and e-mail for development purposes such as networking, advocacy, dissemination and exchange of information, and creative e-commerce initiatives designed to help local artisans and producers to market their products globally. Information-sharing and networking, via the Internet, have become important empowerment tools. The decentralized, interactive and non-hierarchical nature of the new technologies allows women to express their views, interact and establish networks with women and men around the world. ICTs have also greatly increased the range of economic opportunities for some women.

However, millions of the world's poorest women and men still do not have access, to these facilities. Issues such as cost, location bias and time constraints pose impediments to the diffusion of these technologies. A growing number of women, however, use e-mail and the Web for information and communications and repackage information for groups that do not have access to computers and the electronic media.

Since the mid-1990s, women's organizations in the developing world have made great strides in adopting electronic communications and facilitating women's access to ICTs. Since Beijing, various international agencies have also become active in the field of gender equality and telecommunications. WomenWatch, a United Nations Internet initiative jointly established by the Division for the Advancement of Women, UNIFEM and INSTRAW, and, since 1998, a joint project of the ACC Inter-Agency Committee on Women and Gender Equality, provides up-to-date information on the work of the United Nations on behalf of women and establishes a forum in which women around the world may participate in the Beijing+5 process.

On the other hand, women have been slow to enter ICTs-based professions worldwide and have been largely excluded from designing and shaping information technologies. Where women are employed in this sector, they tend to hold low-paying and less prestigious positions. Traditionally, gender differences and disparities have been ignored in policies and programmes dealing with the development and dissemination of improved technologies. As a result, women have benefited less from, and been disadvantaged more by, technological advances. Women, therefore, need to be actively involved in the definition, design and development of new technologies. Otherwise, the information revolution might bypass women or produce adverse effects on their lives. With respect to such adverse effects, incidents of negative stereotyping, discrimination against women and sexual harassment are already evident on-line.

Further actions and initiatives need to be explored and implemented to avoid new forms of exclusion and ensure that women and girls have equal access and opportunities in respect of the developments of science and technology.

H. Towards new alliances and partnerships

The Beijing Platform for Action recognized broad public participation in decision-making at local, national and international levels as one of the fundamental prerequisites of the advancement of women. Effective partnerships involving different levels of government, including national machinery for the advancement of women, civil society including non-governmental organizations, women's groups and academia, international organizations, the private sector and other actors, are essential for the empowerment of women and gender equality. Moreover, effective partnerships of State and non-State actors provide the foundation for more democratic, transparent, accountable and enabling partnerships through which opportunities and benefits may be shared.

The number of non-governmental organizations accredited to the United Nations has increased considerably in recent years, and the global conferences and summits have acted as catalysts for this broadened, and more diverse participation of civil society in the work of the Organization. Unprecedented numbers of non-governmental organizations participated in the Fourth World Conference on Women, and these organizations have remained pivotal in sustaining the momentum for implementation of the Platform for Action. Non-governmental organizations with a focus on women's issues and gender equality have found in the United Nations a political space not always available in their home countries for raising issues of concern to women. This forum has served to legitimize their concerns in a global arena, thereby strengthening their ability to pursue such issues domestically.

The knowledge, skills, enthusiasm, motivation and grass-roots perspectives of non-governmental actors are necessary to complement the resources of official agencies. Civil society groups have been full and sometimes leading partners in implementing programmes to monitor the protection and promotion of the human rights of women, the provision of humanitarian assistance to women, health care including reproductive care and family planning, education and training for women and girls, and the establishment of income-generating activities. Increasingly, non-governmental organizations work in partnership with Governments in sustained efforts over longer periods and seek to advance women's well-being and the achievement of gender equality.

The private sector, media, academic institutions and centres of training and research command financial, intellectual and communications capabilities in all sectors. Private firms and not-for-profit institutions are increasingly providing public services that, until recently, were seen as Governments' responsibility. This transfer of responsibilities from the public to the private sector is accompanied by trends in public administration towards decentralization of decision-making to the beneficiaries, or to the local authorities accountable to them. These trends offer expanded opportunities for productive partnerships among the actors concerned.

The Secretary-General of the United Nations has reached out to constituencies beyond States and civil society in order to build new alliances and coalitions among relevant actors, as attested, for example, by his proposals for a global compact between the United Nations and the world business community. These and other efforts aim at ensuring adherence to commonly held values and to a belief in the principles of human rights, in freedom of association and collective bargaining, in the elimination of forced labour and of child labour, in non-discrimination in employment and in environmental sustainability.

Women have an equal stake in all these issues, and gender equality must be mainstreamed into these and other initiatives.

Notes

[158] *Report of the Fourth World Conference on Women*, op. cit.

[159] E/CN.6/1995/3 and Add.1-10.

[160] E/CN.6/1995/3/Add.1, para. 1.

[161] *Official Records of the General Assembly, Fifty-fourth Session, Supplement No. 1* (A/54/1), para. 220.

[162] *World Survey on the Role of Women in Development*, op. cit.

[163] United Nations publication, Sales No. E.97.II.D.8.

[164] New York, OUP, 1997.

[165] New York, OUP, 1999.

[166] *World Development Report 1999/2000*, op. cit.

[167] *World Survey on the Role of Women in Development*, op. cit. chap. III, sect. A.

[168] Lin Lim, "Flexible labour markets in a globalizing world: the implications for international female migration", paper presented at the Conference on International Migration at Century's End: Trends and Issues, organized by the International Union for the Scientific Study of Population (IUSSP) Committee on South-North Migration, Barcelona, 7 to 10 May 1997.

[169] *World Population Monitoring, 1997: International Migration and Development* (United Nations publication, Sales No. E.98.XIII.4), table 40.

[170] *Official Records of the General Assembly, Forty-ninth Session, Supplement No. 38* (A/49/38), chap. I, sect. A, para. 6.

[171] Report of the Secretary-General on world population monitoring, 2000: population, gender and development (E/CN.9/2000/3, para. 59)).

Annex

Regional distribution of responses to the questionnaire

ECA	ECE	ECLAC	ESCAP	ESCWA
43/52	**47/55**	**27/33**	**25/42**	**12/13**
Algeria	Albania	Antigua and	Australia	Bahrain
Angola	Armenia	Barbuda	Bangladesh	Egypt
Benin	Austria	Argentina	Bhutan	Iraq
Botswana	Belarus	Belize	Brunei	Jordan
Burkina Faso	Belgium	Bolivia	Darussalam	Kuwait
Burundi	Bulgaria	Brazil	Cambodia	Lebanon
Cameroon	Canada	Chile	China	Oman
Central African	Croatia	Colombia	Fiji	Palestine[a]
Republic	Cyprus	Costa Rica	India	Qatar
Chad	Czech Republic	Cuba	Indonesia	Syrian Arab
Congo	Denmark	Dominica	Islamic Republic	Republic
Côte d'Ivoire	Estonia	Dominican	of Iran	United Arab
Djibouti	Finland	Republic	Japan	Emirates
Equatorial	France	Ecuador	Malaysia	Yemen
Guinea	Georgia	El Salvador	Maldives	
Eritrea	Germany	Grenada	Mongolia	
Ethiopia	Greece	Guyana	Myanmar	
Gambia	Hungary	Haiti	Nepal	
Ghana	Iceland	Jamaica	New Zealand	
Guinea	Ireland	Mexico	Pakistan	
Kenya	Israel	Panama	Papua New	
Liberia	Italy	Paraguay	Guinea	
Libyan Arab	Kazakhstan	Peru	Philippines	
Jamahiriya	Kyrgyzstan	Saint Lucia	Republic of	
Madagascar	Latvia	Saint Vincent	Korea	
Mali	Lithuania	and the	Singapore	
Mauritius	Luxembourg	Grenadines	Thailand	
Morocco	Malta	São Tomé and	Vanuatu	
Mozambique	Monaco	Príncipe	Viet Nam	
Namibia	Netherlands	Suriname		
Niger	Norway	Trinidad and		
Nigeria	Poland	Tobago		
Rwanda	Portugal	Uruguay		
Senegal	Republic of	Venezuela		
Seychelles	Moldova			
Sierra Leone	Romania			
South Africa	Russian			
Sudan	Federation			
Swaziland	San Marino			
Togo	Slovak Republic			
Tunisia	Spain			
Uganda	Sweden			
United Republic	Switzerland[a]			
of Tanzania	Turkey			
Zambia	Turkmenistan			
Zimbabwe	Ukraine			
	United Kingdom			
	United States of			
	America			
	Uzbekistan			

[a] Observer Country.

Litho in United Nations, New York
01-40550—August 2001—4,030

United Nations publication
Sales No. E-01-IV-3
ISBN 92-1-130213-7